SECRETS
of
Screenplay
Structure

HOW TO RECOGNIZE AND EMULATE
THE STRUCTURAL FRAMEWORKS
OF GREAT FILMS

LINDA J. COWGILL

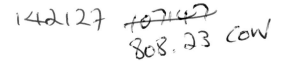

SECRETS OF SCREENPLAY STRUCTURE
How to Recognize and Emulate the Structural Frameworks of Great Films

LONE EAGLE PUBLISHING COMPANY™
1024 N. Orange Drive
Hollywood, CA 90038
Phone 323.308.3400 or 800.FILMBKS
A division of IFILM^{SM} Corp., www.ifilm.com

Printed in the United States of America

Cover and book design by Carla Green
Edited by Janna Wong Healy

Library of Congress Cataloging-in-Publication Data

Cowgill, Linda J.
    Secrets of screenplay structure / by Linda J. Cowgill.
        p. cm.
    Includes bibliographical references and index.
    ISBN 1-58065-004-X
    1. Motion picture authorship. 2. Motion picture plays—Technique.
    I. Title.
PN1996.C8148 1999   98-45740
808.2'3—dc21   CIP

Lone Eagle books may be purchased in bulk at special discounts for promotional or educational purposes. Special editions can be created to specifications. Inquiries for sales and distribution, textbook adoption, foreign language translation, editorial, and rights and permissions inquiries should be addressed to: Jeff Black, Lone Eagle Publishing, 1024 N. Orange Drive, Hollywood, CA 90038 or send e-mail to: info@loneeagle.com

Distributed to the trade by National Book Network, 800-462-6420

Lone Eagle Publishing Company is a registered trademark.
IFILM is a registered service mark.

"Every good idea and all creative work are the offspring of the imagination, and have their source in what one is pleased to call infantile fantasy."

— *C. G. Jung*

For David and Clea

ACKNOWLEDGMENTS

This book would not have been possible without the help of many people who, it is my pleasure, to thank here. Many thanks to:

Joan Singleton and Jeff Black of Lone Eagle Publishing, for giving me the opportunity to add my two-cents to the screenwriting textbook market; and Janna Wong Healy, for helpful comments and editing.

Pat Oliver, of Loyola Marymount University, LA, for allowing me the chance to explore my ideas with a graduate seminar on story structure; and Rick Hadley, also of Loyola Marymount, for encouraging me to pursue the class and lending needed support once it was put on the schedule; Karen Hama, for help deciphering Aristotle.

Andrew Laskos for the film discussions and your incredible movie memory. Geoff Grode for your fact finding and for starting me on this path at AFI; Richard DeBaun for helping me prepare for a teaching career; Steve Sharon for your film discussions and encouragement; Paul Erhman for insightful comments and allowing me to try out my theories with your work; Glen Benest and Bill Bleich, for movie discussions and your lists of favorites; and Cary Vhugen and Chris Tragos for having such vast video collections to lend; and Greg Caruso at 20/20.

Many, many thanks to my graduate students at Loyola Marymount University who inspired me to put these ideas down on paper.

Most of all, I have to thank my husband David DeCrane and my daughter Clea DeCrane, who have put up with all this. Without his encouragement and love, perceptive comments and editorial abilities, and my daughter's understanding and love, none of this would have been worth doing.

CONTENTS

INTRODUCTION

Every year another slew of books on how to write a screenplay hits the market, all promising the secret of screenwriting success. Every one of these books offers something valuable to beginning and experienced screenwriters alike. They usually are manuals on how to write and they could be useful in varying degrees to writers, the way manuals on auto repair introduce the basics to novice mechanics or provide a review to the more experienced. As a screenwriter, you'll want to review these books in a store or library, and take home those that most match your skills, style and the state of your art.

Secrets of Screenplay Structure does not try and tell you how to write a screenplay. It does not lay out structural paradigms to follow. This book does something different: *Secrets of Screenplay Structure* articulates the concepts behind screenplay structure in a clear language based on the study of great film works, from the '30s to today. It is a book designed not only to help screenwriters understand how and why great films work, but directors, producers and development executives, too. Why do the classics continue to move us, to make us laugh and cry? How do their plots and characters manage to keep us engaged, even after multiple viewings? Why do they feel timeless even if they were made over 60 years ago? The goal of this book is to answer these questions.

Rather than viewing this book as the screenwriting equivalent of an auto repair manual or how-to book on building a house, think of it as the screenwriting analog to a survey of great automobiles or buildings, an appreciation of the structural elements that make timeless the best examples of the art. One of the secrets of a great screenplay is its structure, the way form and function combine to bring its story alive. The structure of a film story is as crucial and inseparable from its success as the design of a great automobile or building.

Does it seem strange to think of a film this way? It's not for those who work in the industry and understand Elia Kazan's statement, "A script is more architecture than literature."[1] Film and screenplay structure is not a phantom construct, although it should appear invisible upon the first reading of a screenplay and the first viewing of a film. If the framework is apparent, it often makes a work predictable and weakens the experience of the story. The quickest way into a film is through interesting, well-drawn characters, but the way we hold on to a story is through its structure, through the management of information which focuses the aim of the film for the audience.

Structure can best be understood as the management of information. In order to manage information effectively, through the exposition, incidents, episodes and sequences which construct a plot, a writer must know two things: the focus of his story and the arc of his character. Without this focus and a character who is effected and changed by the plot, a film will always come up short of being great.

What is a screenplay then? It's a story, written on paper, that's told visually, utilizing action and dialogue, about a person (or group of people) trying to accomplish something important to him/her (or them). It is the blueprint for a film, the master plan, the original design.

What is on the palette that a screenwriter uses to construct this master plan?

Characters: protagonist, antagonist; love interest, mentor, foils, confidants.

Setting: subject, arena, locale, mise-en-scene.

Story: plot, back story, main exposition, conflict, plans, stakes, action, midpoint, incidents, events, subplot, obstacles, complications, reversals, crises, climaxes, resolution.

Scenes: dialogue, actions, imagery, sequences.

Theme: the deeper meaning, central premise or question; the underlying, unifying idea.

Clearly, there are many elements a screenwriter uses to tell his story; structure is how he organizes them. In *Webster's New Twentieth Century Dictionary Unabridged*, structure is defined as, "something built or constructed, like a building; the arrangement or interrelations of all the parts of the whole; the complex system considered from the point of view of the whole rather than any single part; something composed of parts arranged in a

particular way; the relationship or organization of the component parts of a work of art or literature." In other words, structure is the relationship of the parts to the whole.

THE DESIGN OF THIS BOOK

The design of this book is simple, and in its own way, interactive. The first two chapters impart the basic concepts necessary
to understand the materials and tools with which to build a screenplay plot, the basis of a great film. The starting point is Aristotle's
Poetics, written over 2,400 years ago. A recent and wonderful
translation by Richard Janko (published by Hackett Publishing
Company in 1987) makes Aristotle's ideas remarkably current
and relevant to screenwriting today. I recommend reading it, but
one doesn't have to in order to understand this book.

Starting with Chapter Two, one or more study films are used
in each chapter to illustrate the points of the section. Before each
chapter, it is recommended that you view the study film. Even if
you have seen it before, *view* it again. Don't rely upon the chapter to refresh your memory. If you can lay your hands on the
screenplay to read first, that's even better. Read the screenplay,
watch the film and find where the film was changed. Ask yourself why the changes were made. Do the changes make the film
better? If the film is stronger than the screenplay, what can you
learn from the changes?

Each chapter then builds on the one preceding it, relating a
new topic to our overall understanding of structure while con-
tinuing to use the study films to illustrate its points. As the number of study films increase, so will our pool of examples. Each
film is discussed by breaking it down to its component parts,
identifying the focus and examining the plot construction and
main characters. By the end of the book, you will see how films
as disparate as *Groundhog Day* and *Se7en* have underlying par-
allels in their structure.

Each chapter ends with a discussion of a late or "final" draft
of the screenplay compared to the completed film. The structure of the screenplay is not always the same as the finished
film; all screenplays go through many revisions in the process
of being realized and a great film is no different. Therefore, if
you can find a published screenplay or studio copy to read, do
so before watching the film. Not only will it be interesting
to see what the writer handed to the director, but it will be

instructive to see how the production of the film improves or perfects its structure.

The analysis of screenplays in screenwriting manuals is often problematic. It is here so many screenplay "scholars" come up short. They use a "final" draft of a screenplay as the basis for evaluating a film without comparing the changes made in production. In *The Screenwriter's Workbook,* Syd Field analyzes *Chinatown* and *Body Heat* based on late drafts, but he fails to take into consideration those changes made in production and editing. These changes are, of course, what we see when we watch the film and they often radically alter the film's underlying structure. As an example, Mr. Field calls the arrival of the real Mrs. Mulwray in *Chinatown* (page 23 of the script) "Plot Point I" and the end of a "very short" first act. But in the film, the appearance of Faye Dunaway's character is really the inciting incident, occurring at minute 17. His analysis of *Body Heat* is just as flawed. The second half of the film veers off dramatically from the screenplay he analyzed in *The Screenwriter's Workbook.* More recently, an article in a screenwriting magazine discussed *Groundhog Day* and *Speed,* but the author used early drafts of the screenplays. He went on to refer to scenes that were never even shot!

This happens often because memory is a very tricky thing. We see a film once, then pick up its screenplay later and it is very close to what we remember seeing. This close association colors our memory so vividly that after multiple readings, the screenplay becomes the film. This is why reading the screenplay (even a published one) before carefully viewing a film can be informative and instructive—the differences become more readily apparent and these differences are often major structural revisions. It is only because we've seen a great film that we know it's great, not because we've read the screenplay. What we learn about screenplay structure should be based on the finished film, too.

I have limited the number of study films and cited other examples outside this pool only where necessary and useful to understanding the point at hand. I consider each title mentioned a great film, or at the very least, a very good one.

The study films in this book are:

Witness
Risky Business
Casablanca
The Piano
Chinatown
Quiz Show
Tootsie
Diner
Parenthood
The Best Years of Our Lives
Grand Hotel
Citizen Kane
Rashomon
The Conformist
Annie Hall
Reservoir Dogs
The Last of the Mohicans
Jerry Maguire
North by Northwest
One Flew Over the Cuckoo's Nest
Groundhog Day
Se7en
It Happened One Night
Thelma and Louise

No doubt any one person will disagree with some of my choices. But these examples will hold up on second and third viewings, becoming even more meaningful, and to us, instructive. As Robert Altman once said, you know a film is great when it's even better the second and third time around.

Endnotes
1. Kazan, Elia, *A Life*. Anchor Books, New York. 1989, p. 380.

1

THE ESSENCE OF DRAMATIC STRUCTURE

The basis of our understanding of classic three-act structure goes back to Aristotle. In his philosophical essay the *Poetics*, Aristotle set out to distinguish what separates a great play from a mediocre one and in the process, he defined the fundamental parameters of dramatic structure which still prevail today. Although his treatise deals primarily with Greek tragedy of his time, his observations and conclusions are not only relevant but surprisingly adaptable to current thinking with regard to screenplay structure.

THE ESSENCE OF DRAMATIC STRUCTURE

In his essay, Aristotle lays out two important concepts for grasping the essence of dramatic structure. He defines tragedy (though, for our purposes, we will understand this as "drama" in general) as the "representation of a complete, i.e., whole, action which has some magnitude." By "magnitude," Aristotle means importance or relevance. Today, we might understand this as "theme," the broader subject matter of the story the writer wants to illustrate. It is the central issue or underlying, unifying idea. A great film, whether comedy or tragedy, must relate to our lives in some way for us to connect with it and find meaning in it.

In the idea of a "complete, i.e., whole, action" we find the beginnings of structure itself. Aristotle continues:

> "A whole is that which has a beginning, a middle and a conclusion. A beginning is that which itself does not of necessity follow something else, but after which there naturally is, or comes into being, something else. A conclusion, conversely, is that which itself naturally follows

something else, either of necessity or for the most part, but has nothing else after it. A middle is that which itself naturally follows something else, and has something else after it. Well-constructed plots should neither begin from a random point nor conclude at a random point, but should use the elements we have mentioned (i.e., beginning, middle and conclusion.)"[1]

This may seem fairly rudimentary. Obviously, a story needs a beginning, middle and end. But what Aristotle is stressing is the causal relationship between the parts of the whole. A beginning starts with a set of circumstances which develops into a specific line of action. This line of action defines the core, or center, of the story. The development of this action then results in a conclusion which ends the story.

All that Aristotle insists upon is that a play has a good and obvious reason for beginning where it begins and for ending where it ends; and that its incidents should follow from one to another in a clear chain of causation, without coincidence and without irrelevance. There should be nothing which is not clearly caused by what precedes, and nothing which is not clearly the cause of what follows. The design of a plot, the story's sequence of events, must seem inevitable—to have both a plan that appears causally inescapable and a pattern that seems artistically unavoidable.

We can conclude from these observations several things. First, there is a basic linear quality to the structure of good storytelling. Second, the arrangement of incidents, episodes and events of the plot must lead to a dramatic solution. And third, if we are to find a dramatic solution at the end, we must have a dramatic problem posed at the beginning.

Basic Aristotelian thought charts dramatic structure like this (although we have no evidence that this is how Aristotle saw it):

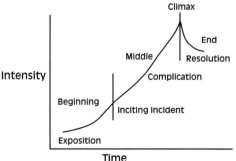

A story progresses through time and rises in intensity to its finish. The beginning consists of the exposition. In the exposition, we find the antecedents upon which the story is based. This is the essential information the audience needs in order to grasp what's going on. In Aristotle's day, playwrights used a prologue, delivered by the chorus, which introduced the main characters and story. The middle, which Aristotle referred to as the complication, is made up of incidents and events. According to him, the important incidents and events of the plot are the reversal, the recognition, and the quality of suffering (or pathos). The story problem's climax and resolution belong to the end.

The purpose of the beginning is to set up the story you want to tell. Certain information must be conveyed to the viewers in order for them to pay intelligent attention to the story as it develops. We call this the main exposition and it consists of establishing time and place, genre, and introducing the protagonist and the basis of the plot problem. Usually, the plot problem is launched in the inciting incident which is often a specific event which has repercussions for the protagonist. It upsets the balance of the status quo, introducing the main conflict and acting as a catalyst. It must create a situation strong enough dramatically to cause the hero to take action. The protagonist's action, which is taken in response to the inciting incident, now begins to sharpen the focus of the earlier exposition into the main plot line.

Another way to think of the middle is as the confrontation. Here the protagonist must confront the problems, obstacles (inner as well as outer), complications and reversals which assail him once he commits to a specific course of action of trying to reestablish the balance which was disturbed in the inciting incident. Our graph shows that as the story progresses, so must the intensity as it approaches the climax.

The main point of the ending is the solution. The climax of the plot leads to a resolution of the story. The problem the protagonist faces must finally be solved.

LINEAR UNDERSTANDING

How and why did this type of structure evolve? Part of the answer lies in the fact that this is how we have always learned stories, starting with the ones we heard on grandma's knee. (First, the setting and the hero are established. Next follows a development or the conflict which gives the hero his purpose and goal.

Consequences and repercussions result, leading to a solution which answers the question the story has posed at the beginning.) If we look at the earliest myths around the world, they follow a similar pattern. (A hero wants something or has a specific task to perform. He takes action and meets with conflict. This leads to a crisis, which results in a climax and finally a resolution.)

The main reason we have always heard stories this way, however, is because we understand and process information linearly. This is not to say we don't understand intuitively, because many of us do at times. But for the most part, we learn in a sequential pattern. You have to have the antecedents to understand the developments which lead to a solution, i.e., there is a beginning, middle and end. Even in nonlinear stories, there is always a distinct beginning, middle and end.

It's important to grasp what seems so obvious because when dealing with a two-hour movie, you have to manage the information you're going to impart. Understanding the specific purpose of each section helps. Trouble often arises when we attempt to define the exact moment when the beginning is done and the middle starts. The same is true about defining where the middle concludes and the ending section begins. With a play, a curtain comes down at the end of the acts, clearly announcing the end of each. But film doesn't employ this technique.

Film is more fluid and sometimes more subtle. But the story information still has to be managed in a way which makes it understandable, interesting and keeps the story moving. The writer must direct and guide the audience through the story utilizing a certain amount of surprise and excitement while at the same time maintaining momentum and meaning.

Before we can understand the significance and power of managing a story this way, let's look at the three sections in greater detail. Our assignment to help us understand the next chapter is to watch the film *Witness*, written by Earl W. Wallace and William Kelley, from a story by William and Pamela Kelley and Earl W. Wallace; directed by Peter Weir and produced by Ed Feldman.

Endnotes
1. Aristotle, *Poetics*, translated by Richard Janko. Hackett Publishing Company, Indianapolis/Cambridge, 1987, p. 10.

THE THREE-PART NATURE
OF SCREENPLAY STRUCTURE
Study film: *Witness*

ACT ONE—THE SET-UP
In the last chapter, we said that the purpose of the beginning is to prepare the story you want to tell and this is done through the main exposition. In modern jargon, we call this simply the set-up. In the set-up, the writer introduces certain elements: time and place, the protagonist and other main characters, the central conflict, and the genre or style of the piece. By genre or style, we mean comedy or drama, sci-fi or western. If it is a comedy, then we must know it immediately, and what kind (satire, farce, romantic?). The audience needs to know as soon as possible if it is expected to laugh.

The Main Exposition
The main exposition must establish your protagonist, though the antagonist only needs to be foreshadowed this early in the film. What is important, however, is that the seeds of the central conflict (or the main plot problem) be planted, and the sooner the better. Why? Because conflict makes us sit up and pay attention. Instinctively, we want to see how the conflict will be resolved. Drama (and comedy) cannot exist without conflict.

The writer must determine what initial information needs to be communicated before he can get the story moving. For example, look at *Witness*. What does the audience need to know at the beginning in order to understand the story that follows? Though the film is a police drama, its central issue is really the clash between two cultures, modern violent America and the religious, nonviolent Amish. Since our audience lives in modern America and is exposed to violence via the media every day, it is the unfamiliar, communal Amish society which needs introduction.

The Amish sense of community, its traditions and religious tenets are suggested with the funeral of Rachel's husband and Samuel's father. This establishes Rachel (Kelly McGillis) as a widow and serves to motivate her trip which will take her into violent Philadelphia. Her father-in-law Eli Lapp (Jan Rubes) and potential suitor Daniel Hochleitner (Alexander Godunov) need to be introduced early due to the integral role each will play later in the story. All of this exposition is established, shown with little dialogue, in the first few minutes of the film. It is the foundation upon which the rest of the story is built.

The Inciting Incident

The main exposition isn't complete until we have a protagonist and a central conflict to give the story direction. Some force must enter the represented world and upset the existing order. In *Witness*, Rachel and Samuel's trip to see her sister takes them out of their world and into another. While waiting for their connecting train, Samuel (Lukas Haas) witnesses a murder in the men's room of the railroad station. The murder of the undercover policeman is the inciting incident for the story. It turns Rachel and Samuel's world upside-down and brings the film's protagonist, John Book (Harrison Ford), into the picture. The murder occurs approximately eleven minutes into the movie. John Book enters the picture at the 13 minute mark and Book and Samuel meet at fourteen minutes into the film.

Though the murder serves as the catalyst for the story, we still need more information to understand the central conflict (or main plot problem) of the film. This will take further developments. But since a conflict is now in place, i.e., a problem has been raised for the protagonist to solve, our interest has also been engaged.

At this point in *Witness*, what is the problem John Book faces? *Can he apprehend the killers?*

Once the main exposition focuses the protagonist's problem on a specific objective, and the audience wants to know what happens next, is the hero now on one path until he accomplishes his goal or fails to achieve it?

The End of Act One

Trying to manage two hours of story without some organization other than a straight arrow plot tends to make a movie feel repetitious and boring. You wonder, why is it taking so long to get to the climax? If the action proceeds in a strictly linear manner, offering no twists or surprises, no new developments or other possible solutions for the dramatic problem, or never allowing the problem to deepen or evolve, the film tends to be one-dimensional. As a result, its meaning will be superficial or, worse, lost.

Meaning is developed in film through the relationships characters form with each other and with the story events. It takes shape often in the subplot which carries the interpersonal story line. If a straight arrow plot progresses from beginning to middle to end, with little interference from other characters or complications, it makes the protagonist seem to exist in a vacuum. The protagonist needs to have the opportunity to interact with others in order to affect and be affected. This helps the audience relate to and care about the characters which leads to deeper audience involvement. It also helps clarify the theme, for it is only within the context of human action that we find meaning. This leads back to Aristotle's idea of magnitude: Great films have a point, a unifying idea, a theme.

Many screenplay theorists think that the main exposition, or set-up, ends with the inciting incident. Once this catalyst engages the plot engine, we are into the main story. But I differ from this view. Though a problem has been framed for the protagonist generally in the opening fifteen minutes (in the case of *Witness*, the problem is: *Can Book get the killer?*), in great films, we find that this is only one component of the dramatic problem. There is a second part which sharpens the focus of the conflict and raises the stakes for the hero.

Whatever constitutes the beginning (the way the problem is first framed for the protagonist) needs to lead to three things while still keeping us surprised and entertained. These are: Development (especially in new developments), story progression and escalation of the conflict.

Development means to expand or elaborate, to evolve. Plot developments fill in other aspects of the story, characters and theme. New developments can be thought of as new problems for the hero as well as for the other main characters. But developments can also come in the form of complications and actions which result from meeting obstacles, or even as support for the protagonist or another main character which then turns the plot in a new direction. How the characters deal with the new developments can add dimension and complexity to their characterizations.

Progression means forward movement in time. If a film develops its elements of character, plot and theme, it moves ahead. However, if too much attention is paid to one area, say to theme and not enough to plot, then the film bogs down. If too much time is spent on the plot, with little consideration of character or theme, the film will be one-dimensional and most likely boring. Development and progression of all the main elements—character, plot and theme—need to be interwoven carefully to create a film that is compelling on all fronts.

Escalation of the drama—the increase in intensity—is also an important element of a compelling film. Escalation means an increase in intensity. The enormity of the consequences for the protagonist and other main characters must rise as the story progresses through time. It is this escalation of the conflict and consequences which keeps the audience on the edge of its seat.

When we left *Witness*, the dramatic problem raised for Book was: *Will he get the killers?* But to understand the true central conflict (main plot problem) of the film, we need more information through further developments, progression in the action and the escalation of the conflict. Let's look at the main thrust and development of this section of the film to see how it's done.

John Book proceeds along police procedures, essentially taking Rachel and Samuel into his custody, holding Samuel as a material witness and totally disrupting their lives. Rachel bristles, but can't resist the "law" though she wants no part of it. When Samuel can't identify a suspect, Book arranges for mother and son to stay another day. At the police station, Book shows Samuel a police line-up and mug shots. So far, Book pushes the action forward as he tries to solve the crime. The new and important development comes when Samuel finally makes an identification, but not of a felon. Samuel sees the photo of an honored policeman, Lt. McFee (Danny Glover), on the wall of the police station. Book takes this news to his superior and mentor, Capt. Schaeffer (Josef Sommer), who tells Book to sit tight and not say anything yet. Book returns home where McFee is waiting for him (another new development and an escalation of the conflict). They exchange gunfire. McFee flees and Book is wounded (yet another development). With the knowledge that his former partner and mentor Schaeffer is also "dirty," Book must react to save Rachel and Samuel, as well as himself.

Now the central conflict of the film is truly defined. The problem Book faces is no longer: *Will he get the killers*, but can he get McFee and Schaeffer and save Samuel and Rachel before they get him? Act One ends with Book, wounded, asking his partner Carter (Brent Jennings) to destroy any paperwork leading to Rachel and Samuel's whereabouts and spiriting mother and son back to the Lapp farm. He intends to leave them, but loses consciousness and cannot move on.

Though there are other points made during this section of the film, these are the main beats on which the plot is structured. In a later chapter, we look at the development of Book's character in relationship to structure.

ACT TWO—THE CONFRONTATION

The middle section is often called the rising action because as the plot progresses, the story tension escalates. In most films, it escalates because the conflict set up in the beginning is now out in the open. The middle section is the confrontation between these opposing forces.

The middle consists of obstacles, complications, reversals, subplots, crises and climaxes the protagonist and antagonists encounter in the pursuit of their goals. Along the way, plans are set in motion and characterizations are fleshed out. In effect, these are your materials and your tools for building the plot to carry the story, so let's define them for a clearer understanding.

Obstacles

An obstacle is whatever stands in the way of the protagonist's progress toward his goal; it is the clearest form of conflict. The best obstacles incite the most action from the characters. Once an obstacle becomes apparent, it should aim a direct threat at the protagonist.

There are basically four kinds of obstacles:
1. The antagonist;
2. Physical obstructions;
3. Inner/psychological problems;
4. Mystic forces.

The antagonist best represents the conflict. Though a film can exist with only a psychic or internal conflict, a specific antagonist lends clarity and power to the dramatic structure because his primary function is to oppose the protagonist. He doesn't necessarily have to be evil, but he should personify the protagonist's obstacles. Frequently, the antagonist initiates the protagonist's (and the drama's) crucial problem. In *Witness*, Schaeffer and McFee are the antagonists; McFee creates the problem for Book by murdering the undercover cop.

Physical obstructions are just what they seem—material barriers standing in the way of the protagonist. These can be rivers, deserts, mountains, a dead-end street or a car causing a crash—anything that presents a substantial obstacle for the protagonist. In *Witness*, Book's gunshot wound which must heal and the car's dead electrical system are concrete problems to be overcome.

Inner obstacles are intellectual, emotional or psychological problems the protagonist must overcome before being able to achieve his goal. For example, dealing with fear, pride, jealousy, the need to mature fall into this category. In *Witness*, Book's inner problems manifest themselves in the hard outer shell of his personality. Though Book is a good man and honest cop, he is initially insensitive toward Rachel and Samuel's plight; he is also prone to violence. Book's internal odyssey begins with the wound which almost kills him. Nursed back to health on the Lapp farm, Book's awareness changes. His respect for Rachel, Eli and Samuel and for the Amish culture grows. But because of his violent nature, he is unable to truly fit in among the Amish. His brawl with a local brute leads directly to being found by Schaeffer and McFee, and puts Samuel, Rachel and Eli in jeopardy. However, it is with his new understanding of nonviolent means that he ends the confrontation with Schaeffer.

Mystic forces enter most stories as accidents or chance but they can be expressed as moral choices or ethical codes which present obstacles; they can also be personified as gods or supernatural forces which the characters have to contend with. In *Witness*, Book must adhere to the Amish code. Having his gun is an obstacle to that so he hands over to Rachel his gun and bullets. This action leaves him unarmed when the antagonists arrive. (In a film like *Ghost*, the protagonist has to deal with a paranormal world in order to reach his lover.)

Obstacles are important because when properly conceived and handled, they force the major characters to make decisions about what to do and whether to do it. Such decisions produce dramatic action, and this produces a compelling film.

The Plan

The protagonist usually has a plan he starts implementing once his problem has been introduced; it may be conscious or unconscious, carefully thought out or arbitrary. The plan often finds its way into the protagonist's dialogue soon after the main action begins so the audience will know his intention. The plan also allows us to grasp how the protagonist initially sees the conflict and anticipates the results. As the plot progresses, the gap between the protagonist's expected results and the reality of the main conflict often produces story surprise and leads to a greater struggle; this adds more suspense to a film. As the protagonist perseveres, he reveals his true character and the audience gains insight into the meaning of the story.

In *Witness*, Book clearly demonstrates different plans at different times. In the beginning, he plans on using Samuel to identify the killer so he can make an arrest. Once Samuel has made an identification, Book discusses options with Schaeffer, his mentor and superior, unwittingly tipping his hand to the antagonists. Once McFee challenges Book in the garage and shoots him, Book's plan is to flee. He bundles Rachel and Samuel off, calls his partner, Carter, and tells him to destroy the paperwork on the case so mother and son can't be found. Then he drives them to the Lapp farm. He clearly intends to leave, but his wound prevents him. Once he is on the mend, his plan is to get out of there as soon as he's strong enough and go after Schaeffer and McFee. When Schaeffer and McFee kill his partner, Book directly tells Schaeffer he's going to "get" him.

Complications

Complications are just what they sound like: any factor entering the world of the film which makes matters more difficult for a major character and causes a change in the course of the action. They differ from obstacles in that they don't immediately pose an apparent threat. A complication generally arises when an unexpected problem confronts the protagonist (or antagonist) and creates repercussions which must be dealt with later in the plot.

It is only later when the full extent of the problem's ramifications arise. The best complications are credible but unexpected and add tension to the plot line. (Viewers usually anticipate the hero's inevitable reaction to a problem, whether major or minor, but, in any great film, since they cannot predict what that reaction will be or how it will play out, it tends to add tension.)

Almost anything can cause a complication. For example, the sudden arrival of a character, an unanticipated set of circumstances, a mistaken identity, misunderstanding or discovery, all can cause an abrupt turn in the action. Often a complication triggers the subplot. The major contributions complications make to the plot are surprise and story extension.

Think about *Witness*. What kinds of complications do we find? Book's gunfight with McFee represents an obstacle to the protagonist; his gunshot wound, however, is a complication. Out of the gunfight grows Book's new plan: to save Rachel and Samuel by getting them away. But his wound worsens and he faints as he drives off, crashing his car into the birdhouse. The wound complicates Book's plan and goal, but the fact that he's wounded also creates a problem for the Amish. They want to take him to the doctor, but Book has communicated the danger of such a move to Rachel and she argues to let him stay and recover.

This complication leads directly into the subplot. Book's recovery on the farm causes a closer association with Rachel. As a result, his feelings for her grow and complicate his task. Rachel's feelings for him threaten her ties to her community.

Previously, we defined as an obstacle Book's handing over of his gun to Rachel. (The gun is an obstacle to his fitting in on the Lapp farm. Book makes a moral choice—to give it to Rachel and leave himself unarmed—and by doing so he overcomes what the gun represents to the Amish and part of what stands between him and them.) But giving up the gun is also a complication in the truest sense, paying off later when he is unarmed and the antagonists arrive.

Another example of a complication growing out of Book's inner obstacles is illustrated in his inability to transform his violent nature. After learning that his partner Carter has been murdered, Book cannot contain his emotions. When confronted by the local punks who harass Daniel Hochleitner, Book violently punches one man as much for the man's disrespect to Daniel as to express his own rage at what has happened to Carter. This action leads to Schaeffer and McFee finding him.

Unless it is the antagonist who recurs, obstacles usually arise once and are immediate impediments to the hero's story objective. Complications undulate through a story, arising at different points to engage the hero—sometimes leading to an obstacle to overcome and other times as a lingering character or circumstance which must be dealt with in some way, deepening our understanding of the hero.

The Subplot

A subplot is a secondary story line which supports the main story, usually by adding dimension to the protagonist and antagonist and/or by filling in details important to the plot. In great films, the secondary line of action is often the personal story and it is often what audiences remember best. Again, think about *Witness*. What is most memorable about the film? For most people, it is the relationship between Book and Rachel, rather than the details of the police melodrama. Because the subplot in most great films carries the personal story, it is also a main carrier of the theme. In the relationships between the characters, the film's true meaning is portrayed.

For a subplot to be truly effective, it must be intricately related to the main plot. It can't be a tangent, which goes off on its own course, showing different aspects of the protagonist's life but having no bearing on the main plot. It must be built around one or more of the major characters and dramatically impact the main plot at some point, usually in the second half of the film.

This is why a complication facing the hero in pursuit of his goal is often used as the starting point of a subplot. A good subplot presents a problem to the protagonist and other characters and creates initial tension: Can the characters solve or deal with the problem or not? But since the main objective of the subplot is generally to flesh out the protagonist and secondary characters by showing how they handle the problem and how their relationships develop (thus filling out the theme), their immediate problem (of relationship) is generally solved early enough to make them allies for the second half of the film. Even so, more problems may threaten their alliance in the subplot as the film moves on.

Again, in *Witness*, Book's near-fatal wound complicates not only his life, but Rachel's, Samuel's, Eli's and the rest of the Amish community's, too. The problem facing Rachel and Book is clear enough: If the Amish elders send Book to a doctor, the renegade police officers will find him, and Samuel, and kill them both. For her son's safety, Rachel prevails upon the elders to let Book stay at the Lapp farm. Now Rachel has to hope and pray that Book doesn't die, for if he does his death will create still more problems for her. The subplot begins in earnest which deals with their relationship and how their world views collide, meet and finally intersect.

Most subplots develop similarly to the main plot: There is a problem which must be dealt with by the characters involved in it. As this problem is dealt with, new developments occur. Strong subplots usually progress and intensify. Once the subplot impacts the main plot in the second half of the film, it is tied to that line of action and will resolve generally around the same time the main plot resolves.

In *Witness*, the subplot develops Book's relationship with Rachel on the Lapp farm as he recovers from his wound. During this time, their relationship encounters obstacles; these impediments are illustrated in various ways. Book's delirium, when he utters a wild string of profanity, shows how deep the division is between Rachel and him. The scene where Rachel catches him showing the gun to Samuel illustrates another conflict in their world views, but Book overcomes this obstacle by giving her the gun and bullets for safekeeping. Once he makes this sacrifice, the main obstacle to their relationship deepening is removed because his action tells us that he respects and has accepted, while he is in their house, the Amish way.

The subplot in *Witness* develops the relationship between Book and Rachel resulting from his presence on the farm. It raises the question, though subliminally at first, of what will happen between them? Through the course of specific scenes which show how they handle what stands between them, Book and Rachel's feelings for each other intensify. Toward the end of the subplot and movie, it becomes clear that Book intends to leave. At this point, Book and Rachel act upon their mutual feelings. But before anything else can happen, Schaeffer and McFee arrive, pushing the story to its conclusion.

Reversals

A reversal is one of the most important plot tools a screenwriter has at his disposal. Aristotle noted its significance in the *Poetics* and his definition still holds today. A reversal is "a change of the actions to their opposite." Generally, a reversal is when something good turns bad, or something bad changes to good. As a result, it spins off the plot into a new and often startling way. Because it's unexpected, a strong reversal surprises the audience; it helps keep them guessing about what will happen next as well as about the final outcome of the film.

Since a reversal changes the direction of the action, the protagonist cannot go ahead as he planned; instead, he must deal with the situation created by the reversal. Sometimes a reversal causes a setback. Other times, it is a revelation of unexpected facts involving the characters or story action. Whatever it is, a reversal almost always leads to new and unexpected developments (obstacles, complications or support) which the protagonist must deal with in order to move forward.

In *Witness*, we see an expert use of the reversal. After Samuel identifies McFee as the killer, Book goes to his superior, Schaeffer, with the information. Remember, Schaeffer tells Book not to say anything for the time being. Book's expectation, and the audience's, is that his job will now be to apprehend McFee. But in a twist, Book is set up by Schaeffer, resulting in McFee trying to kill him in the garage. Book manages to escape death, but now he knows he's in trouble and must flee. The reversal here destroys our expectation that the film will be about Book apprehending the bad cop. Instead, the reversal turns the film in a new and unexpected direction.

A reversal is a strong tool for two reasons. First, it inevitably demands a response from the protagonist. His reaction pushes the plot forward, often accelerating the momentum. And second, a good reversal leads to greater audience involvement because a it surprises viewers. Any bias they may have formed about the direction of the film becomes irrelevant after the reversal. Now they must pay close attention to what's happening on screen in order understand how the pieces fit together. Audiences are always, to some degree, anticipating a film's plot. Consciously or unconsciously, they try to make sense out of the events transpiring before them. When a film is predictable, it is unsatisfying. The use of one or two well-placed reversals within the structure of a film can help keep the audience on its collective toes, and staying with the film all the way through to its surprising finish.

Revelation

Another important tool is the revelation. Aristotle noted its importance in the *Poetics*, although he called it the "recognition of a hidden truth." Revelation means something revealed or exposed, especially a striking disclosure, of something not previously known or realized. In great films, and all great fiction, there is a moment when information important to understanding the story cannot be concealed or withheld from the characters or the audience any longer. This information often comes as a shock but it always makes sense. Often, it sheds light on one of the main characters and explains what's going on in the story, relative to motivations and/or back story. Sometimes, it is a sudden realization or epiphany the protagonist has about his life as a result of the events experienced in the film. Sometimes, it is a realization or insight the audience has about the protagonist of which he remains ignorant.

In film and theater, this is the "revelatory scene," or the moment when the writer chooses to let the audience in on the secret motivation behind the characters and the story. The revelatory scene is a scene or group of scenes during which the truth is finally let out or forced into the open and the characters, especially the protagonist, must cope with it. Now, we, the audience, understand why actions were taken despite the risks and we realize what the film is really about.

Story revelation is most often character revelation. It takes place generally in the second half of the work and is more powerful when linked with another element, like a reversal or crisis, climax or resolution. The main revelation usually occurs near the climax of the second act, although it can come as early as the end of the first act. *Witness* has a shocking revelation at the end of the first act when Book discovers that Schaeffer is part of the murder he is investigating. Many action films or thrillers employ this technique of using an early reversal to jump-start the plot and get things moving. Wherever it comes, a revelation tends to act as a catalyst and propel the plot into the next portion of the film.

A strong revelation always has consequences, frequently drastic. Sometimes the startling information causes the protagonist to doubt himself before he finds the strength to recommit to the goal and story. Or the recognition of an overpowering truth confirms the protagonist's struggle, sending him and the film rushing toward its conclusion. Seeing these responses dramatized allows the audience to glimpse the protagonist's true character.

A revelation aids in creating suspense and offers entertainment by giving crucial but unexpected answers to the characters and the audience. Revelations are most powerful when they are simple but surprising.

New information is best revealed in action and through conflict. Revelation, too, is best when actions dramatize it or conflict forces it out into the open and not when given in expository speeches or flashbacks. A flashback must be essential to the whole structure and not just a means of exposition. If it is only in the film to visually tell something but does not utilize conflict or action, it stalls the forward momentum of the story.

The same is true regarding an expository speech. If the protagonist has changed or realized something important, that change must be dramatic. A character who says, "And then I realized ..." will be dull. If the realization is a true revelation for the character, it will be important to him and there will be emotion surrounding it. A good writer finds action to dramatize the change and emotion to lend drama to it.

The revelatory moment or scene is an important element of the overall structure of a successful film. Revelation confers meaning to the characters and the story, going back to what the story is really about.

Crisis

In drama, a crisis occurs whenever one of the main characters confronts an obstacle; it is an incident or event in the plot showing the active conflict that results from meeting the specific obstacle. Generally, a crisis shows the protagonist taking an action while another character tries to obstruct that action, though a crisis is not limited to the protagonist. Other major characters may experience crises during the time span of the film. The action may be an attempt to reach an objective or capture a stake, but because of the obstacle the character cannot achieve his goal, for the moment. During the time span of the crisis, the outcome is uncertain. Since the final resolution remains undetermined until the climax, crises naturally arouse suspense.

This meeting of opposing forces generates conflict, and conflict is what keeps the audience engaged in the film. If there are too few crises for the main characters to cope with, the plot loses momentum and the audience loses interest. A crisis involves some combination of physical, verbal, emotional and intellectual activity on the part of one or more of the characters. A crisis can be a physical fight, a verbal argument or an introspective search, depending upon what kind of obstacle the character faces.

A well-conceived crisis forces decisions upon the characters, who must decide how to meet the obstacle, i.e., whether to fight or run, and so on. When properly structured, a crisis always produces dramatic action as well as forces a turn in the plot. In a great film, the crises build, and in this momentum, the action and intensity escalate toward the main climax.

Witness has a wide variety of crises for all the important characters to face. How many crisis scenes can you identify?

Think about the first scene of violent conflict where Samuel is in the train station men's room. Because he is in a stall during the murder, he winds up in danger from the antagonist, McFee. McFee is Samuel's obstacle to staying alive. By scurrying under the wall into the next stall, he maneuvers around the obstacle and remains undiscovered.

The next crisis belongs to Rachel. She wants to continue with Samuel to her sister's home in Baltimore, but Book prevents them. Book is Rachel's obstacle to seeing her sister. Although she does not physically fight him, she verbally spars with him; her attitude also shows she has met an obstacle she cannot get around.

The next big crisis arises when McFee attacks Book in the garage. The protagonist and antagonist are in active conflict. McFee wounds Book but doesn't kill him. Book is able to bundle off Rachel and Samuel and direct Carter to destroy Book's paperwork to cover up their trail. His wound causes him to pass out just after he leaves Rachel and Samuel at the Lapp farm, but before he can flee. This forces another crisis, this time for Rachel. She realizes what Book has done (he has saved Samuel's life). If she allows the Amish elders to take Book to the hospital, Schaeffer and McFee will be alerted to their whereabouts and her son will be endangered. She convinces the elders to let Book stay on the Lapp farm. This turns the action in a new direction and raises the stakes for all concerned.

Witness, like most great films, is chock-full of crises for all of the main characters, some forceful, others muted. This variety creates a multilayered conflict because it utilizes the four types of obstacles described above: the antagonist, physical obstructions, inner emotional problems and moral codes. As characters from separate walks of life collide, conflict arises and produces crises for all to face until the main story problem is solved.

Climax

In today's screenwriting lexicon, "climax" is often used to refer to the main climax of a film, the moment when the central conflict is finally settled. But in truth, climaxes occur throughout a film but now we call the most important ones "turning" (or plot) points. A climax always follows a crisis, for in it a conflict (just not the main conflict) is in some way settled.

Let's look at *Witness* and the scene where McFee attacks Book in the garage. The attack causes a dramatic crisis for Book. His life is in danger. Book meets McFee (an obstacle), causing a scene of active conflict for the two foes. Book defends himself and McFee flees, unable to accomplish his mission. McFee's flight climaxes the crisis he started for Book. The present conflict is settled, for the moment. It's followed by Book realizing that he's wounded and realizing Schaeffer's involvement. This pushes the action in a new direction and defines the main conflict for the rest of the film.

A climax is an intense moment when a conflict is settled. It is strongest when the characters discover or realize something important to the overall story. Often, a climax acts as a reversal, changing the direction of the plot and/or the audience's expectations, hence Linda Seger's name "turning point" (see: *Making a Good Script Great*). A climax can be major or minor in impact, depending upon the type of crisis it follows; it can be a full scene or a moment in a scene, defined by a line of dialogue or silence; or it can play out over several scenes. A climax can settle the crisis in the protagonist's favor or go against him. In many films, the climax of a crisis in the second half of Act Two ends badly for the protagonist. For a moment, the hero looks beaten until a development occurs to push the hero into action once more.

Above, we commented upon Rachel's crisis facing the Amish elders over whether or not to take Book to the hospital. Once the elders allow Book to stay, the scene climaxes and that conflict is settled. A new conflict begins for Rachel as she tries to insure that Book will survive.

Most films have a minimum of three or four major climaxes in their structure before the final main climax, as well as a series of minor climaxes. We generally see them in the inciting incident and the last development of the beginning section (Act One) which taken together truly define what the film will be about. Then during the middle section (Act Two) we see one around the middle (midpoint) and near the end of this section. The final, main climax is the key point of the ending section (Act Three).

Climax Aftermath

Sometimes a climax is followed by an aftermath scene (or scenes), in which the result or response to the action is shown. This allows the character and audience to absorb the events. Act One of *Witness* climaxes when McFee tries to kill Book. Now we know what the true conflict of this film is. But in the aftermath, we follow Book as he races to escape with Rachel and Samuel and get them home, then passes out when he tries to drive away.

The End of Act Two

How do we know when Act Two is ending and Act Three is beginning? Above, we discussed the end of act one as "framing" the dramatic problem for the protagonist in such a way as to lead to new developments, to story progression and to an escalation of the conflict which flesh out the middle and define the theme. Almost the opposite happens at the end of Act Two. In most great films, the focus is once more on the protagonist's dramatic problem (the story goal), but this time, instead of leading away from the main conflict (at least momentarily in the new developments the protagonist encounters and the subplots which begin), the focus points directly to the inevitable confrontation which must take place between protagonist and antagonist (escalation of the conflict). This is what resolves the film and is the point of the last section.

As Act Two ends, the plot construction takes up the major threads of the central conflict (the protagonist's problem) and dramatically sends the line of action hurtling toward the final climax and solution. If there is an important subplot, it has impacted the main plot by this point so that the two story lines have merged into one. Even though there is one main plot line, a couple of scenes may still be necessary to close Act Two and set up Act Three.

Can we find in *Witness* a clear ending of Act Two and a beginning of Act Three? Let's look.

In the middle section, Book has several problems. Besides recovering from his near-fatal wound, he must cope with being framed for the murder of the undercover policeman (at the inciting incident). As the film shows what happens to him while he recovers in Rachel's care, it also tracks the police story line. Throughout the second act, the film shows Book contacting his partner Carter for help; it also shows Schaeffer and McFee trying to locate Book. Carter stands by his partner but Schaeffer and McFee increase the pressure on him. In a very strong scene, Book learns that Carter has been killed. Stunned, Book calls Schaeffer and tells him directly he's coming after him. Then, unable to suppress his emotions, Book reacts violently to the local punk who is harassing Daniel Hochleitner. The Amish restrain Book but the damage is done. In the aftermath, a local busybody informs a policeman about the incident, including information on who Book is staying with. We assume this information is passed onto Schaeffer because earlier we have seen him in contact with the local police trying to find Book.

Book returns to the Lapp farm, now resolved to leave. We learn of his decision through Rachel's eyes. First, she sees Samuel playing with a handmade wooden toy, a special present from Book. Then she sees Book and Eli working on the birdhouse. When Eli enters the kitchen, she asks him if Book is leaving. Eli tells her Book will go in the morning. Upset, she leaves her cap on the kitchen counter and goes to Book. In the fading light, they give expression to their desire for each other.

With these scenes, we see and infer information which climaxes the two important lines of the plot: Book is now focused on a course of action; and, Schaeffer and McFee, we can infer, are set to react. The Book/Rachel story line finally climaxes when they act on their feelings for each other; however, the first to take action are Schaeffer and McFee.

ACT THREE—THE SOLUTION

The purpose of the ending is to resolve the conflict by solving the story problem and to confirm the theme of the film. To do this, the focal points of Act Three (the final crisis, main climax and resolution) are introduced.

The third act takes off and builds on the scenes which end the second act: A development or result from the previous crisis at the end of Act Two creates a situation which now sets in motion a line of action leading directly to the final crisis and main climax. Above, the term "crisis" was discussed in detail. There is little to add here. In the final crisis, the main combatants involved in the film are locked in a conflict which must lead to the main climax.

The Main Climax

In a film, the moment when the final crisis reaches the greatest intensity and resolves the conflict is the main climax. It is the decisive point of the plot and the most meaningful in relationship to the conflict and theme. Here, not only should the problem be solved but the premise or theme must be clarified.

Synthesis between action and theme is best shown in the climax of the film. The climax makes the theme concrete in terms of an event. By focusing the action of the film upon a definite goal, which ends at this event, an integrated movement is created. In this way, the climax becomes a reference point to test the validity of every element of the structure. If a scene is not developing or leading up to this conclusion, it needs to be reconsidered and reworked or thrown away.

The climax is the key to dramatic unity. It determines the worth and meaning of everything which has preceded it—the decisions, actions, obstacles, complications, crises. If the climax lacks power and inevitability, the theme or premise has not dictated the progression of the conflict toward it as the goal. Somewhere, the meaning has become obscured to the writer. In the climax, the writer drives home the point of the story. Simply put, in the climax, *who* succeeds and *why* determine the ultimate meaning of the work.

The climax is not necessarily the final scene, but it is the one in which the conflict reaches its final stage. Though it is discussed as a point in the action, it is not limited to a single scene. Depending upon the story, the climax may be very sudden and abrupt or it could be a complex event combining many lines of action over several scenes.

In film, the climax must be visual and visceral, not internal. Though it does not have to end in screams, shoot-outs or car chases, an ending that incorporates strong actions is more powerful and memorable than one which is restricted or confined. In great films, the protagonist's emotional response to the end of the conflict is often included in the climax. Showing the emotional response keeps the drama in human terms and makes it more understandable and satisfying to the audience.

Let's look at *Witness*.

Act Three begins at dawn with Schaeffer, McFee and Fergie (Angus MacInnes), guns in hand, walking down the road to the Lapp farm. From this moment on, we know we are into the final confrontation, although it is staged in several different crises for the various characters involved. First, Schaeffer discovers Rachel in the kitchen and says he won't hurt her boy but wants to know where Book is. She is too frightened to tell him anything. Eli comes out of the barn, spots McFee and Schaeffer. He turns toward the barn and shouts to Book as McFee strikes him.

Book, warned, now sees McFee and Eli. He turns with Samuel and runs, sending the boy to the Hochleitner farm for help while he tries to figure a way to save Rachel, Eli and himself. McFee and Fergie split up, each taking a different level of the barn as they search for Book. Fergie sees Book, gets off a shot, then follows him through a trap door to the lower level. An open door to the silo shaft catches Fergie's attention. He goes in and Book gets the drop on him. Book throws a lever and grain rushes down in a golden shower, knocking Fergie off his feet. Fergie suffocates in the grain but not before firing a couple of shotgun blasts.

Fergie's shots alert both McFee and Schaeffer. McFee follows the sounds and rising dust and calls Schaeffer. Schaeffer leaves Rachel and Eli in the kitchen to try and see what's happening in the barn. At this moment, Samuel appears in the spring room, just off the kitchen; he returned to the house without making it all the way to the Hochleitners. Schaeffer, without seeing Samuel, orders Rachel and Eli outside but before Eli goes, he motions for Samuel to ring the farm bell.

Outside, Schaeffer herds his hostages toward the barn while inside the kitchen, Samuel approaches the bell rope. Meanwhile, in the barn, Book works his way back to the silo to get Fergie's shotgun before McFee kills him. Book is able to break into the silo and get the shotgun in time to shoot and stop McFee. Now the bell starts ringing.

This is all very climactic but the conflict is not over. Book and Schaeffer have yet to resolve their dramatic problem. The theme seems to hold with violence winning out over nonviolence. But let's go on.

Schaeffer sends Eli to stop Samuel and, holding his revolver to Rachel's head, tells Book to put his gun down. Schaeffer takes Book prisoner but from across the fields, running, answering the Amish call for help, come the members of the Amish community, the Hochleitners, the Stoltzfus family and others. Thirty or so men, a few women and children, all approach the Lapp farm and come face-to-face with Schaeffer, Book and the others.

Now the final climax comes. Schaeffer tries to take Book away. He explains he is a police officer and that Book is wanted for murder. Here, the lines are clearly drawn: a violent man ready to use more violence, opposed to a group of unarmed farmers.

Book has had enough and whirls away, asking if Schaeffer is going to kill them all? Schaeffer is forced to put the gun down, defeated. The climax is complete; the main conflict is over. This is where the main story has been heading since Book escaped Philadelphia with Rachel and Samuel. The Amish culture has played a part in the end of the film. The final conflict is solved by nonviolent means.

By the climax returning to the clash between the two worlds, it focuses the film's theme on this opposition. As we look back over the scenes, we see the film has really used the contrast between these two societies to examine the place of violent confrontation within our culture. Though the film validates nonviolence by having the Amish succeed over the violent, bad men at the climax, it does not totally reject the use of violent force. This climax was only made possible by Book killing Fergie and McFee, allowing enough time for Samuel to ring the bell and call for help. These scenes provide a strong finish to the film. The characters' emotions, attitudes and actions force the conflict to culminate. The theme is finally spelled out through the conflict, though it's been hinted at all along. Looking back, every scene contributes to the inevitability of the ending. Thus, the climax feels satisfying.

The Resolution

After the climax comes the resolution, or the falling action. It is called the falling action because the tension decreases as a result of the struggle culminating at the high point of the climax. This final part of the structure realigns the parameters of the film's world as a result of the climax, fixing the fates of the main characters involved in the struggle, especially those the audience is most interested in. The certainty of the climax results in a specific set of circumstances. Because the hero wins or loses, reaches his goal or doesn't, all the other characters are affected. Often, in the best films, the resolution bestows one last insight into the story which helps define even further the theme declared in the climax.

The final crisis in a great film generally brings together the major characters. The climax then closes all meaningful involvements (fixes the fates) of these characters, as far as the film is concerned. The resolution simply shows the resultant situation.

The resolution in *Witness* plays out quickly. With the arrest of Schaeffer, Book accomplishes his goal. All that's left to resolve is his relationship with Rachel. First, he says good-bye to Samuel; we hear Book acknowledge what Samuel already knows—he's leaving and not ever coming back. The two embrace, acknowledging Book's bond with the boy. Then, Book goes to see Rachel. The scene plays with the screen door closed between them, showing there is still a wall between their worlds. Book cannot stay on the Amish farm, because violent force is too inherent a part of his identity. Both Rachel and he know this. They say nothing to each other but their expressions tell us how hard their parting is for them.

Book heads for his car to leave. But before he goes, Eli hollers after him. "You be careful out among them English!" he says. And in this line, Eli also acknowledges the connection these two men have made. As Book drives off, he passes Daniel Hochleitner walking down the road toward Rachel's house, indicating that Daniel will take up where he started, courting Rachel.

This short but powerful sequence deals with all the major characters and shows that order has been reestablished on the farm. Book is going, Rachel will stay and Daniel will reaffirm his interest in her. Life will get back to normal. The resolution provides a truly untraditional Hollywood ending to the film for it says, "Love cannot solve everything." Love cannot bridge the gap between Book's and Rachel's two worlds. The resolution underlines the difference between the two societies, reinforcing the theme stated in the climax.

SPECIAL NOTES

Every screenplay that becomes a film goes through many revisions in the process of being realized. *Witness* is no exception In 1985, this film went on to win Academy Awards for Best

Screenplay and Best Editing. These two awards recognized the structure of the story as well as the beauty of its telling. But they are even more closely linked. The film *Witness* is a wonderful example of how a good screenplay is made even better through the contributions of all the talent, especially the film editors.

I add these final notes based on comparing a late version of the screenplay, including revisions through June 15, 1984, to the final film. For more information on the evolution of this great movie, see Chapter Eleven in Linda Seger's excellent book, *Making a Good Script Great*.

The June 15th draft (102 pages) includes nearly everything we see in the film, and more. Many of the scenes are fuller, longer, providing more detail to the story, back story and relationships between the characters. In the film, however, many of these scenes are trimmed so that they are, in fact, reduced to their essence. Lead-ins to important exposition contained in scenes are often cut or trimmed so that the thread of the main story stays in the forefront of our attention. For example, it takes nearly 40 pages of screenplay to get to McFee's attack on Book in the parking garage; in the film, the attack comes at the 27-minute mark. Almost twelve pages have been cut (one page of screenplay is generally considered to correspond to one minute of film).

The screenplay also includes several scenes involving and contrasting Rachel with Book's sister Elaine in the first act. These scenes, while interesting and well-written, were cut because they did not further the main story. Likewise, an early scene introducing Schaeffer with Book outside the train station just after the murder investigation gets underway is cut. Even though the scene foreshadows Schaeffer's involvement and provides a little exposition regarding what the murder was about, it slows Book's investigation. As the movie shows, it's enough for the audience to know that an undercover cop has been murdered; they don't need the added explanation in order to understand what is going on at this point. The audience has enough information to follow the story.

As a result of these cuts in the film, the movie stays focused on the plot problem facing the lead characters, revealing these people within the context of the conflict. This keeps the tension up, along with our interest. By cutting the scenes which have little bearing on the initial plot problem, the dramatic momentum picks up. The changes in the second act also keep the momentum moving, pulling us into a story which ultimately contrasts the two different cultures.

In Act Two, several scenes bearing heavily on the main plot (which show Schaeffer and McFee trying to find Book) are moved up, partially as a result of the 12 pages cut from the opening 40, but also because of structural considerations. In the screenplay, the scene where Schaeffer comes to Elaine's house and tries to intimidate her into revealing Book's whereabouts, comes on page 57; in the film, it comes at 31 minutes into the story, moved up by 26 minutes. In the screenplay, this scene comes after Schaeffer calls the Lancaster Sheriff's office; in the film, it is more forceful because it is Schaeffer's first response to the problem Book has presented him. The scene between Schaeffer and the Undersheriff of Lancaster County, which starts in the screenplay on page 51, plays better as a second response. Shortened and more direct in the film, it starts 12 minutes sooner, at 39 minutes. The scene where Schaeffer interviews Carter in the screenplay is on page 74; in the film it starts at minute 62.

These film scenes are almost identical to what is on the page, though sometimes shorter. Because they are moved up in the film, they increase the tension, as well as strengthen and tighten the plot structure. The reordering and moving up of the scenes keep the focus of the film on the conflict between Book and Schaeffer even as it explores and contrasts Amish culture with American society.

Another big change involves how Carter's murder is handled. In the screenplay, the actual murder is shown, intercut with the barn building sequence. The film keeps the barn building sequence intact and the murder offscreen. The emphasis stays on the Amish culture, how the people help each other, work together. Playing Carter's murder offscreen produces a surprise for the protagonist and audience and creates a new crisis for Book, shown when he learns of the news and in how he reacts to it.

3

FIVE KEY FOCAL POINTS

Study Film: *Risky Business*

The last chapter laid the groundwork for understanding screen-play structure by defining the materials and tools and by illustrating how they are used in a great film. In this chapter, we expand our view of structure by examining how film segments are designed and by looking at the primary movements of each act.

SCREENPLAY MODELS

On paper, a very basic model of screenplay structure often looks like this:

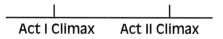

This model denotes a three-act structure, but it gives the idea that there are only two main supports holding up the entire screenplay.

If we add the inciting incident and the Act Three climax, the diagram takes on a little more dimension:

Inciting   Act III
Incident   Climax

Act I Climax   Act II Climax

This model shows us that there are at least four important points in the construction of a film story.

Study the diagram for a moment. Although there seems to be a certain symmetry to it, the middle is much longer than the first and last segments. The middle, generally the longest act in any film, is often the most unwieldy in a screenplay due to its length. Many films as well lose momentum or even fall apart in this section because the various lines of action tracked in the second act may not be sufficiently organized around the dramatic problem motivating the protagonist and pushing the plot. The result is a lack of focus and a muddled middle.

Great films have a point in the middle which orients the structure of the plot in this section and helps support the whole film. We call this the midpoint. If we add it to our diagram, the model looks like this:

```
     Inciting                          Act III
     Incident         Midpoint         Climax
       |  |              |              |    |
     _____
       Act I Climax      Act II Climax
```

The Midpoint

If we compare this new diagram with the ones above, we see it is more complex. It tells us that there are at least five key focal points which support the structure of a film. A midpoint links the action of the plot in the first half of Act Two (and the first half of the film) to the second half of Act Two (and the last half of the film). It is an incident or episode in the plot which culminates a line of action on one hand and, on the other hand, pushes the plot forward toward the second act climax.

An effective midpoint is one that is active and dramatic, either solving a problem or crisis, or creating more of them. The midpoint often takes us to a surprise, reversal, discovery or new complication, at the same time strengthening the relationship between the first half of the second act and the last half. It does not have to come exactly at the halfway mark in a film, but it generally occurs somewhere in the middle.

Look at *Witness*. Can you find a point near the middle which links the first half of Act Two to the second half? The first half of Act Two deals with the result of John Book's wound and his initial recovery as it affects Rachel and her family. The second half of Act Two shows how Book's recovery on the Lapp farm affects him, his growing relationship with Rachel and his inability to do anything about Schaeffer and the crooked cops. A strong midpoint for this story might deal with one of two lines of action. If the emphasis of *Witness* was on the melodramatic crime angle, then the midpoint would have something to do with that story line. However, *Witness*'s emphasis is on the contrast between two cultures—one violent, the other nonviolent—and how these worlds cannot meet. The midpoint should have something to do with this story line. Can you think what it might be?

Approximately 52 minutes into *Witness* (the film is one hour 42 minutes), Book gives Rachel his gun and bullets for safekeeping. This scene is the midpoint. Because the gun represents Book's violent nature and culture, this action initially solves what separates him from Rachel; it is a turning point in their relationship. He symbolically gives up his violence, at least while he's in Rachel's house. Giving the gun to Rachel paves the way for their relationship to develop and deepen in the second half of the film and so it intensifies his crisis when she is taken prisoner by Schaeffer. The audience too experiences this heightened intensity because through Book and Rachel's relationship viewers become more deeply involved with the characters and the story.

THE STRUCTURE OF FILM SEGMENTS

The importance of the five focal points underlying film structure can best be understood in terms of plot construction. In great films, we find a strong causal (cause and effect) relationship between inciting incident, first act climax, midpoint, second act climax and final climax. The thrust of the plot appears at the inciting incident, causing the protagonist to act in response to some force. This response pushes the protagonist on toward the end of the first act, where his problem or conflict for the film is more fully defined and the set-up is completed. Once this main conflict is established, the protagonist acts again in response to the new and greater problem, encountering opposition and dealing with these setbacks through the course of the film. The thrust of the first half of Act Two takes the film up to its midpoint. Whatever happens at the midpoint provides the drive to push the plot to the Act Two climax, which pushes the plot to its conclusion. These focal points upon which the plot line hinges are the events and incidents most dramatically relevant to the story. The scenes in between build and develop the plot to these points.

If the thrust of the plot at the inciting incident is pointed solely at the final climax and not toward the end of the first act, a film loses dimension and depth as well as momentum. As we saw in the last chapter, the set-up of a film needs to lead to three things: Developments, story progression and an escalation of the conflict. And these generally take more than one incident to establish. An inciting incident alone does not have sufficient intensity and force to drive a film from this point all the way to its conclusion. A look at films like *City Hall* illustrates the difficulty of maintaining interest in a story when a plot problem never truly evolves past what is set up in the inciting incident, or does so only very late in the game.

Great films effectively manage information by breaking down the plot—the story's sequence of events—into segments. There are at least five segments of varying lengths, but often as many as nine, depending on how long a film is. These segments focus the line of action for the viewer so that he can see a progression in the plot as the story develops and the conflict escalates. There is a strong cause and effect relationship between them; one is built upon the one preceding and leads directly to the one following. Each segment has a specific bearing on the main plot of the film. Even if the segment seems to veer off in a different direction and picks up a subplot or focuses on characterization, its meaning will become apparent by the end of a great film.

In many films, we find that the first act is made up of two important segments, from opening to inciting incident and from inciting incident to Act One climax. Act Two becomes a little more complex. The first half of Act Two, taking us up to the midpoint, can be made up of two or even three segments. The same is true of the second half of Act Two: the segment from midpoint to second act climax can be constructed of two or three distinct segments. Act three might have one or two segments which lead to the climax and resolution. It all depends upon the film.

A segment is not to be confused with a scene sequence, which is a group of scenes linked around a single idea or action, becoming a mini-plot line within a movie. Scene sequences play a major role in the construction of a film segment, however, since they keep the plot focused on the action—on what's happening—as the characters work to achieve their goals. In the second half of a film, scene sequences tend to make up larger and larger portions of each segment, until, in many films, the entire third act is one long scene sequence that builds to the climax. (See Chapter Eleven.)

Structuring a plot into segments of film time strengthens the causal relationship between the scenes in a movie, and therefore a film's momentum. It helps the audience stay focused on the action pushing the plot ahead even as the story tracks the characters' emotions, motivations and reactions to what they encounter in the story. Audiences understand stories in terms of cause and effect: this happened and so that happened. Segments help the audience better follow a story by keeping the cause and effect relationships clear.

A segment has a specific focus or objective; generally to move the characters in one direction or another with regard to the overall plot goal and the theme of the film. To understand the purpose of each segment, one must first grasp the broader overall story movements that the plot rests on.

The Primary Movements of the Acts

Each act of a great film has its own movement and purpose; We can see these clearly in the overview of their plots. The movements are generally very simple and can be easily stated. If we look at *Witness*, we can understand the movements like this: The purpose of Act One is to set the characters and scene, then move John Book from a cop chasing bad guys to a cop being chased by bad guys. Act Two continues to track the crime story (showing Book being pursued by the bad guys), but the real movement is in the relationship between Book and Rachel. The purpose of this act, then, is to show how these two people from different worlds find a way to come together. The last movement, Act Three's, is the confrontation between good and bad guys, which then leads to the resolution between Book and Rachel.

In many great films, when we reduce the plot to its simplest movements, we see thematic issues rising to the foreground and dominating one of the various acts. The core humanity of the story is often the reason why a film rises to a new level. Thematic issues play a key role in the design of the plot. The theme is illustrated in the plotting of the film's action and is not relegated to speeches characters make; it is dramatized, acted out, in the interrelationships between the characters.

It sometimes takes several drafts for a writer to distill enough of the story to see the ideas of the plot in simplified terms. It doesn't matter how long it takes a writer to see the broad movements. But once a writer becomes aware of them, he must make use of them consciously to reinforce the structure of the screenplay. If he doesn't, he can only hope that the director does.

Risky Business

Risky Business, written and directed by Paul Brickman and produced by Jon Avnet and Steve Tisch, was released in 1983 and made a star of Tom Cruise. Essentially, the 94-minute film is the story of a high school senior's coming of age. But Mr. Brickman's use of his backdrop, a materially oriented society, elevates the film above many similarly told tales.

If you haven't already viewed *Risky Business*, now is the time to do it. Then let's see if its overall structure supports the concepts of midpoints and structured film segments, and examine whether or not there are broader, primary movements directing the construction of the plot.

ACT ONE—THE SET-UP

The opening of *Risky Business* sets up a film which deals with the coming of age of a young man, Joel (Tom Cruise). The opening dream sequence establishes the tone and style of the film, that narration will be used and that Joel is anxious about his future (he's afraid of screwing up his whole life).

The Main Exposition

The last chapter defined the main exposition as the initial information the audience needs to understand the story and how it develops. It is the foundation upon which everything else is built. In *Risky Business*, what are the antecedents we have to know to understand the story which follows?

Besides establishing Joel's character as sexually inexperienced and anxious about screwing up his future, we need to know that his parents (Nicholas Pryor and Janet Carroll), are leaving town for a week and he will have the house to himself. This one action is the basis of the entire story. Joel also has a friend, Miles (Curtis Armstrong), a Harvard-bound high school student, who expresses the idea that Joel needs to loosen up and take a chance. Taking chances, says Miles, leads to opportunities. Last, but just as important, is the set-up of Joel's school project for the Future Enterprisers, which provides the forum the screenwriter needs to explore his ideas on society and capitalism.

All this is put into motion right up front, in the opening ten minutes of film. Six minutes in, Joel's parents are heading out of town, leaving him with a bundle of responsibilities and a list of things not to do. He is not to play with his father's stereo or drive the Porsche. Already, tension is mounting. As soon as the audience hears these restrictions placed on Joel, they start anticipating whether or not he will listen. The film answers this question in the scenes immediately after he drops his parents at the airport by showing Joel doing things his way: he drinks scotch with dinner, sets his father's stereo system his way, takes his father's Porsche out for a spin. Joel breaks the rules.

The Inciting Incident and Act One Climax

If we had to identify the point where the story and plot for *Risky Business* engage, what would we look for? We'd look for the first hint of the problem Joel faces in connection with the main conflict. And what is the main conflict of the film? It involves Joel returning his house to the way it was before his parents left, i.e., retrieving the Steuben Egg from Lana (Rebecca De Mornay), and, at the end, getting all the furniture back from Guido (Joe Pantoliano).

If the main conflict involves Lana and Guido, can we find the point when the plot clearly begins moving toward this end?

The action which sets the plot on its course originates with Joel's friend Miles, who calls the hooker. It is a specific action. Miles calls the hooker at 16 minutes into the movie, then leaves. Once the hooker is called and Joel can't stop her from coming, the film is off and running and is narrowing its sites on its true plot line. The events seem to be telling us this film is going to be about a guy losing his virginity (will Joel or won't Joel get laid?). But Miles' calling the hooker is only one important factor affecting the whole set-up of the film. Let's look at what follows.

Left alone to deal with hooker, Joel panics. He doesn't want to let her in, especially since she looks suspiciously like a he. But Joel has to deal with the transvestite Jackie (Bruce A. Young) and does so with respect by giving her/him $75 to cover the time and car fare. Jackie knows what Joel wants and gives him Lana's number. This new development occurs at minute 20.

Now the question is, what will Joel do with Lana's number? He vacillates, showers, reads the sex ads. He dozes dreaming of another sexual encounter which ends in disaster. But his hormones are raging so he calls Lana and makes a date. This is the result of the earlier development and it causes another, thus furthering the plot. Now Joel waits. The question set up when Miles called Jackie is answered 25 minutes into the movie, when Lana arrives to claim Joel's virginity.

The next development occurs the following morning. In the cold light of day, reality sets in. Joel must deal with the real Lana. She is a shrewd, high-priced call girl and he doesn't have the cash on hand to pay her. Joel solves this crisis by going to the bank and cashing a bond to pay her. His naiveté causes him to make his first mistake: he allows Lana to wait for him alone in his home. When he returns, 30 minutes into the film, Lana is gone and so is his mother's Steuben Egg (another crisis). Now Joel really has a problem.

We can see from this discussion that there are two segments which lead to the definition of Joel's problem for the film. The first, starting at the opening, sets Joel's character and takes him up to the point where, with parents gone, we see how he acts: Joel breaks the rules. This segment builds effectively because his parents place distinct limits upon him while Miles challenges him and it immediately sets up a question in the viewer's mind: Will Joel obey or not? The segment ends by answering this question, no.

But this plot line is not strong enough to drive a 94-minute film. Enter Miles, who sets the next segment in motion by calling the hooker. This action leads to the main conflict. However, if the film began with this segment, without laying the foundation for Joel's character and his parents' conditions, the film would lose a dimension, plus many of its complications, and the resolution of the conflict would suffer at the end. The beauty of the writing is in how it sets up questions in the viewers' minds which create tension and keep the audience guessing as to what will happen next.

The primary movement of the act is clear, too. It's about Joel losing his virginity, both literally and figuratively. Joel is about to be forced out of the womb of his upper middle-class existence and initiated into the real world—of sex, dollars and cents—to retrieve his mother's egg.

ACT TWO—THE CONFRONTATION

In the middle, the story tension escalates because the conflict set up in Act One is now clearly defined: we have the problem, the conflict that drives the plot. And the stakes for the film are established. In *Risky Business*, Lana takes the Steuben Egg and Joel must get it back. In *Witness*, the end of Act One defines Book's problem (Can he get the killers before they get him?).

The strong Act One climax poses a problem for the protagonist which requires the character to react and therefore take action. The plan of action begun by the character in Act Two turns the plot in a new direction. Once on this new path, the protagonist (in trying to solve his problem or reach his goal) meets more obstacles and complications which must be dealt with, not only to fill out the plot, but also to clarify the full meaning of the work. As characters implement plans, form relationships and make commitments, we come to understand who they are and what they stand for and these add to the meaning of the film.

Obstacles, Complications, Plans, Crises

Joel's problem, that Lana has taken his mother's prized possession, starts the story in earnest. Lana is the obstacle he faces to getting the egg back. What we thought was going to be a film about a guy losing his virginity turns out to be about what happens when an extremely naive guy loses his virginity with a shrewd young call girl who takes off with his mother's valuable egg.

The first segment of Act Two starts Joel's quest to find Lana and get the egg back. He has a plan. With Miles in tow, he heads for the Ritz Carlton where, according to Jackie, Lana hangs out. Sure enough, Lana is there. But Joel doesn't know what to do about it. This is as far as his plan goes. However, a new development occurs. Lana runs out of the hotel after Joel and Miles because she needs Joel to get her away from Guido, her pimp. Guido enters the scene at the film's 32-minute mark. He is the film's obvious antagonist; and, Lana owes him money. Joel manages to elude Guido in a car chase and rescue Lana.

This leads directly to the next segment, which starts the following morning at Joel's house. Joel wants his egg back and Lana needs a place to stay until she figures out what to do about Guido. Again, Lana is the obstacle to Joel achieving his goal, but now she creates a complication. Joel needs to get to school, but he has learned something from his previous dealings with Lana; he cannot trust her, even if he has slept with her once more. He doesn't want to let her stay in his house alone because he's afraid she'll take something again. A crisis ensues. Their stalemate is finally resolved (a climax) by Joel agreeing to let her stay for a couple of hours and Lana promising to return his mother's egg. He warns her, though, if anything else is missing, he'll call the police.

But while Joel is in school, worrying about what Lana is

doing, a complication develops: she cases his house, takes his father's Porsche and drives to the train station, returning with her girlfriend Vicki (Shera Danese) before Joel gets home from school (a new development). When Joel discovers that a class-mate has paid to sleep with Vicki in his house, he kicks the girls out.

In order for the story that writer/director Brickman wants to tell to work, however, Joel and Lana have to be united. But the union of inexperienced schoolboy and worldly-wise call girl has to be believable; they must be forced back together. This is achieved at the end of this segment, the midpoint for the film.

The Midpoint and Reversal

As the girls leave, Guido arrives (another development). Joel watches from his upstairs bedroom window as the confronta-tion on the driveway turns violent. With neighborhood children watching, Joel chivalrously defends the girls. Guido doesn't fight Joel but he does warn him. "In a sluggish economy," he says before leaving, "never, ever, fuck with another man's livelihood."

As a result of this encounter, Joel lets Lana and Vicki stay, for one night, with Lana again promising to get the egg back. This occurs at approximately 46 minutes into the film. The mid-point results in a strong reversal of the action and gets the film back on track. Just previous to the midpoint, Joel has kicked the girls out; after the midpoint, they are back in his house again.

From this point on, Lana has her own agenda for Joel. She wants to get their "friends" together, using Joel's house as the meeting place (or brothel), and make some real money. This be-comes the focus of the last half of the second act. The screenwriter's challenge now is figuring out how to orchestrate the action while believably uniting Lana and Joel in Lana's scheme.

The End of Act Two

Mr. Brickman brings Joel and Lana together by carefully design-ing the next segment to give Joel a reason to go along with Lana's plan. The segment starts off innocently enough: Lana invites Joel to come for ice cream with Vicki and her. This scene also introduces in more detail about Joel's free enterprise workshop and the underlying ideas about free market systems, something Lana truly believes in. The power Lana holds over Joel is clear: she's beautiful, smart and sexy. When we next pick them up, they are parked above Lake Michigan, stoned, eating ice cream and talking. When Joel and Lana talk alone on the pier, we get a look into her character. What she wants in the scene is to convince Joel to go along with her plan to bring their "friends" together. In the process, she reveals her background which helps make her sympathetic and contributes to the audience's understanding of her.

The overall orchestration of the scene has two halves. In the first half, Lana proposes her plan and Joel rejects it, although it's clear he hasn't taken her seriously (he's too stoned). The halves are split by a beat which shows Lana return to the Porsche for her purse. Not only does she accidentally knock the gearshift into neutral, she locks the car doors, too. The second half of the scene exposes Lana more directly when Joel asks questions about her life. This exposition is presented naturally; it's normal for Joel to be as interested in her answers as the audience is. But when she finally explodes, viewers are as stunned as Joel. Her anger seems to come out of the blue, but Lana's reaction is fueled by her own defenses: she's not happy about what she's doing but feels it's the only way she can survive.

She storms off, leaving Joel confused. But when he starts after her, moving away from the front of the Porsche, the car begins its slow roll toward the lake (complication). The scene is masterfully crafted, keeping the outcome in suspense until the last possible moment.

The segment doesn't end here but continues to pick up steam. The next scene shows Joel at the Porsche dealership and realizing the extent of the damage (another complication); then we pick him up at school, trying to convince the school nurse to give him an excused absence so he won't fail two midterms and wreck his grade point average. (Remember, Joel is afraid of screwing up his future.) His desperation causes him to cross a line with the nurse and; instead of an unexcused absence, he ends up with a two-week suspension (yet another complication). As his friends note, she has "trashed his whole record." With nothing left to lose and no other way to get the money he needs, Joel goes to Lana and commits to her plan—one hour into the film.

The Primary Movements of Act Two
Looking at the segments like this, we can see how each leads unavoidably to the next until finally Joel is motivated to go along

with Lana. But how would you characterize the primary movement of Act Two? If you are unsure, check the progress of Joel's character from the start of Act Two through to its end.

At the beginning of Act Two, Joel is still an innocent but the egg has been cracked; he has lost his virginity and gotten himself into a peck of trouble as a result. But he still thinks he's in command. In fact, through the midpoint, Joel thinks he has a handle on what's happening. He rescues Lana from Guido, not once, but twice. He's the all-American boy as hero—though still as sexual innocent, so not a whole man. But by the end of Act Two, Joel is so desperate for money, he's ready to partner with a prostitute and turn his parents' home into a brothel.

Joel is inexperienced, he doesn't understand the "real" world. (In fact, Joel is naively idealistic. Remember, early in Act One, Joel questions his social group's materialistic focus on making money. When asked what he wants to do with his life, he answers: "Serve my fellow mankind." He must make a joke out of his response to save face with his group, but clearly Joel is questioning the values of his group.) Guido warns him never to "fuck with another man's livelihood" in a "sluggish economy." But Joel doesn't listen. He doesn't know the rules of the world. Act Two destroys Joel's illusions about "real life"— or life outside the family cocoon. What he needs is experience. And this he gets, in spades, from his involvement with Lana, and, in turn, Guido.

ACT THREE—THE SOLUTION

The principal thrust of Act Three is always moving toward the final climax—the peak moment—and the resolution. Driven by the outcome of the second act, the line of action builds to the final crisis and climax where the main conflict is resolved and the theme is confirmed. The solution to Joel's problem which is laid out at the beginning of Act Three is getting his father's car repaired without his father finding out. He goes into business with Lana to accomplish this.

Act Three of *Risky Business* basically has two segments. The film slips into a new gear—changing both tone and style—as this segment starts at the beginning of his business venture with Lana (a development). Returning to narration, Joel explains the set-up while we see the action. Lana takes care of the organization ("production") by contacting girls, renting beds, setting up the house. The Steuben Egg is even returned to the mantle. Joel concentrates on sales by becoming the consummate salesman and selling the ultimate commodity—sex—to his male friends.

This segment continues into the night, showing what happens: the call girls come. The boys come. And Joel and Lana rake in the dough. The segment also contrasts Miles with Joel, showing that Miles is unable to bring himself to go inside and get laid. (While Miles can talk the talk, he can't walk the walk.) More significantly, Joel deals coolly and calmly with the arrival of the Princeton alumnus, Rutherford (Richard Masur), who has come to interview him (complication). Resigned to being rejected by the university, Joel relaxes, and in so doing comes off as self-assured, far better than the uptight high school senior we saw at the beginning of the film. Later, he even handles his parents' phone call, getting off the line before he further incriminates himself in their eyes. The segment comes to a close, after the party, with Joel and Lana heading out and making love on the train. Joel is a different person as a result of his encounter with Lana.

The Main Climax
The next segment begins at the Porsche dealership as Joel picks up the car. He carefully drives it home. When he enters the house, it takes him a minute to register that everything, including his mother's Steuben Egg, is gone. Here, the main climax begins. Guido pulls up with the moving truck overflowing with Joel's family belongings. At this moment, Joel's parents arrive at the airport. It costs Joel every cent left from the night to buy back his parents' property. He barely gets it all in place before his parents return. But Joel doesn't get off scot-free: His mother's Steuben Egg has been cracked—just like the warm cocoon of his upper middle-class existence. Joel is unable to avoid trouble entirely. He knows there is another side.

The Resolution
The film's resolution plays out over several short scenes. Joel gets into Princeton, making his father happy and learning a valuable lesson about how the world works. He even sees Lana once more and asks if she set him up with Guido to pay her ex-pimp back. At first, Lana doesn't answer, but finally she says no. We're not sure if Joel believes her. And we're not sure if it matters. The film returns to narration, flashes quick cuts of

the Future Enterprisers Competition, then ends with Joel's voice: "My name is Joel Goodsen. I deal in human fulfillment. I grossed over $8,000 in one night." He pauses, then continues sardonically, "Time of your life, eh, kid?"

SPECIAL NOTES

Paul Brickman's *Risky Business* was released in the summer of 1983 and captured the tenor of the changing times wrought by the Reagan era. The dark and satiric film was an immediate hit, launching Tom Cruise's career and making him a major star.

The fifth draft of the screenplay, dated June 8, 1982, contains a substantial number of still later revised pages, the latest dated July 2, 1982. And, almost everything in the screenplay is in the film. The screenplay had been trimmed and reworked while in pre-production and reflects these changes: it contains many "A" and "B" pages, as well as shots which have been omitted.

There are a number of changes from this draft of the screenplay to the film (some are small cuts while others reorganize entire sequences) and all definitely enhance the end product. Many of them are minor line edits or changes, further scene deletions or those which hone in on the heart of the scene (cutting the opening and ending lines, possibly while editing the film).

The first significant change involves the second dream sequence which starts on page 10 (shot 18), touching again upon Joel's anxiety. In the movie, this scene sequence is moved back and appears after Jackie leaves but before Joel decides to call Lana. In its original position, it halts the forward momentum of the film because it is too similar to the first dream sequence, in tone and theme, to come ten minutes into the film and so it feels redundant. The filmmakers instead cut to his parents leaving. This moves the story ahead more directly, establishes Mom and Dad and their rules and then gets them out of the way. The scenes detailing the parents' leaving show Joel's world and set up a good portion of his conflict. Playing the second dream sequence later, after Joel's hormones have been stirred up, reinforces the earlier anxiety and heightens the sense of his fear and desire.

The next important change involves the Princeton alumnus Rutherford. In the screenplay, Rutherford is put on the spot by Lana during Joel's interview. She challenges his ideas about who's smart enough to get into Princeton and who's not. The film, however, keeps the focus on Joel. Joel's new "What the fuck" attitude frees him to deal with Rutherford as an equal. In the film, this scene ends with Joel putting on his sunglasses, mugging and delivering the memorable line: "Looks like it's the University of Illinois!" But this line is not in this screenplay. Also, the screenplay shows Rutherford return and engage in a heated discussion about capitalism and who gets into the best schools; this discussion is cut from the film. But in the film, Rutherford stays, clearly taken with the "goods" the party has to offer.

In the screenplay, after Lana blows off Rutherford in Joel's interview, she tries to apologize to Joel; the scene is played on the back patio. In the film, the scene plays after Rutherford leaves; the setting is in the attic where Joel's toy trains are set up. This locale returns to the idea of Joel's youth and reinforces how young he is. Lana tries to make him feel better by telling him she's his girlfriend (or lets him believe it). Filmmaker Brickman interrupts their interaction, as passions rise, with a call from Joel's parents which Joel handles expertly, and then he sets up the late-night train ride which occurs after the party ends.

Another change is the deletion of a major scene during the party, in which Joel takes exception with Lana for agreeing to sleep with one of the young customers. In the screenplay, it becomes a real issue between them, again illustrating Joel's naiveté. The film wisely avoids this, allowing Lana the role of "Madame" for the party (instead of just another trick), and thus portraying them as partners in this venture. In fact, the entire party sequence flows and builds far more succinctly and naturally in the film. While conflicts tend to be overstated in the screenplay, they are perfectly understated in the film and this allows viewers to have their own opinions about what's happening.

A number of Joel's voice-overs during the party are juggled around. Many of the exchanges are completely cut and replaced by more natural ones. Much of the party is characterized by what we see on the screen as opposed to lines delivered. The whole party sequence comes to an end on Joel's voice-over line: "Trust. It seems to me, if there were any logic to our language, trust would be a four-letter word." In the screenplay, this line comes in the middle of the party sequence.

A scene is added when Joel realizes the house is empty. In it, he calls Lana but Guido answers. He first must swallow his anger and pride and then Guido will deal with him.

Also, in this draft of the screenplay, Joel does not get into Princeton. The screenplay shows Joel raking leaves; the film adds his father appearing with the news that Joel has been accepted. Many considered this a cynical move but it accurately reflects the feelings of the time.

Joel's last line of the film is also changed from the screenplay. In the screenplay, Joel ends with "Isn't life grand?" In the film, Joel repeats Guido's earlier line (from the midpoint), "Time of your life, eh, kid?" Delivered with irony, it evokes just the right tone for the ending.

CHARACTERIZATION'S RELATIONSHIP TO STRUCTURE

Study Film: *Casablanca*

In film, or in any fiction, the best stories are told within the context of human relationships. In great films, it is not so much what happens on screen that affects us, but what happens to whom. Great films are about characters we care about, who embody our emotions and, at some level, even our thoughts; they are about people caught up in events, having to make difficult decisions and choices which affect other people. Timeless stories are about people, not about effects, no matter how big and loud they are. The greater the film, often the more difficult the choice the protagonist has to make—and the consequences of action, or inaction, add a moral dimension to the story which raises the stakes for the characters and audience alike. At a very basic level, film stories are about characters making choices and forming commitments to each other in difficult circumstances and what these characters are willing to do to keep their commitments. It is only through the commitments a character makes and struggles to keep that we find out who that character really is.

How we effectively move a character, and therefore the audience, depends upon a number of things. We could sum them up like this: how strong the idea; how innovative the plot; and how effective the characterizations. Wonderfully drawn and observed characters are not enough to make a masterpiece, but without them, a film will suffer and fail live up to its potential greatness, no matter how good the idea and inventive the plot. Characterization must serve the plot of a film. It must be intricately woven with the other threads of the story (plot and theme) to develop meaning and increase the audience's involvement.

WHAT CHARACTERS WANT AND NEED

In the book, *Theory and Technique of Playwriting*, John Howard Lawson says that drama cannot deal with people who are weak-willed; who cannot make decisions of even temporary meaning; who adopt no conscious attitude toward events; or who make no effort to control their environment. In drama, characters (specifically the main characters) must be active to drive the plot. If they are not, the drama (film or play) will fail. The protagonist must be committed to something and be forced to take action because of that commitment.[1]

Before a plot can be constructed to serve the characters, the screenwriter must know three important things about the protagonist (and each of the other main characters):

1) What does the character want?
2) Why does he want it?
3) What does he need emotionally or psychologically?

The *want* refers to the story goal: The protagonist's want creates the action of the story that drives the plot; it is what the character wants to achieve. The *why* relates to the character's conscious motivation: These are the reasons he understands and gives for the pursuit of his goal. The character's *need* differs from what he wants: it refers to his unconscious motivation and comes from a depth of his psyche of which he is often ignorant. In a sense, it can be considered what he unconsciously needs to become whole and is what can compel the character to act in irrational ways. The character's conscious and unconscious motivations push him through the story while the goal pulls him. In *Risky Business*, what Joel wants is to get his mother's egg back. Why? Because if he doesn't, he will be in big trouble with his parents. What he needs is experience to mature. Both his conscious and unconscious motivations push him through the plot while the goal pulls him.

In some cases, however, the protagonist's need opposes his stated goal. When this happens, the character's need contributes to the inner obstacles he faces. Part of the conflict results from the disparity between the stated aim and the subliminal need. In *Witness*, John Book wants to get the corrupt cops and he specifically threatens to kill Schaeffer. He needs, however, to develop his emotional side and be able to relate more completely and compassionately to others. His stated goal, rooted in violence, is diametrically opposed to his unconscious need of relationship.

A screenwriter uses the answers to the questions of *want*, *why* and *need* to define the protagonist, antagonist and other main characters as well as to build a plot. The other main characters' wants and needs should conflict to various degrees with the protagonist's wants and needs; they should become obstacles and complications for the protagonist to deal with and overcome. In film, characters who want something definite are more active and therefore more interesting than passive characters. A successful feature film must be driven by an active protagonist, one committed to achieving his goal in order for him to last though feature's two-hour length. If he is not active, the film will flounder and the audience will fall asleep.

Some films, however, bend these rules to some degree and still succeed. Let's see how.

Need Driving the Story—Casablanca

If the character's want doesn't drive the story, his need must. In *Casablanca*, written by Julius J. Epstein and Philip G. Epstein and Howard Koch (adapted from the stage play *Everyone Goes to Rick's* by Murray Brunett and Joan Alison), directed by Michael Curtiz and produced by Hal Wallis, Rick (Humphrey Bogart) says he wants to remain neutral in the face of the greatest conflict facing the free world in the twentieth century. He doesn't want to take action. He wants to be passive. So what keeps the film so compelling? Many scholars and critics say that Rick actively pursues his neutrality and therefore he is active. But it is really Rick's need that drives his part in the plot. Let's take a moment and think about what Rick needs in *Casablanca*.

Rick needs to know what happened in Paris and he needs to know Ilsa (Ingrid Bergman) still loves him. (Rick loved Ilsa so deeply and fully, and believed she loved him, that he can't understand how she could have left him.) He can only think the worst about her which invalidates everything they had together. But deep inside, he knows there has to be a reason why she left— good or bad. Until he knows it, he is incapable of moving on, of becoming involved with other people, of returning to his true, former self.

This need drives Rick within the plot. Act One establishes his character as a bitter ex-patriot who sticks his "neck out for nobody" while tracking the stolen Letters of Transit (announced in the film's opening) until they find their way into his possession. Since Rick doesn't want anything except to remain neutral, his actions are limited to responding to other characters around him—Ugarte (Peter Lorre), Ferrari (Sidney Greenstreet), Renault (Claude Rains), his girlfriend, Yvonne (Madeline LeBeau), the Nazis, his staff—while running his popular saloon.

It is not until he hears Sam (Dooley Wilson) singing "As Time Goes By" and sees Ilsa that something more powerful grips him and starts directing his actions. He begins drinking, something we have heard he never does. When Ilsa returns after-hours to explain why she left him in Paris, Rick's bitterness forces him to attack and push her away. It is only later, when he's sobered up and realizes how much he still feels for her, that he tries to find out what happened. But Ilsa has felt the sting of Rick's hate and won't tell him anything. After a nasty crack Rick makes about her and Laszlo (Paul Henreid), Ilsa drops her bomb: she was already married to Laszlo when she knew Rick in Paris. This is the first indication Rick has that there may have been a bona fide reason why they had to part.

It is not until the beginning of the third act, when Rick gets his explanation from Ilsa, that he can take definitive action. This action, then, drives the plot to its ultimate climax and defines Rick's character—he will not remain neutral

Of course, *Casablanca* is filled with other characters who are more than willing to take action. Ilsa wants the Letters of Transit to save her husband whom she respects. But she still loves Rick and needs him. Laszlo wants the Letters ostensibly to save himself and continue fighting the Nazis, but also to save Ilsa. Ultimately, it is her safety that he is more concerned about. Maj. Strasser (Conrad Veidt) wants to stop Laszlo from leaving Casablanca and send him back to the concentration camp because of his duty. Even smaller characters, Renault, Ugarte and Yvonne have wants that direct their actions and call for responses from Rick.

What a character needs is often the psychological key to understanding his inner obstacles; it therefore deepens the levels and meaning of the story. How the character copes with these inner obstacles forms the basis of his development through the film because the psychological or emotional problems force the character into corners which demand new and different responses if he is to conquer the outer obstacles and attain his goal.

CHARACTER DEVELOPMENT

Characterization is most effective when it charts the growth or development of the characters. In our own lives, many of us have come to realize that people are changed, for better or worse, when they encounter extraordinary events. Most films force dramatic, life-changing situations on their characters. From the audience's own experiences, they know the characters must be affected. The screenwriter's job is to weave into the plot how the characters are influenced by events. How they are affected causes the plot to move one way or another, i.e., because they stand up to oppression, they reclaim their dignity; because they run away from persecution, they die like dogs. It is in the interaction between characters and plot that meaning is developed and it is through the characters' movements that we understand what the film is about. This character movement is called the transformational arc or, more simply, the character arc.

The Transformational Arc

In great films, one or more of the characters is transformed significantly by the events of the story. Most often, it is the protagonist who undergoes a profound change, but not always. Sometimes the protagonist changes little, but he causes other characters to change. The transformational arc charts the progress, growth or development of the character who is changed by the story. For our purposes, we relate the character's arc only to the protagonist.

Once the protagonist is committed to his goal and meets the conflict, the film becomes a test of his commitment. As he struggles to reach his goal, he must make choices. The harder the struggle becomes, the more the character's commitment to his goal is tested. If he finds or has the courage to stay committed in the face of tremendous obstacles, the choices he makes push him to discover qualities within himself that compel him to grow. This growth allows him to solve the problem and reach his goal. Growth can also come as a result of failing to solve the problem adequately but realizing greater truths in the process of trying.

All great film characters enter a plot with specific attitudes, relationships and ideas about the world. As a character moves through the plot, encountering problems, obstacles (external and internal), complications, new developments (often in the form of other characters), he must grow or mature in some way to accomplish his objective in the film. It is often the character's starting attitude, relationships or ideas which have to be changed in order for him to achieve his aim and come to a proper solution. The character's inner obstacles (emotional or psychological problems) have a direct relationship to how he changes in the plot.

The character's change, interestingly enough, is often what confers the most meaning on a film. When we see a character grow in the face of conflict, to be able to resolve the problem at the end in a satisfying way, we make sense of the film because we draw conclusions based on what we've seen. The specific qualities the hero has gained through the course of the plot, the realizations, the revelations, inform our understanding of the story.

Effective character development also leads to greater audience involvement. First, because a character feels more true to life if we see a progression of emotions which lead to change (positive or negative). But also because character transformation helps keep the audience guessing about the final outcome of the film. Often we think we understand the main character of a film but showing that character in conflict and how the conflict affects him casts doubt on what he will finally do. In the film *The Searchers*, written by Frank Nugent and directed by John Ford, Ethan (John Wayne) searches five years for his niece who was abducted by the Indians after they massacred his brother's family. Ethan's only intent is to kill her when he finds her because he feels that she is tainted, no longer white. When he finally finds her, he first avenges his family by scalping the Indian who led the raid against his brother. With this action, Ethan's anger and revenge are spent so when he locates his niece at the end, he can't kill her. Instead, he gathers her into his arms to take her home.

At its best, drama examines the costs of the protagonist's actions, usually in terms of personal relationships. Part of the drama comes from what he leaves behind or forsakes in order to gain his goal. In *Witness*, the protagonist Book trades his gun for acceptance in the nonviolent household which leads to a change in his values. In *Risky Business*, Joel leaves his bourgeois middle-class morals behind to get himself out of his predicament and in the process, loses his innocence but gets the girl (at least temporarily). In *Casablanca*, Rick recommits to life and the good fight, but loses Ilsa. These costs are trade-offs; gains come from losses, losses from gains. Audiences then ask of these trade-offs: "Were they worth it?"

Character transformation can be major or minor. A film can chart a profound change in a character. In *Witness*, Book starts out hard, insensitive, alone. By the end of the film, he's receptive, more feeling, capable of having relationships. Joel, in *Risky Business*, loses his innocence and his youthful idealism but he gains maturity and a new outlook on the world. In *Casablanca*, Rick is reborn: he changes from a bitter ex-partisan to a recommitted patriot.

Transformation can also be more modest. We can see it simply in the progression of emotions a character goes through, i.e., from indifference to anger, from friendship to passion. However, this has more to do with strong cause and effect plotting than in orchestrating a consequential change to a character's fundamental personality. But there is progression that can be seen in the character relating to the plot. Successful melodramas (thrillers, science-fiction, murder mysteries) often work because they employ this technique, although no one is truly changed by the experience of the story in the end. Think of such films as *Scream* or *Air Force One*.

THE CHARACTER ARC'S RELATIONSHIP TO PLOT STRUCTURE

The process of character transformation in the plot depends upon how pronounced the protagonist's inner problem is. Let's look at our three films so far to see how the protagonist's problem and his transformation are incorporated into their respective plots.

Witness

In Act One of *Witness*, Book is a tough, honest, hard-working cop. On the job, he is in command. He is a violent man living in a violent world. On the personal level, he has a tendency toward self-righteousness and is rather insensitive toward others. He's been a cop too long: unmarried, he hasn't had the softening presence of a woman in his life. He lacks the tact and discretion a relationship with the opposite sex can produce. His problem is so remote to him he isn't even aware he has one. How do we know this? We see it in his behavior in scenes which show his character and his inner problem. Think back to the film. Which scenes in the first act give us clues to his character?

When we first meet him, he's in command of the situation. He talks with Samuel gently, but clearly lets Rachel know he's in charge. When the officers think they have a suspect, they put Samuel and Rachel in the back seat of their car and they set off to find him. Book and his partner Carter laugh and joke in the front seat with a sort of gallows humor until Rachel lets him know she doesn't appreciate it. Book apologizes, saying he knows this must be very difficult for her and her son. A few moments later, though, Book allows his anger to explode as he slams the suspect up against the car for Samuel to see, scaring the boy and his mother. His violence is brought into high relief by contrasting him with the nonviolent, religious Amish mother and son.

A moment later, Book brings Rachel and Samuel to the home of his sister Elaine without so much as a phone call, then gives Elaine grief about having a man over while her two sons sleep upstairs. Later still, we hear, through Rachel, what Book's sister really thinks about him: he's a judgmental lout who believes he's the only cop on the force who knows how to do a good job, and he's afraid of the responsibility of having a family of his own.

These scenes give clear indication of Book's character. How, then, would you characterize Book's inner problem? He's been hardened by the violent world he lives in. It's made him self-righteous and insensitive to others. It takes a gunshot wound to throw him into a different realm, a more gentle world based on cooperation and nonviolence, in order for him to have an opportunity to change.

At the start of Act Two, Book is unconscious. Rachel understands the jeopardy Samuel would face if Book were taken to a hospital so she convinces the Amish elders to allow him to stay on the Lapp farm. Knowing he has risked his life for Samuel and her, she will try to save his. Psychologically, we understand Book's near-death experience as a shattering blow to his all too rational ego. His macho sense of himself must be broken down before healing and transformation can begin. He must be exposed to a different environment which embraces a moral code contrary to his beliefs. At first, his violent, profane world spews from his lips in his delirium. But with Rachel's care, he improves.

As soon as he's conscious, he wants to leave, but his body tells him otherwise: he is too weak to do what his head commands. While recuperating under their roof, Book's transformation begins when he accepts the Lapp's values and puts his gun away. Book begins to understand and appreciate the differences in their cultures only after Rachel tells him it is not his gun she objects to with her son, but what he stands for.

Gradually, we see him become more receptive to the Amish and their communal life. He helps with the chores, he uses his carpentry skills around the Lapp farm and at the barn raising. He takes time to relate with Samuel who recently lost his father. And most of all, he comes to appreciate Rachel and her caring. He becomes more sensitive and opens himself up to a relationship.

Rachel, too, is affected by Book's presence. She responds to his courage, to the changes she sees him, his gentleness, his deference. She allows herself to dance with Book, even at the cost of Eli's anger and the threat of shunning. Her feelings are so strong, that she offers herself to him after the barn raising. She knows what Book has done for Samuel and her. At the end of the second act when she discovers that he intends to leave, she symbolically puts her Amish code aside and gives into her feelings for him.

It's important to note, that though Book does change, he cannot change his violent nature. He responds to the crisis at the end of the second act—when he learns of his partner's murder—with more violence, thereby causing Schaeffer and McFee to discover that he is at the Lapp farm. Book grows a bit, but not enough to fit into the Amish world.

Though he cannot escape his violent culture, Book learns lessons about the importance of relating to others. Act Three returns to the confrontation between the one good cop and the three rogues. Though Book still must resort to violence to stop two of killers, it is in self-defense: when Rachel is threatened, he throws down his gun and allows Schaeffer to take him. Then at the end, when he has the opportunity to kill Schaeffer, something he has said he's going to do, Book chooses a nonviolent solution. Though he doesn't get the "girl", John Book has been transformed by his experience.

Risky Business

In *Risky Business*, Joel also undergoes a striking transformation of character. Act One sets up Joel as anxious and indecisive. We know this because, even though he lusts after his neighbor and friend Nancy Kessler, he is afraid to take a chance with her. Though honest, he's sexually innocent and suffers from a juvenile idealism which leaves him open to exploitation by a more wily hustler.

How do we know all this? The scenes at the start of the first act illustrate it. The opening dream sequence describes Joel's anxiety over sex and his future. The following poker game exposes his innocence and honesty. We see his youthful idealism in the scene with the other Future Enterprisers when he asks if money is all they want. Even the imagery just before and just after Lana's arrival—the blowing leaves, the bike falling over in the driveway, the childhood photos of Joel—underscores Joel's youth and innocence.

At the end of Act One, Joel gets a blast of reality: the price for his fantasy night is much higher than he anticipated. His last naive action of the first act—leaving Lana alone in his house while he goes to cash a bond given to him by Grandma—costs him his mother's Steuben egg. Metaphorically, we can read into these scenes that initiation into the sexual realm leads to a separation from the safety of the adolescent world. Eggs are often associated with initiation because, upon hatching, they represent a second birth. The experience of sex has changed Joel, whether he wants it or not.

Act Two shows Joel first taking responsibility for what has happened and then taking action. He must get the egg back but he has to wise up and not panic. It is when he goes into action to try to find Lana and the egg that his real journey and growth begin. His rescue of Lana and escape from Guido intensifies the course. In defending Lana, his feminine counterpart, he grows (and his sexual encounters increase, too).

By the midpoint, Joel has defended Lana and her girlfriend Vicki from Guido again, and this makes him feel more of a man. But trouble arises because he is still too naive to see through Lana and what she's after. (Lana wants and needs money to repay Guido to get him off her back.) If Joel wasn't so naive, and the power of sex so strong, he would have held to his original aim of getting both Lana and Vicki out of his house; instead, he yields to the women.

As the complications escalate to crisis proportions, Joel is forced to take actions he never dreamed of in order to solve his problems. He has nothing left to lose, except his parents' trust, so he teams up with Lana for one night.

In Act Three, Joel's whole attitude is different, from the clothes he wears to the way he combs his hair to how he deals with his peers. Though he affects an air of experience, Joel still has one important lesson left to learn: who can he trust?

Throughout Act Three, Joel's new attitude serves him well. He handles his peers, Princeton's Rutherford and his parents' phone call in the middle of the party. But because he still doesn't know who to trust, he leaves himself open to be double-crossed.

In the climax, Joel makes it through his ordeal by ignoring his parents' phone calls and sticking to his task of replacing all the furniture. Though he gets the house back together before his parents return, Joel cannot totally escape the consequences: his mother's Steuben egg has been cracked and he loses some of her trust as a result. (Read as a metaphor, Joel's egg has been cracked; his world will never be the same as a result of his experiences with Lana.)

When he meets Lana again, he is a changed man: he's lost his innocence. He suspects she set him up from the start, but he's gotten into Princeton only because he joined forces with her. He's had a lesson in how the world operates more valuable than anything the Future Enterprisers could have taught him and we sense that he's ready to meet the world on his own.

Casablanca

Looking at *Casablanca*, we again see similar attention paid to the emotional side of the story. Rick's character is clearly set up in Act One. We see how he coldly and unsympathetically deals with people, Ugarte, his lady friend Yvonne, the Germans. He tells us so in his line, "I stick my head out for nobody." But we also see how well he treats those who work with him, Sam in particular. So despite his coldness, we know he is at least loyal. We also get an indication of his back story, that he was a gun runner in Ethiopia and fought the fascists in Spain. When Renault suspects that Rick is a secret sentimentalist but something has happened to change him, Rick assures the man that he is not interested in helping anyone other than himself. All of this, of course, changes when Rick lays eyes on Ilsa at the end of Act One. His immediate response is to have a drink, something he doesn't normally do as Renault informs us. Act Two begins with Rick getting drunk and remembering what happened in Paris, something he's tried to forget. He bares his bitterness and hostility when Ilsa returns after the saloon has closed to explain what happened.

But as the story moves along, Rick's need surfaces. He needs an explanation from Ilsa; he needs to understand why she left him. When he has sobered up and meets Ilsa again (the midpoint) he apologizes for his ugly behavior the previous night and then wants to know what happened in Paris. He speculates about her reasons for leaving and even asks her to come back to him. But Ilsa, still hurt over the things he said the night before, will tell him only that at the time she knew Rick, she was already married to Laszlo. This is the first indication we have that there may have been a legitimate reason for her leaving him. But Rick still needs to hear the story.

The first evidence of real change in Rick comes when he helps the young Bulgarian newlyweds in their struggle to raise money to leave Casablanca, winning praise from his staff but curses from Renault. However, it is followed by Rick's refusal to sell Laszlo the Letters of Transit, telling Laszlo to ask his wife the reason why he won't. The scene is cut short by the Germans singing "Wacht am Rhine" and Laszlo responding by leading the French and all other ex-patriots, orchestra included, in a rousing version of "Marseillaise" while Rick looks on.

At the end of Act Two, Ilsa tries, at gunpoint, to get the Letters of Transit from Rick. He tells her to shoot him: "You'll be doing me a favor," he says. Rick can't go on living without her or with such bitterness in his heart. Ilsa breaks down and declares her love for him.

Act Three begins with Rick getting the explanation he has needed all along. Now he understands why she left him: loyalty to Laszlo and a cause greater than their love. His bitterness leaves him but not his cynicism. Next, Rick learns that Laszlo, who understands they both love Ilsa, will sacrifice himself for Ilsa's safety. Laszlo, knowing Rick won't sell him the Letters of Transit, asks him to take Ilsa and leave Casablanca. Just before Laszlo is arrested, Rick sees how much Laszlo loves Ilsa.

Now Rick begins operating on a whole new level and it is only at the end that we realize how much he has changed. He orchestrates a plan to leave Casablanca but, at the last minute he sends Laszlo off with Ilsa while he stays behind with Renault to join the Resistance. With this action, Rick rejoins the world of the living: he sacrifices what he has held dear for a more important cause.

One of *Casablanca*'s wonderful accomplishments is seeing how unexpectedly all the relationships are resolved at the end. Because Rick has been depicted as self-involved—still reeling from his love affair with Ilsa—we can believe he intends to set Laszlo up. When he doesn't, we understand how deep Rick's transformation, or rebirth, has been.

Character Growth and Structure

Characters enter films with certain emotions and attitudes. At the beginning, their attitudes define them; their emotions come into play, so to speak, as they encounter the plot's conflicts. It is only after the characters respond to the conflicts that their true personalities are revealed. Who the character is at the beginning determines his specific choices and decisions and the specific actions he initially takes. Sometimes these are the right actions, but often, especially when they meet with strong resistance, they aren't. Wrong choices are indications, however subtle, that the character has still to grow and change to resolve his conflict. Often, it is his inner obstacles which must be overcome before he can change or mature enough to successfully resolve the conflict.

This aspect of the film is most often dealt with in the subplot, which carries the personal story for the protagonist, while developing similarly to the main plot line (see Chapters Two, Five and Eight). In fact, one of the functions of the subplot is to fill in the characters. But understanding how the protagonist's inner obstacles impede his progress toward his goal and incorporating into the subplot how he is forced to deal with these problems deepens the story and increases the audience's interest in the film. Because, whenever conflict arises, audiences pay greater attention.

The progression of scenes which make up the subplot, showing the changes needs to be causally related. There must be a strong cause-and-effect relationship between these scenes, starting with an initial set-up to the subplot problem. This focuses the protagonist and the character who will help him change on a conflict which must be dealt with in some manner before the protagonist can move onto his main goal. As this plot line develops, the characters are forced to interact on different levels which bring about compromises, changes. These incidents are orchestrated to illustrate the character's change.

The resistance the protagonist faces to the conflict forces him to make new decisions and choices, to try a new course of action. To be able to make the new choices, the character must grow. In great films, it is not enough just to persevere—unless that's the true point of the story—it's about what happens to the protagonist in the face of immense obstacles. Or how he changes.

This doesn't mean that the protagonist must always change 180 degrees in order to solve his problem; however, by the conflict's resolution, the audience must understand that he has changed, or at least that he has learned something. By meeting the conflict in a new way, the character often discovers unknown inner resources, or the conflict forces him to open himself up to the influence of others. These changes can be incremental. As they add up over the course of the film, they make up his transformational arc and show the progress or deterioration as he moves from one position to the next.

In Act One, filmmakers spend time establishing who the main character is. This is the point from which the protagonist starts to grow and bloom or disintegrate. In Act Two, the pressure of the conflict begins to assail the character. Obstacles standing in the way of his goal force him to stop: he can no longer continue on his old course because the emotional or psychological cost is too great. He must take a new course, and because he does, he is forced to change, for better or worse. In great films, this makes up a part of Act Two, but the character's change forms the heart and soul of a story. Act Three shows the result of the change in how the protagonist overcomes the problem of the film and succeeds in his goal, or how the problem overcomes him.

Incorporating the emotional/psychological side of the characters into screenplays deepens stories and causes them to resonate with their audience. The best films have both inner and outer problems for the protagonist and other characters to face. In *Witness*, we see the outer problems clearly in the antagonists Book faces. The inner problems are shown in his rigid, self-righteous personality. In *Risky Business*, the outer obstacles are Lana and Guido, but Joel's inner ones are his own naiveté and need to mature. Rick in *Casablanca* faces the Nazis as his ultimate external problem. But he must overcome his bitterness and cynicism before he can commit to take them on. In real life, no man could remain the same through a series of extreme conflicts. Likewise, in drama, characters encountering life-changing conflicts must either be changed by the experience and interaction with them or die.

Character transformation develops over the length of the screenplay and film. It affects the story and influences the action because, as the character changes, so does the way he relates to his problem and goal. We see this transformation in the way the protagonist chooses to meet the conflict as he grows and how he responds to changing situations, both intellectually and emotionally. We see it, most of all, in how he is affected and moved by others to take actions contrary to who he has earlier shown us he is.

The Agent for Change

Characters rarely change without help. That help comes from the protagonist's experiences within the story and the influence of other characters. Most often, though, help comes in the form of one character in particular, who can be seen as an agent for change.

The agent for change generally enters the film as a new element in the protagonist's life. This character has a different point of view toward the conflict which, often, initially clashes with the protagonist's. Only later in the film does the hero come to appreciate what this character stands for. The agent for change introduces new issues that the protagonist at first resists but later learns to value. The agent for change has goals or is compelled by the story to set them. He must determine strategies to achieve these goals and struggle to accomplish them. However, unlike the protagonist, he does not have to change though his situation may.

In wrestling with the problems and issues the agent for change raises and dealing with them, the protagonist acquires what he needs to meet the conflict appropriately. Hopefully, he will solve the problem in an unexpected though satisfying manner. We can look at the agent for change as an active representation of what the protagonist needs to face in order to grow. If he can't face it, then the character will deteriorate. (This is often the basis of tragedy.)

Each of the films we have viewed so far has a strong agent for change. Can you identify them?

Witness has Rachel. *Risky Business* has Lana. *Casablanca* has Ilsa. Each one of these characters has a strong point of view which clashes with the film's protagonist. Rachel belongs to a religious sect valuing nonviolence and cooperation. Though her feelings for Book provoke questions about her allegiance to the Amish community, she does not leave it and so reaffirms her beliefs. Lana is a cynical, streetwise hustler. She chips away at Joel's naiveté, but she doesn't change. Ilsa's commitment to a man and a cause so important to the survival of the free world forces Rick to confront his own pain and recommit to the struggle against the Third Reich.

In other films, the protagonist and the agent for change are often transformed by the give-and-take of the relationship. Think of Rose Sawyer and Charlie Alnutt in *The African Queen*; Danny Dravot and Peachy Carnehan in *The Man Who Would be King*; Barbara and Oliver in *The War of the Roses*. The interaction of these characters with each other and with the other forces of the story creates the chemistry with causes them to be changed. Again, these changes are shown in how the characters deal differently with problems and situations which arise than they did earlier in the film. The changes in attitudes, ideas and actions are related causally to each other in the plot.

Marking the Character's Growth

In film, change in a character is marked in various ways. The strongest, however, is when the protagonist confronts a situation after everything else he has tried to secure success in his goal has failed. The protagonist must now take new action which is based on a new understanding or a new emotional response. It is saying, in fact, that the old ways aren't working anymore. The protagonist, to be a true hero, must try something different, new. And, to try something new means he must change, or grow in some way.

Structurally, the strongest places to mark change in a character are near the most significant points in the plot: the key focal points (Act One climax, midpoint, Act Two climax, Act Three climax). These changes are presented in reaction to whatever has happened in the crises surrounding these points. But character change doesn't have to be strictly linked to these turning points. Any response to a strong crisis scene, wherever it occurs in the plot, is an opportunity to see the protagonist adopt new behavior in order to illustrate new emotions.

Above, the study films have been briefly sketched, highlighting the main characters' growth. Review these sketches now to see if the major beats of the character changes hinge upon the key focal points underpinning the structure of the film.

In each case, characters respond with modified behaviors to the crises at or around the structural focal points.

THE MORAL DIMENSION

All great films are about characters forced to make difficult choices. In these films, the characters are shown finding the courage to make their choices, and/or having the courage to stand by them once they are made despite obstacles and complications.

In the most powerful films, there is a moral component to the story. It isn't as simple as good vs. evil, or even right vs. wrong, although one cannot ignore such moral certainties. There are situations where we know the right thing to do, but we also understand the difficulty in doing it. When a character does the right thing under hard circumstances, however, it engenders respect from the audience because we witness a hero in action and admire his courage.

If we look at *Witness*, we can find two very important decisions Book makes which determine his core character as a heroic and moral human being. His first is risking his life to save Samuel's. Though wounded, he makes sure Schaeffer and McFee won't be able to trace the boy and his mother to their farm and then he drives them there. He has no intention of staying with them, for he knows this could put them in more danger. He stays only because he passes out from his wound and crashes his car.

The second important decision he makes is at the end when he lays down his gun and trades his life for Rachel's. However, Book isn't the only character capable of moral behavior. The Amish won't allow Schaeffer to take Book away to kill him. And so, the Amish too, are willing to give up their lives for Book.

In *Casablanca*, we love Rick because he sacrifices his love for Ilsa to save Victor Laszlo's life. He understands Laszlo's importance to the fight against the Third Reich. At the end, he commits to the struggle to preserve the free world.

Emotion and the Importance of Audience Identification

Let me end this chapter discussing the considerable role that emotion plays in making the audience care about a film and its characters. The emotional/psychological life of a character is probably the most important aspect of characterization (next to want, why and need). Here, motivations are born and characters are made into flesh and blood. Yet, it is usually the most neglected aspect of writing—even by many advanced writers. Many mediocre films could have been greatly enhanced if only more attention had been paid to the core emotional responses of the characters. Instead, emotional reactions to the story's dramatic events have been glanced over, represented only with tears and anger, or totally ignored.

True emotion is the source of our connection to other people. We see someone in pain and it elicits feelings of sympathy; we watch people celebrating and their joy makes us smile. Emotion is one of the great universals, connecting human beings to each other despite sexual and ethnic differences. Emotion is the basis of the audience's identification with the characters in the film. If we see a mother defending her young, whether she is the Vietnamese woman in *Platoon*, the French prostitute in *Les Miserables* or the wolf roaming the Canadian wilds in *Never Cry Wolf*, our response is the same: we root and hope and feel for her. We become involved in her crisis.

Audience identification is established if your characters create emotions viewers can immediately recognize. These are universal emotions such as love, joy, hate, jealousy, fear, humiliation, etc. This is why period pieces such as *Lawrence Of Arabia*, *Dances With Wolves* and *Sense and Sensibility* succeed. The characters are recognizable through their emotional responses to the situations and obstacles they face. The reason? We have all encountered some type of unkindness, embarrassment, neglect or cruelty in our lives and we never forget these experiences. The same is true of compassion, generosity and love. They affect us as they affect the characters.

Stories are told in terms of relationships, which are matrices of emotions we share with others. If a character's pursuit of a goal affects no one, he won't affect the audience. He must relate to other characters, positively or negatively, in order to stir and sway the audience. Just as in our lives, relationships on screen have meaning only to the extent they engage and arouse our emotions. We love or hate, care or feel disdain for someone; in drama, these emotions color our reactions. Great writers—screenwriters, novelists, playwrights—understand that this is the source of a character's true motivation and will find actions which are both logical and surprising to represent the emotion. When their writing succeeds, we call them inspired.

By the end of *Casablanca*, we have shared a wide range of emotions with Rick, Ilsa and Laszlo, from bitter hate to selfless love. We have suffered Rick's pain of betrayal and Ilsa's misery, as well as the passion of their reunion; we have felt Laszlo's loyalty to freedom and to his wife. And when Rick's transformation of character is complete, we have experienced the altruism of his sacrifice for a greater cause. These emotional truths expressed in *Casablanca* are what has kept the movie timeless and universal since the day it was made.

SPECIAL NOTES

Considered by some to be the best Hollywood movie ever made, *Casablanca* took home three Academy Awards in 1943, for Best Picture, Best Director and Best Screenplay. Many books have been written about *Casablanca* telling the behind-the-scenes story of how a film without an ending wound up with one of the strongest finales ever made.

The little I want to add to the literature written about *Casablanca* is simply to point out changes that were made from screenplay to finished film. The screenplay I used for comparison is dated June 6, 1942. It is a carefully written shooting script, 158 pages, showing the input of the director. Scenes indicate close-ups and full shots. Almost all of the scenes written in this draft are included in the film. The biggest change we see is in the editing of these scenes and one significant addition.

The opening sequence in the film has been edited and the scenes slightly rearranged. As soon as the narrator finishes and we have arrived on the streets of Casablanca, a new scene is inserted. A police official puts out a bulletin to all officers, detailing the murder of two German couriers and the stolen documents. The official instructs his men to round up the suspects. The film cuts right into the police action and the suspects being taken into custody, picking up the pace of the film. The addition clearly defines the reason for the police round-up and builds the film's momentum. A brief scene introducing the Bulgarian newlyweds is eliminated, keeping the pace strong..

In the screenplay, more attention is paid to supporting characters. For instance, the plight of the Bulgarian newlyweds trying to leave Casablanca is shown in much greater detail, forming a true subplot in the screenplay. It specifically details the young newlywed's problem with Renault. In the film, all these scenes have been drastically edited or deleted until the Bride's final scene with Rick when she asks him what she should do; sleep with Renault or not? The previous scenes in the film do little more than establish the couple's presence and desire to leave Casablanca. We already know of Renault's attitude toward young and beautiful refugees and what they must do to earn his aid. In the film, it's not necessary to dramatize this point. It takes away from the main conflict surrounding Rick, Ilsa, Laszlo and Strasser.

Scenes showing the interplay between other soldiers belonging to Renault and Strasser also have been edited down to brief exchanges or cut altogether. Several scenes exploring the motif of pickpockets combing the streets of Casablanca for easy marks have been eliminated. Many of the changes in the film come as edits to scenes, removing anything off the main topic of the action directing the plot.

Although the screenplay is 158 pages, the film is only 102 minutes. In the screenplay, Ilsa enters on page 42, but in the film she walks into Rick's at the 23-minute mark. Part of this is due to the way the screenplay is written; it includes full, medium and close shots, reverse and side angles indicated within scenes. These shot descriptions lengthen the script, and the reading process. In the screenplay, it seems to take a long time for the story to engage. (It is not until page 54 that Rick hears Sam singing and sees Ilsa.) In the film, this comes 31 minutes in, heralding the main conflict for Rick (how to deal with Ilsa and make sense of his past). Once this line of action engages in the screenplay, the story takes off.

The plot of *Casablanca* relies on dialogue more than action to tell its story. But the dialogue is extremely well-written and delivered, with a couple of exceptions (the Rick/newlywed scene, for instance). Most of the characters, from Sam and Ugarte to Rick, Ilsa, Renault and Laszlo, have their own voices and specific traits which make them seem like real people. For the most part, these voices have been created in the writing.

Endnotes
1. Lawson, John Howard. *Theory and Technique of Playwriting and Screenwriting.* Garland Publishers, New York, 1985, p. 168.

5

THEME'S RELATIONSHIP TO STRUCTURE

Study film: *The Piano*

All great films have a broader subject matter than just the story the writer wants to tell. This is known as the theme, the underlying unifying idea and is what the film is really about. Theme gives direction to the plot, defines the key issues for the characters and ultimately determines the depth of meaning for a work. It is the integrative force behind a great film and is essential for understanding what makes a great film great.

People around the world are basically similar, despite racial and ethnic differences. We all love and hate. We tell the truth and we also lie. We all have hopes, yet often we must settle with failure. In our core, we dream the same dreams and have the same fears. Everyone moves through the same rhythms of life—through childhood, adolescence, maturity. We're born, we live and we die. This journey forms the basis of our understanding of existence and ourselves.

The earliest myths deal with the journeys of life, trying to understand who we are, where we come from and where we're going—what the experience of life is all about. The best stories we tell are similarly grounded. They are efforts to relate the human experience. What makes us human? The capacity to feel, to understand, to change. Emotion—from anger to affection, desire to revulsion—directs people from every walk of life. (Jealous obsession can lead to catastrophe whether one is black or white, Muslim, Jew, Hindu or Christian.) The ideas and issues affecting our lives—honor, ambition, responsibility, compromise, questions of identity—must be dealt with the world over. Understanding is the mental process we use to perceive and assign meaning. In the transformations we undergo, we discover the convergence of feeling and understanding. When feeling and understanding collide, people are affected and therefore must respond. The response is often growth. In drama, as in life, when people can't grow and change, they stagnate and die. So, themes are concerned with universal emotions, concepts and issues. For example, love, honor, revenge, greed and guilt are all experienced worldwide. The universality of these ideas and emotions helps insure an audience that can relate to the material on a level deeper than just via the plot.

Without a theme, a film is an aimless story, having little significance for the audience. Without the unifying focus of the theme, there is no purpose, no depth to the work. The theme is the ultimate subject of the film. Even "good triumphs over evil" or "love conquers all," though broad, tell us someone's point of view toward the world, which the audience can agree with or not.

Witness tells the story of an honest cop being chased by bad cops who hides among nonviolent Amish. The broader subject of the film concerns the place of violence in society and what it does to those who live with it.

Risky Business is ostensibly about a young man's first encounter with a prostitute. The deeper topic of the film, however, is how the effects of unadulterated capitalism corrupt innocence.

Casablanca is the story of what happens when a cynical expatriot encounters the old flame who caused his bitterness. Its deeper meaning explores the selflessness of true love.

In great films, plot structure, characterization and theme cannot be separated. They expose and illuminate different aspects of the same story. Plot tells us what happens, characterization relates how this action affects the main characters while the theme integrates the entire experience.

HOW THEME RELATES TO PLOT STRUCTURE

The plot of a film is a carefully orchestrated sequence of actions and counteractions, rooted in a conflict between (at least) two forces and arranged to achieve an intended effect. Plot is constructed of actions, incidents and events, progressing to a climax and resolution. It is the form or the vehicle that carries and communicates the content of the story—the substance or meaning of the film—by illustrating what happens in the action. Theme is the unifying force. It illuminates what the plot events stand for, what they communicate when added up in the mind of the viewer at the end of a film.

Theme relates to plot structure the way characterization does—it develops. If we knew from the beginning what a film was about, it would destroy the surprise of discovery and cause the film to become predictable. In order for a film to be effective, the audience needs to be as uncertain about the true meaning of the film as it is about the outcome. As plot progresses from the beginning toward the climax, the emotional lives of the characters (seen in their needs and often shown in the subplot), generally carry the theme. As the characters meet the challenges (obstacles and complications) standing between them and their goals, their qualities, either intrinsic or developed along the way, define the audience's experience of them. How a character responds to the conflict, whether he succeeds or not, illustrates his core traits. How these qualities affect the actions which create the plot determines how the audience understands the story.

In the first act, the protagonist's *want* or *goal* is established: it is what he struggles to achieve throughout the film. The first act also sets up, or at least hints at, the character's *need*. We can think of this as what the character needs to learn or understand about life or himself. This need, which the character is often unconscious of, directs part of his actions making up the plot. These actions create other problems or complications for the protagonist. Until he learns his lesson or deals with his need, he is not going to succeed. This is how the interior life contributes best to the subplot.

Just as the first act of a film sets up the plot and characters' starting point, it sets up the thematic premise, too. This set-up describes the characters and situation, including the beginning of the central conflict. In so doing, a thesis or proposition is set forth. In *Casablanca*, the first act describes a world torn by war, where individual freedom is threatened and human lives are essentially sold on the black market. Rick, a cynical saloon keeper and "man with a past," takes center stage. Although he clearly knows which the side is worth fighting for and he is capable of helping, he wants no part of the world's troubles; he only wants to be left alone. Rick is set up as completely self-absorbed, we might as well say selfish; he has nothing but contempt for the world. Two things happen in the first act which create Rick's situation in the film. First, Ugarte asks Rick to hold the Letters of Transit and then is killed. Second, Ilsa (with her husband Victor Laszlo) walks through the doors with hopes of buying those same letters. Since Ilsa is the source of Rick's suffering, he will be forced to confront his pain over his previous loss of deep love.

What, then, might be thematically posited in the incidents of the first act of *Casablanca*?

Look at the key character traits which define the protagonist in the first act: Rick is a confidant but cynical man; he was once quite heroic but now cares only for himself. Yet, at the end of the first act, we see him shaken by Ilsa's presence, the woman from his past. It's as if the story is positioning opposites: cynicism vs. love. What will result from their meeting?

The plot question may be: "Will Rick remain neutral?" as many screenwriting texts assert, but this is not the theme. Theme ought to be defined more by emotions and needs interacting with ideas.

Act Two starts with Rick trying to drown his pain in alcohol and the memories stirred tell of a deep love which ended abruptly. Now we know the reason for Rick's bitterness: love betrayed. His hurt has grown into a cynical shell preventing anything from reaching him. Only Ilsa's arrival provokes an uncharacteristic response.

As outlined in Chapter Four, Rick's need for an explanation, and to know that Ilsa still loves him, takes over the midsection of Act Two. The man whom no one could touch in Act One becomes vulnerable in Act Two. Even though he acts tough, he has a need and it is for Ilsa. He tries to force a confrontation with Laszlo to divide husband and wife, but Laszlo is above taking the bait. When Ilsa comes for the letters at the end of Act Two, she says she's prepared to kill him for them. Rick tells her to do it, thereby saying that he can't go on living the life of the cynic: he would rather die. Ilsa collapses into his arms, declaring her never-changing love for him. By the end of Act Two, we see cynicism and love coming together.

By the end of *Casablanca*, at the climax of Act Three, the action illustrates the selfless quality of true love. Love has overcome cynicism in the most amazing way.

As a character's transformational arc evolves through the plot and subplot of a story, so does the theme. The incidents which shape the character's transformation provide insight into the meaning of the work because they show what affects him. The

67

character's resultant choices define him. The last chapter states that the "screenwriter's job is to weave *how* the characters are influenced by events into the plot. How they are affected causes the plot to move one way or another." Meaning develops as we try to understand what happens to a character in the face of conflict, how the character handles the conflict or is beaten by it. The ubiquitous question living within each of us, uttered first when we are children, is *"why?"* "Why is the sky blue? Why are we here?" We are all innately curious and want to know why things happen. "Why?" is always at work in us, even when we see a film, whether we contemplate the greater meaning of it or not. When we are satisfied by a film, we have accepted the characters' motivations as true and have found their actions credible. When it works, a film *feels* right and it resonates with us, if not consciously then unconsciously. Even if we don't fully understand a work, our unconscious feels the meaning and we connect with it.

In a great film, theme declares itself in the climax. It is the sum of all the dramatic elements, of characterization, mood, action and, most importantly, transformation, which come together in the shape and end result of a particular climactic movement.

How Theme Unifies a Screenplay

Just as *why* constitutes part of our innate psychological makeup, so does our search for meaning. From the beginning of time, humanity has sought the answers to the riddles of life. Storytelling has been but one way we try to make sense of our lives. It is no coincidence that all the great philosophers and religious teachers use parables, simple stories illustrating religious or moral lessons, to relay their messages. Their stories are defined by the conflicts and the choices the people in them make.

Great writers and filmmakers understand these same concepts. So, when the main conflict is laid out and defined, we have the basis for understanding the significance of the work. How the final meaning is determined depends upon how the conflict plays out. In winning or losing, all is made clear.

This is true, however, only if the point of view is valid. The theme must hold true for more than just the author. "A return to innocence makes us whole" is an invalid theme because it's impossible: once innocence is lost, it's gone forever. Many unsuccessful films have untrue themes (or none at all), mainly because no one has paid attention to the point or to the levels of characterization which guide the work and determine its meaning. Many well-made films fail because the screenwriters and directors don't understand the themes suggested at the beginning, and so don't carry them through to the climax and resolution. Or, the theme that emerges at the final climax has never been set up at all, causing the film to feel disjointed and confusing to the audience. *Primary Colors* is an example of a film which seems to be on one thematic track in its first half, but then careens to another theme in the last act. This shift in focus usually alienates viewers because they feel like they've stepped into a different movie.

Once conflict is set up in the first act, the topic is fixed for the film. The protagonist is good, the antagonist evil; one is authoritarian, the other a nonconformist; one a corrupt cop, the other an naive crook. Your screenplay is going to deal with these concepts whether you want it to or not. The theme will develop with the introduction of new elements, but the ultimate meaning will be determined by how the forces interact and oppose each other to the bitter end.

THEMATIC UNITY IN TERMS OF CLIMAX

The synthesis between action and theme is best shown in the climax. Let's now examine the 1993 film, *The Piano*, written and directed by Jane Campion, produced by Jan Chapman.

The Piano

In a note at the beginning of the published screenplay for *The Piano*, Jane Campion writes:

> I think that the romantic impulse is in all of us and that sometimes we live it for a short time, but it's not part of a sensible way of living. It's a heroic path and it generally ends dangerously. I treasure it in the sense that I believe it's a path of great courage. It can also be the path of the foolhardy and the compulsive.

Campion tells us that the film is about the "romantic impulse," but how do we determine what its underlying meaning is to us? To understand a film's central theme, we must identify its main conflicts set up in the first act, the characters' dominant traits, their wants and needs, and then see how they develop through the film to the climax. Can you think what these elements might be?

Right from the start, we learn that Ada (Holly Hunter) is mute and has not spoken since she was six. She tells us, in her mind's voice, what her father says of it: "...it is a dark talent and the day I take it into my head to stop breathing will be my last." Her father has married her off to Stewart (Sam Neill) a New Zealand farmer, whose apparent charity she mocks in her opening introduction. Clearly, she is not happy with the situation but has no power to alter it. Her strongest feelings are saved for her piano; she communicates her deepest emotions through her playing. Now, with her daughter Flora (Anna Paquin), she leaves Scotland to meet her new husband.

Ada is willful, stubborn, unhappy. Obviously, something traumatic (though we don't know what), happened to her as a child that has made her guarded, difficult, unconventional; it causes her to withdraw from the world. She is suspicious of anyone trying to get close to her, except her daughter with whom she enjoys an almost childlike relationship. Through her piano, Ada seeks to communicate what she feels—her deepest passions, her spiritual being. And, her playing makes her truly unique. The only problem is that her mode of communication is one-sided, allowing no reciprocity, so she is inherently lonely. What she needs, desperately, is some sort of connection with someone.

Stewart is also lonely; he marries Ada because he wants a wife and family. He, too, needs connection. But Stewart is very different from Ada. He is grounded in the earth, in the here and now. He is trying to build a farm, acquire land, make something for himself. Stewart is far more conventional and materialistic than Ada. In his own way, he is as stubborn and egocentric as she is. But he lacks sensitivity. This is first shown when he meets Ada and comments that he never thought she would be small. A moment later he says to Baines (Harvey Keitel) that he thinks Ada is stunted. She has not lived up to his expectations. The inciting incident is when Stewart refuses to transport Ada's piano to his farm. When he leaves it on the beach, despite her desperate protests, he shows his insensitivity again. But, at the end of Act One, when he trades the piano to Baines for land, he betrays Ada and shows his true colors. What he truly values is property over his new wife and her feelings.

How can we distinguish the way these characters are set up in the first act? Look at the key character traits which define the protagonist and antagonist. Ada's most dominant trait is her defensiveness. She is afraid of connecting, for fear of being betrayed. Everything else, from the spirituality of her piano playing to the stubbornness of her will stems from her desire to protect herself. In so doing, she has cut out the world and lives a very solitary existence.

Stewart's dominant characteristic is his egocentrism, a typical male trait of the Victorian era. His conventional attitude and materialistic desires are derived from his egocentric world view. Sacrifices must be made for the good of the group, the family, but he will make all the decisions. They further his wishes, not necessarily anyone else's.

The film positions a defensive character opposite an egocentric one and seems to ask: How will they get along? Both characters need to find some kind of connection with the opposite sex to complete their lives. Stewart is consciously trying to but he betrays himself when he fails to consider his wife's feelings over his own wishes. Ada's need to connect is totally buried; she fights it at every turn. What will become of them once Stewart so unfeelingly trades Ada's piano to Baines at the end of act one?

There is one other element that must be considered in order to understand how the film develops, and that is Baines. Neither protagonist nor antagonist, Baines fulfills an important role in the film. Can you think of what it is? Introduced in the first act with Stewart, Baines has a half-finished *moko*, a Maori tattoo, on his face. He has given up his culture but he is not completely native, and so does not fully fit in either place; he is an outsider. He, too, is lonely and wants a connection. More empathetic than Stewart, Baines can see that Ada looks tired from her journey. He has no expectations and so sees more clearly. He is more sensitive than Stewart, too, and responds to Ada's pleas to go back to the beach and check her piano. When he hears her play, sees and feels the intensity of her passion, Baines knows he wants her. What is Baines' dominant trait? It's his empathy, his feeling.

What role does Baines play in the film? He functions as Ada's agent for change. His part in the constellation of characters becomes clearer at the beginning of the second act when he offers Ada his deal: the piano for her body. The deal he makes with Ada forces her to relate to another human being—to touch, feel and finally connect. Through the physicality of touching and Baines' appreciation of Ada's music (or soul), a deep and simmering eroticism takes hold and a connection is forged which changes them both. At the beginning of Act Two, Ada agrees to Baines' deal, trading her body for her piano, because she will do anything to get her piano back. By the midpoint, Baines returns the piano. He releases Ada from their bargain because her inaccessibility is making him "wretched" and her a "whore." His feelings for her cause him to suffer: he cannot continue unless he knows that she truly cares for him. It is in losing Baines that Ada realizes what she has come to feel: love. Baines becomes more important than her piano and now Ada suffers the burning passions in her heart.

What is truly original about *The Piano* is how Jane Campion allows Ada's need to connect, born in her relationship with Baines, to drive the film from this point on. Think about what is happening at this point: The typical mainstream film would have the protagonist recommit to her goal, despite a series of obstacles and complications which have made this goal more difficult than anticipated to achieve. But Ada actually changes her goal. Even though she has her piano back, she is not interested in playing it. Her need to connect takes over. Then, when she can no longer see Baines, she comes to Stewart, her husband, making a strange though erotic attempt to connect with him. In this act, she makes Stewart the sexual object and assumes a position of power in their relationship.

Toward the end of the second act, Ada learns that Baines is leaving and attempts to tell him of her love. She directs Flora to deliver her message, written on a key from her piano. Though she can't leave Stewart, she can express her feelings to Baines. But Flora, who has accepted Stewart as her father and who wants and needs a family, is jealous of her mother's relationship with Baines and sides with Stewart. She takes the note to Stewart and sets off an explosion of passion and violence which ends with Stewart chopping off Ada's finger.

What has brought us here? What has unleashed this hunger, pain and brutality, the highly-charged eroticism of the situation, introduced by Baines (the agent for change)? Ada now explores with Stewart the transforming eroticism that she experienced with Baines, leaving Stewart vulnerable and exposed. However, Ada does not have any true feelings for Stewart, so her actions do not serve to bind or connect them. Sexual jealousy then ignites a rage which harms and stuns them all. At this point, the film focuses upon the tragic damage done by living the erotic impulse. But Act Three is yet to come.

When Stewart's emotions calm, guilt arises and he realizes that he can't live with Ada or with what he has done. He wants the whole thing to be nothing more than a dream. He sets her free to leave with Baines who takes the numbed Ada, Flora and all their belongings on a treacherous sea journey. It becomes apparent immediately that the piano, perched precariously on the canoe, is making the boat dangerously unsteady in the choppy waters and that all the Maori oarsmen want to dump it overboard. But Baines will not hear of it, knowing how important it is to Ada. Suddenly, Ada tells Baines to throw the piano over the side. She doesn't want it anymore. Baines won't listen so she unties the instrument herself, making it completely clear what she wants.

The relationship Ada had to her piano has been forever altered by her mutilation at Stewart's hands. The one way she had to feel and fully express her emotions has been "spoiled." Ada now rejects the piano, the cause of so much suffering, and wants it thrown over the side. The piano, which has been the center of her being, a symbol for her Self, no longer serves that purpose; it no longer holds her together. Pushing the piano over is akin to killing herself.

Baines has the oarsmen stop rowing; they push the piano off the boat. As it begins to sink, Ada slips her foot into the coil of rope attached to the piano that is furiously unfurling, and she is pulled over the side. Down she sinks, seeking death as her escape, the result of this tragic interplay of forces. As the eerie silence envelops her, she takes in what it means. Then Ada awakens and struggles, against the depths and ropes, against death. She fights her way free and makes it to the surface, choosing life.

What does this action tell us? In the climax, Ada's true struggle with life is brought into high relief. The interaction with Stewart has been just one more in a long line of life's disappointments. Stewart represents conventional society that Ada will never be a part of, a society that betrayed her and that she has shunned since she stopped speaking as a child. Now physically crippled as well, she rejects life. The piano, the center of her being, has been "spoiled." The sum of her experiences, starting before the film opens and moving through all that we have seen to the climax, leads her to attempt suicide. But in confronting death, she discovers that she wants to live, despite all the suffering she has experienced. The connection she has forged with Baines, a fellow outsider, has given her something worth living for. Ada's choice affirms her journey which has taught her the value of reaching out, of touching, with her heart, and enables her to go on with Baines. The erotic impulse, born of Baines' feelings for Ada, enables her to change.

In the resolution, we find that the whole environment is changed. In contrast to the gloomy pall hanging over Stewart's place, their new home is light and airy, happy. We see that Ada is learning to speak. She is even playing the piano again, with a metal finger Baines has had fashioned for her. By accepting what Baines offers, Ada's life is transformed.

THE "MESSAGE IN THE BOTTLE"

Themes grow out of who you are and what you believe. The best themes come from your emotions, experiences and insights about yourself, people and the world. For a theme to be compelling to an audience, it must first have compelled you in some way: to understand, to believe, to share, to tie your individual beliefs to a collective ethic. It must be important to you. You must believe in it; if you do not, no one else will.

It is not essential to have the theme completely worked out when you begin, but it must be present by the final draft. The theme may emerge or change in the process of writing. It may take several drafts before you discover the theme of your piece. But whenever your theme emerges, it is best to let it help unify the story. The closer your story stays to its theme, the easier other choices related to it will be.

The topic of theme is always controversial. How it comes into being, when and who defines it, whether it is important at all, have all been debated. Films are first and foremost entertainment. But even in comedies, which are supposed to make us laugh, the best always comment on our condition. Think how much more satisfying *Groundhog Day* is than *Tommy Boy*. Stories should always be about something. The more conscious the writer is about what he is saying, the more powerful the pull of the message and the more effective the film. But don't beat anyone over the head. A good rule is to think of your theme as another writer's tool, not a message to be conveyed by your work, even though that is the ultimate goal.

SPECIAL NOTES

The Piano, an absorbing tale of alienation, passion and transformation, was nominated for eight Academy Awards in 1994, among them Best Picture and Best Director. It won for Best Actress (Holly Hunter), Best Supporting Actress (Anna Paquin), and Best Original Screenplay (Jane Campion).

At the end of the published screenplay is a chapter titled "The Making of The Piano," containing many interesting insights by Campion, producer Jan Chapman, actors Holly Hunter, Anna Paquin, Sam Neill, Harvey Keitel who also describe the genesis of the film.

The format of the published screenplay is different than a shooting script of a film, having more in common with a play than a screenplay. But despite the formatting differences, the content is the same. And this script contains everything we see in the film and more. Again, what we see are dialogue and scene, in some cases scene sequence, deletions from the screenplay and, in a few other cases, the reshuffling of the order of scenes to make a dramatic point. In the first half of the film, a scene introducing the Blackbeard play is moved to set up this line of action earlier.

One sequence cut entirely from the film starts just after the Act Two climax. It shows how Baines comes into possession of the piano key and how he must go to the local school to find someone who can read Ada's inscription to him. The film, instead, stays on the drama at hand: Flora follows Stewart's instructions by going to Baines with Ada's finger and telling him to never see her mother again. This keeps the momentum moving and building after the striking Act Two climax.

Another sequence which is edited to good effect has to do with Baines bringing a piano tuner to his hut to care for the piano. In the screenplay, he brings the man in after Ada hears the piano badly out of tune. In the film, these scenes are cut to two lines, and the piano tuner comes before Ada's initial visit. When she arrives for the first time and expects the piano to be out of tune, she is surprised when it isn't. This editing makes Baines more sensitive to Ada and more sympathetic to the audience.

The screenplay has more intercutting between Ada's story

75

line with Baines and Stewart's with the Maoris and their land. In the film, some of the scenes between Stewart and the Maoris have been cut and others grouped together, increasing the plot momentum by strengthening the cause-and-effect relationships between the scenes. The same is true of the Ada/Baines plot line. Grouping the scenes as they build to each new point in their relationship strengthens their story line. In the case of the Maoris, the screenplay gives them more attention than the film. But they are not crucial to the film; *The Piano* is the story of Ada, Baines and Stewart, not Ada and the Maoris. All of these changes serve to tighten the plot and keep the momentum moving to its final climax. And, in so doing, they strengthen the theme.

6

THE STRUCTURE OF PLOTTING
Study Film: *Chinatown*

Great films tell great stories. They are powerful and compelling, sometimes hilarious, but always engrossing. They demand our involvement. We become involved not just because the story is great but because it has wonderful characters and something important to say. The screenwriter has fashioned the telling of it into a great plot. Structuring the plot of a great film is distilling from all the elements of screenwriting—concept, characterization, theme, story, action, obstacles, etc.—a sequence of scenes that builds suspense, utilizes surprise and logically makes sense of all the factors while saying something meaningful by the end.

Constructing a believable, unpredictable and exciting plot ranks up there next to creating deep characterizations as one of the hardest aspects of screenwriting to master. The plot of a film must follow the rules of logic and still be unpredictable. It has to work on the audience's emotions without being manipulative. It has to weave together outer story problems with inner character dilemmas so that by the end every thread and every line of action relate to each other and no moment is wasted. The plot of a great film takes you on a journey, leading you down a path filled with highs and lows. There are unexpected obstacles as well as joys. Sudden complications often bring surprising advantages. When this plot arrives at its final destination, the tale it has told stays with you and leaves you enriched.

Chapters Two and Three laid out a rough structural plan defining very basically the acts—beginning, middle and end—and explaining the elements we usually see in them and how they relate to each other. Plotting is the way we "connect the dots" of a story to make it active. In film, we don't want to be told a story. We want to see it unfold.

STORY AND PLOT

Story and plot are not synonymous, although they are often used interchangeably. According to the *Concise Dictionary of Literary Terms*, story is a sequence of events, either true of fictitious, designed to interest, amuse or inform hearers, readers, or in our case, viewers. Plot refers to the arrangement of events to achieve an intended effect, a series of carefully devised and interrelated actions which progresses through a struggle of opposing forces to a climax and resolution. A story tells you what happens while a plot shows you via a causally related chain of events.

E.M. Forester made the distinction between plot and story in *Aspects of the Novel*:

> We have defined a story as a narrative of events arranged in their time sequence. A plot is also a narrative of events, the emphasis falling on a causality. "The king died and then the queen died" is a story. "The king died, and then the queen died of grief" is a plot. The time sequence is preserved, but the sense of causality overshadows it.

Plotting is the selection and arrangement of scenes. It organizes the narrative line around a rising action, orchestrating the characters' actions—how they go about trying to achieve their wants and needs—as they move through the story. As the characters attempt to reach their goals, they collide with each other. As the end nears and the protagonist and antagonist approach their goals, the conflict rises to generate maximum suspense and excitement. Plot uses such factors as conflict, tension, suffering, discovery, reversal, suspense, etc., as well as obstacles, complications, et. al., in its overall arrangement to build momentum and arouse curiosity. A strong plot goes somewhere; films without a clear plot often feel aimless, a mere sequence of events leading nowhere. Story may be the starting point but the goal in any film story is the creation of a plot made of scenes with strong cause-and-effect relationships.

Plot and the Total Narrative

Plot is a more specific form of story which shows what happens and comprises part of a total narrative. The total narrative consists of all the situations and events pertinent to the film but includes many that are not shown on screen. All the events previous to the beginning of the film, plus those enacted during the film, make up the narrative. The total narrative of *Witness* begins with the corrupt cops who stole the drugs years before the initial killing takes place which brings John Book to the scene. It ends when Book defeats Schaeffer and deals with the relationships he has formed as a result of his ordeal.

The following illustration represents the difference between narrative and story.

A   B   C

"A" is the beginning of the narrative; it might be considered the back story. The important events in the narrative leading up to the opening enter the film only as exposition after the film begins. "B" is the start of the story and the opening of the film (plot). "C" is the ending of the narrative, story and film.

In *Risky Business*, the total narrative begins with Joel's mediocre high school career. It ends when Joel gets into Princeton and meets Lana one last time to ask if she set him up.

In *Casablanca*, the total narrative begins with Rick's gun-running in the Spanish Civil War and Ethiopia. It ends when he puts Ilsa on the plane with Victor, shoots Maj. Strasser to keep him from stopping them, then walks off into the night with Renault to take up the good fight.

The total narrative of *The Piano* begins with whatever caused Ada to stop talking at age six. It ends when she looks death in the eye and realizes life is worth living after all and starts talking again.

Why are these distinctions important?

Because we have to determine the best place to start a film. A screenwriter wants to begin with a gripping situation rather than with the exposition needed to get to it. Understanding what is back story and what is the current story helps to create tension and maintain momentum because it allows the screenwriter to telescope certain events, to reorganize or restructure time within the plot and to build transitions to cover and yet not dramatize certain events.

Plot Unity

The ancient Greeks defined the parameters of Greek tragedy in the "three unities"—unity of time, place and action. For the Greeks, this meant a play's action was set in a single locale and took place during the course of a single day. Aristotle provided the rule for the unity of action in the *Poetics*.

> ...the plot, since it is a representation of an action, ought to represent a single action, and a whole one at that; and its parts (the incidents) ought to be so constructed that, when some part is transposed or removed, the whole is disrupted and disturbed. Something which, whether it is present or not, explains nothing [else], is no part of the whole.

Aristotle is saying that material not absolutely key to the plot's development doesn't belong in the work.

Long ago, theater shed the necessity of observing all three of these rules to tell a story, but realized that at least one was needed in order to focus the ideas of a story into a meaningful whole. A locale, a cast of characters, even a time span can provide the basic unity for a film story. But most often in film and theater, unity is provided by action. At a fundamental level, this is why most films and plays use a single protagonist with a specific goal to move the plot. It is the protagonist's pursuit of his objective which provides the story's unity of action and keeps the audience oriented to its basic meaning, which is, will he or won't he succeed? (Chapter Nine discusses different forms of plot unity at length.)

In order for a film to be truly great, it must have strong dramatic unity, which can be characterized as a synthesis of thematic unity and plot unity. The plot unity serves to create the spine for the action while the thematic unity provides the meaning.

THE ROLE OF CONFLICT

Action in drama depends upon conflict, which is defined as the opposition of persons or forces, the struggle in a plot which grows out of the interaction of opposing ideas, interests or wills. Conflict is the essence of storytelling; it is the starting point of all drama.

Conflict defines the parameters of the plot. Without it, a great story cannot be told. In storytelling, writers play upon our instinctive desire to watch other people fight it out: we all want to know who wins and who loses. Look at how people follow sports, court cases, wars. A film may be about the selflessness of true love, but unless it emphasizes a strong conflict to overcome, it will not hold an audience's interest. Conflict creates tension. It keeps people sitting in their seats wondering how it will all turn out in the end. But while we are vicariously absorbed in the fight, we also want to understand the nature of the conflict and so our minds constantly jump ahead, trying to make sense of it, to find meaning. It is meaningful conflict, i.e., one that is related to and dependent upon the other factors of the story (characterization being the most important), which keeps viewers on the edge of their seats.

In great films, the role of conflict is to keep the audience engaged and interested in the work while the film explores other larger issues and themes important to our lives.

Unity of Opposites

In a great film, conflict rises, reaching a higher and higher intensity as the plot unfolds. In order for the intensity of the conflict to increase, the protagonist and antagonist must be locked together with no compromise possible between them. They must be characters with purpose and strong convictions who will fight for what they want. They must be united by what opposes them.

Unity of opposites is the unbreakable bond that exists between protagonist and antagonist. It stands for whatever binds the characters together, forcing them to clash. In the best film, theater and fiction, none of the characters can compromise. Only a change in the situation or at least one of the characters can stop the conflict. Often, conflict can only end in the "death" of a dominant trait or quality of one of the main characters. However, "death" doesn't necessarily mean the death of a person. For instance, the breaking of family ties can be very powerful; think of *Ordinary People*. Ending a relationship often hurts; look at *Annie Hall* or *Husbands and Wives*.

Unity of opposites can be achieved when characters have the same goal but only one may win (*Raiders of the Lost Ark*). Family relationships can keep conflicting characters in constant association (*He Got Game*). Love can bring opposites together

(*Annie Hall*). The stronger and more specific the unity is, the harder it is to break.

What creates the unity of opposites in *Witness*? Samuel. (Book wants to protect the boy; Schaeffer and McFee want to kill him.)

What provides the unity of opposites in *Risky Business*? The Steuben egg. (Lana has taken it and Joel must get it back.)

In *Casablanca*, what is the unity of opposites? The Letters of Transit. (Ilsa and Victor must have them to save their lives and Rick withholds them to punish her for hurting him.)

In *The Piano*, what keeps bringing the conflicting characters together? Ada's piano (Baines wants it because he knows it will bring Ada to him).

Samuel, the egg, the letters, the piano, all stoke the conflict of their films by providing specific reasons why the characters in conflict must interact with each other until something significant changes in the situation that holds them together.

A specific object or character which the antagonists struggle over often strengthens a plot and film because it provides a strong tangible reason for the conflict, one that the audience can easily understand. The bonds of relationships (familial or romantic), are also immediately understood. In all great films, the unity of opposites is specific, clarifying what fuels the conflict and what characters must surrender in order for a resolution to be found.

Types of Conflict

Conflict in film does not always mean murder and mayhem. Conflict can be subtle—emotional, sexual, intellectual—as well as physically violent. Audiences often relate far more quickly to emotional conflict than physical violence because we have all experienced emotional friction in our lives. Very few adults have escaped life without emotional scars. In *Casablanca*, the conflict between Rick and Ilsa is based solely upon emotion: a broken love affair and a broken heart.

However, physical violence represents the meeting of uncompromising positions and so makes for good drama. Film will always rely on violence to tell stories, just as dreams (even for the unproductive dreamer) often use violence to get attention and illustrate their messages. In many great films, physical violence is an intricate part of the story and its success. In *The Piano*, the emotional conflict between all of the characters escalates until it finally erupts with such physical violence that it leaves both the characters and audience stunned.

Of course, conflict does not have to be physically or emotionally violent to illustrate a successful story. *Risky Business* is loaded with conflict that is not particularly emotional or violent. Still, it creates a predicament and engages the audience's interest by setting up a likable protagonist, one whom we want to see solve his problem.

Conflict Rises in Waves

To be effective in plot construction, conflict needs to rise in waves. Along the way there may be temporary solutions or cease-fires, but they shouldn't last. *Risky Business* careens from one temporary solution to another. Joel's first crisis arises when the black hooker arrives and he doesn't know what to do. He solves this problem when he agrees to pay for his/her time and car fare and he/she gives him Lana's number. This leads to Joel calling Lana later, initiating his next crisis when, in the morning, he can't pay the $300 he owes her. He leaves the house to cash his bond and upon returning home, she's gone with his mother's Steuben egg, creating an even bigger crisis. He solves this problem when he finds and rescues Lana from Guido and she promises to return the egg. This allows the two of them to interact on more friendly terms—until the next crisis arrives.

In *Witness*, Book and Rachel clash until Book hands over his gun for safekeeping. This produces a cease-fire which allows their relationship to grow and brings the audience deeper into the story.

These short-term solutions delay the audience's arrival at the moment of final confrontation with the antagonist. Delaying the confrontation can build tension but it also allows the writer time to fill in important details about the main characters. Therefore, we better understand the characters, the main conflict and the final meaning. These details help to influence the audience's relationship to the characters and story. A plot deepens and grows by including scenes which dramatize the main characters' reactions to the conflict of the plot. When we see John Book realize that his mentor has tried to kill him, we feel his betrayal. When we see Ada's reaction to the news that Stewart has sold her beloved piano, we experience her pain and rage. When we see Rick watch Victor Laszlo lead the club in "Marseillaise," we sense his admiration grow for his rival. As with real relationships in life, we need time to understand the allies we have and the foes we face.

Probability, Not Predictability

When conflict is properly conceived and handled, a film has a better chance of fulfilling the audience's expectations. Not because viewers are able to predict the outcome, but because the inevitability of the conclusion feels true to them. At the beginning of a screenplay, anything is possible. But after the first scene, the possibilities of what can happen become increasingly limited. Once the beginning indicates a specific situation, group of characters and conflict, the screenwriter leaves the realm of the possible and enters the realm of the probable. Logic must take over. As the plot unfolds, the characters must follow one or more lines of probability in reaction to the conflict so that, by the end, the screenwriter is limited to only what is necessary. Because the characters have said and done specific things, there can be only one necessary resolution.

This doesn't mean that the climax is inevitable from the start. Far from it. A good screenwriter constructs a plot to get the audience wondering what will happen next and what the final outcome will be. The plot of a film must appear as though it is changing directions in order to keep the audience guessing about what may happen. Otherwise, the audience will lose interest. (How many times have you heard "predictable" used as a criticism of a movie?)

Look at *Casablanca*. At the beginning, Rick is cynical and bitter. As events proceed and he learns important information about Paris, he begins to soften. He witnesses the heroics of Victor Laszlo on more than one occasion and can't help but be affected. By the end of Act Two, Ilsa has come back to him and they make plans to leave together. At the beginning of Act Three and until its end, Rick appears to be selling Victor out. But Rick is really orchestrating Laszlo and Ilsa's escape. At the end, when Rick sends her away, it makes sense he would act this way because of all we have seen (even though it goes against everything he has said during the film).

As the protagonist faces obstacles and complications, he must alter his course to get what he wants. New characters bring new possibilities to the plot. Misunderstandings, missed opportunities and failures cast doubt on the story's outcome. In fact, some of the best surprises in films come from the transformation of character. A character changes or grows to do something right or something wrong, and in so doing affects the plot of the film. It is the screenwriter's job to incorporate and orchestrate these changes into the plot in order for the audience to accept them.

One last note: problems with a film's ending do not indicate trouble with one or two final scenes, but rather, trouble with a plot that has disintegrated—and characters not logically realized—far before that. Audiences often leave a theater saying they liked a film but didn't like the ending. As a screenwriter, you should know there are problems long before the end.

THE PRINCIPLES OF ACTION

In the best films, the action of the plot is based on the characters, who they are, what they want and need, what their motivations are. They desperately want to achieve their goals. The plot of a great film depends upon the protagonist pushing the action forward, either from his own design or as a reaction to a situation. The protagonist and antagonist are always committed to their goals. If they aren't, the audience won't be. A great plot orchestrates the conflict via a chain of events which rise from specific characters who are locked in a particular situation (or conflict). Then, it is developed through one episode after another to a climax and resolution. Plot is structured action, and structure in drama is crucial. Arbitrary form in a screenplay is deadly.

No one section of the plot (beginning, middle or end) is more important than the rest. All are equally significant. Yet, if the beginning set-up doesn't poise the protagonist in the middle of a situation which demands a strong reaction, chances are the plot will lose steam in the middle as the protagonist loses motivation and direction. The opening section of a film (Act One) must create a character in a situation who will take action powerful enough to drive a plot to its dramatic climax. Without a dramatic problem, the plot cannot sustain the character's or audience's interest.

Think about the films we've looked at so far. Every one of them creates a dramatic situation in the first act which demands a personal reaction from the protagonist. The set-ups get the films up and running, demanding responses not only from the protagonists but from the antagonists as well.

This demand for a response from the protagonist and antagonist is key to understanding the principles of action. All great plots are based on causality. One action causes another and another and so on. The audience understands and processes information this way, causally ("a" causes "b" which causes "c"). We need to see a relationship in what's happening, the chain of events, to become fully involved in the plot. In a great film, the threads of action and reaction weave everything together, creating a tapestry of character, emotion, plot and theme.

Narrative momentum, too, depends upon causal relationships between scenes. If there is no obvious connection between the scenes, the plot breaks down because the audience must struggle to find the meaning. The right conception and arrangement of scenes engages the audience's interest and curiosity in a character and situation and carries the momentum of the plot forward, keeping the audience involved in the story.

Plot is not a complex structure created out of thin air and then handed over to a group of characters to act out. Plot develops as a writer turns the general theme and characters into specific details—actions, dialogue, circumstances, time and place. Good plot evolves naturally from the reaction of a certain character (or characters) in a specific situation.

A screenwriter creates strong causal relationships by thinking in terms of:

a) cause-and-effect scene relationships
b) rising conflict (move and countermove)
c) foreshadowing of the conflict.

Cause-and-Effect Relationships

In a cause-and-effect relationship, each scene advances the action of the plot and causes a reaction in the following scene (or scenes). In other words, scenes are related through action and reaction. Since the protagonist's overall story goal isn't resolved until the end of the film, writers dramatize the pursuit of that goal and what happens as a result of pursing it. However, the successful film plot does not focus solely on scenes showing the active pursuit of the goal or only on the points of active conflict between the antagonists; it also includes the reactions of the main characters, especially the protagonist, to the obstacles, complications, losses and even successes encountered—the costs emotional and otherwise. Irwin Blacker writes in *The Elements of Screenwriting*, "Plot is more than a pattern of events; it is the ordering of emotions."[1] In all great films, this is true; emotions come into play and the action of the plot changes as a result. When viewers see the characters' reactions to the conflict, they are better able to identify with them through their own emotional responses to the action. The audience becomes more deeply involved. Emotion allows the audience to empathize with and understand the characters better.

When the emotional side of the story is left out, the characters feel less true and films lose dimension. A plot pushed by action and not characters' emotions manipulates the characters like puppets, making viewers less likely to fully embrace them. If plot is all action and little real emotion, a film turns into melodrama. Director Sidney Lumet said in *Making Movies*, "drama is when characters move the plot; melodrama, when the plot moves characters."[2]

Cause and effect, action and reaction, drive the plot ahead. Let's look at the opening 20 minutes of *Chinatown* (written by Robert Towne, directed by Roman Polanski and produced by Robert Evans), a film which might easily have disintegrated into melodrama, but instead rises to the highest levels of tragedy because of the depth of the characterizations. Here, the relationships between the scenes are masterfully handled. Sequences built on actions and reactions keep the film focused and moving ahead.

Chinatown—Cause and Effect Relationships

Chinatown opens in the office of the protagonist, Jake Gittes (Jack Nicholson), as he gives bad news to Curly (Burt Young), an obvious working-class man who has hired Gittes to find out if his wife is cheating on him. Contrasted with Curly, Gittes immediately is set up as successful, self-assured, cocky. He understands human nature and is confident of his ability to read people.

The second scene starts the story. Gittes meets with Mrs. Mulray (Diane Ladd), wife of Hollis Mulray, who is Chief Engineer of the City of Los Angeles Department of Water and Power. She wants to find out if her husband is "seeing another woman." Unable to dissuade her, Gittes takes the case. Now the story can be told and plot begin.

In the third scene, Gittes attends a City Council meeting where exposition is introduced about the drought hitting Los Angeles, the proposed dam and the conflict over whether to build it or not. This is Gittes' first response to being hired by Mrs. Mulray.

The next scene shows Gittes following Mulray to the Los Angeles riverbed where he again watches the City Engineer, but this time from a distance. Again, this is a response, a reaction, to being hired. He sees Mulray talk to a Mexican boy on horseback. Later, this action will be revisited when Gittes meets and talks to the boy about Mulray.

Gittes then follows Mulray to the beach. As he watches Mulray, he is caught in a stream of water rushing down a culvert to the ocean. This, too, is important exposition which will pay off later as Gittes tries to make sense of the case.

In the next scene, Gittes, wet and irritated, sets a cheap pocket watch under Mulray's car tire to determine how long the man stays at the beach. He takes this action as a result of getting wet.

In the next scene, Gittes is back in his office meeting with his associate who has also followed Mulray and taken photographs of him. The pocket watch is on his desk, showing that Mulray didn't leave the beach until late into the night. This ties the present scene specifically to the preceding one. It is clearly action and reaction. (We saw Gittes put the watch into play in the last scene, now we see what happened to it in this one.) More exposition is given in this scene, via the photos showing Mulray arguing with an older man who will turn out to be Gittes' chief antagonist—Noah Cross (John Huston). But at this point, we don't know who the man is. In fact, Gittes is annoyed because they have found nothing. Then the phone rings. It is Gittes' other associate. He has found Mulray with a girl. This is what they've been looking for.

The following short scenes show Gittes and his associates photographing Mulray and the girl. They have solved the case. This seems to be the final response to the action presented in the second scene: the cause (Mrs. Mulray hiring him) and the effect (photographing Mulray with the "cute little twist").

However, the next scene shows that the photographs have ended up in the newspaper with Gittes named in the article. This now begins a whole new set of problems for Gittes. Before the pictures ended up in the newspaper, his problem (of discovery) was solved. Now, with the publicity, he finds himself the center of a new dilemma. With the newspaper in hand, the scene shows Gittes in a barber shop having to deal with the effect of the photos landing in the paper. A man severely criticizes him for his role in the scandal. Put on the defensive, Gittes reveals how he views his work—he makes an honest living and tries to help people. This is Gittes' emotional response: he's upset about what has happened, but he's not going to take it lying down. Gittes is ready to take the man, a mortgage banker, outside and pop him. It is his barber's quick thinking and funny joke which mollify Gittes.

The next scene shows Gittes arriving at his office, bursting with a new joke to tell—the one he's just heard. Again, this is cause and effect. (The previous scene shows him hearing the joke, the next shows him telling it.) His staff, unable to stop him, listen to the joke, all the while knowing that the real Mrs. Mulray (Faye Dunaway) is waiting for Gittes. (This happens about seventeen minutes into the film.) Evelyn Mulray threatens to sue Gittes since she clearly didn't hire him. This is the inciting incident of the film. Now Gittes really has a problem, one that puts his own career in jeopardy. The scenes move ahead to the climax of the first act, the discovery of Mulray's body.

The scenes here are all related, one to the next, by action and reaction, cause-and-effect relationships. They are wonderfully crafted so that the connections linking the scenes seem to effortlessly pull us forward with the plot as it unfolds. You can pick out any section of *Chinatown* and find the same thing, scenes relate to each other seamlessly, and that's what keeps the action moving ahead.

When scenes do not affect the ones immediately following them or the reactive influence of one scene is not shown until many scenes later, momentum is lost and the audience loses interest. In great films, one action causes another action and another and so on, and this keeps the transitions strong and the characters from becoming boring. All good stories concern themselves with characters' emotional responses to the plot action. Good writers know they must show this side of the story to keep the audience relating to the material. It helps us understand the characters' motivations and feel empathy for them.

Rising Conflict
Rising conflict is also based on causality. But it is distinguished from mere action and reaction by the nature of the conflict. Rising conflict orchestrates the actions between protagonist and antagonist as they conflict with each other over what they both want to achieve. One makes a move, the other counters it. One attacks, the other counterattacks. After the action has been set up, the attacks and counterattacks usually become increasingly

more serious and threatening to the protagonist as the plot progresses, especially in the second half of the film. As the attacks and counterattacks escalate, they lead directly to the last crisis and climax.

Again, this type of conflict plays upon viewers' natural inclinations to be drawn to discord and strife. If we see a scuffle on the street, our natural tendency is to stop and look. How many times have you been in a traffic slowdown on a freeway, expecting to see an accident ahead? When you come to the accident, it's on the other side of the freeway. The cause of your slowing has been everyone's desire to see what has happened. Rising conflict takes that inborn propensity and focuses it upon the drama at hand.

Again, let's look at *Chinatown*.

Chinatown—Rising Conflict

What is the first action the antagonist takes which directly affects Gittes?

One could argue it is the fake Mrs. Mulray hiring Gittes. But if Gittes' name had been left out of the newspaper article, conceivably the whole mess might have avoided him. Once the photographs end up on the front page with his name, causing the real Mrs. Mulray to take action, Gittes is drawn into the plot. His reputation is at stake. Gittes' first move is to try and talk to Mulray himself, but Gittes only catches up with the man after he's dead. This is the end of the first act. Our story now becomes about murder.

Gittes investigates, trying to track down clues to what happened, who used him. Conflicts are set up with Lt. Escobar (Perry Lopez), Gittes' former partner when he was a police officer, and with Escobar's assistants. Gittes' investigation leads him to the Oak Pass Reservoir where he runs into two thugs. They get the jump on Gittes, threaten him and slit his nose as a warning.

This attack spurs Gittes on: from this point, Gittes is determined to get to the bottom of the mystery. It is as much a matter of pride for him as it is discovering the truth. When he convinces Evelyn Mulray that her husband was murdered and she hires him to find out what happened, he draws a second response from the antagonist: Noah Cross, Evelyn's father, invites Gittes to his hacienda on Catalina Island. Cross tries to influence Gittes' view of his daughter and hires the detective to find the girl who he says was Mulray's girlfriend.

After further digging, Gittes makes the connection between the water run off, the real estate in the Valley and the Mar Vista Inn and Rest Home. At the rest home, as the plot becomes clearer to him, he's confronted by the two thugs he met at the Oak Pass Reservoir. But Gittes, with Evelyn's help, gets away from them.

The antagonist's next move is to have Ida Sessions (Diane Ladd), the actress who pretended to be Mrs. Mulray, killed, leaving the photographs Gittes took in her apartment. This draws in the police: they think Gittes is extorting money from the real Mrs. Mulray who killed her husband. Here, a key detail comes out: Mulray had saltwater in his lungs. Gittes' reputation and position are on the line when Escobar accuses him of being an accessory to the crime. He buys some time and heads off to find Evelyn. She's not at home and the house is being closed up, but he learns that the backyard pond contains saltwater and he discovers the bifocal eye glasses. Thinking he knows what's going on, Gittes calls Cross and tells him he has found the girl. Gittes is ready for a big payoff.

As a result of what Cross and Escobar have added to his investigation, Gittes believes he has figured things out. Wanting to hang onto his license, he drives to the home of Evelyn's maid, accuses Evelyn of killing her husband and confronts her about the girl. Instead, he learns the truth about Evelyn, the girl and Cross: her father raped her and the girl is her daughter. All Gittes wants now is to save Evelyn from her father.

After ditching Escobar, Gittes meets his true antagonist, Cross, at Mulray's home. Believing he has Cross for Mulray's murder (with the bifocals as his evidence), Gittes gets the rich and powerful man to admit his past actions and what he's doing in the Valley. However, Cross and his thug have the drop on Gittes. At gunpoint, they force Gittes to take them to Evelyn. Here, in Chinatown, the climax unravels. Police are everywhere, having followed Gittes' associates, and Evelyn is unable to get away. In the chaos, Gittes can't save her from the forces at work. After wounding her father, she tries to escape but is shot and killed by a cop. Cross takes the girl away and Escobar lets Gittes go, because he understands it's "Chinatown."

A film doesn't need an unrelenting rising conflict to be effective. A great film always has more than just the main conflict between protagonist and antagonist going on. Other obstacles stand in the protagonist's way as he pursues his goal. Complications arise along the course of the plot which the protagonist must cope with. The subplot usually presents obstacles and problems to be overcome. How the protagonist meets these problems, obstacles and complications helps deepen his characterization as well as the full meaning of the film.

Yet, there's no escaping it—the main conflict defines the plot. It is the spine which determines the main action of the story. Understanding the main conflict in terms of moves and countermoves, attacks and counterattacks, allows the writer to interweave these plot lines into an overall pattern of events. This keeps the audience interested in the other aspects of the film, which may hold the story's real importance.

Foreshadowing the Conflict

To foreshadow means, literally, to show or indicate beforehand; to prefigure. In drama, we use the term in reference to conflict, meaning, the promise of conflict to come. Foreshadowing is also based on causality but the effect is not felt until later in the story. Foreshadowing usually comes in the first half of a film, closer to the beginning, when the conflict is being set up but tension is necessary to provide a narrative hook.

For instance, in *Risky Business*, Joel's anxiety dream hints at some hidden conflict within the protagonist that will come into play later in the film. Another example is when Miles calls the hooker: we know she's coming; we're waiting now for something to happen and to see how Joel will respond to the problem.

In *Witness*, Samuel identifies McFee, a police officer, as the killer. Because he is a policeman, we expect some kind of trouble.

In *Casablanca*, Sam doesn't want to play "As Time Goes By" for Ilsa. When she forces him to, we know something is going to happen.

In *The Piano*, we hear the tone of Ada's inner voice as she tells us her father has married her to a man in New Zealand whom she has never met. We know there is going to be conflict.

In *Chinatown*, when the phony Mrs. Mulray hires Gittes to get the goods on her "husband," the head of Water and Power, we know this means trouble for someone.

Foreshadowing alerts the audience that something threatening is lurking in the wings. This sense of foreboding grabs our attention. Now we wait, expecting something to take shape.

Lajos Egri writes in *The Art of Dramatic Writing* that any uncompromising character can create expectancy in the mind of the audience. He goes on to say:

People distrust strangers. Only in conflict can you "prove" yourself. In conflict your true self is revealed. On the stage, as well as in life, every one is a stranger who does not first "prove" himself. A person who stands by you in adversity is a proven person. No, you cannot fool the audience. Even an illiterate knows that politeness and smart talk are not signs of sincerity or friendship. But sacrifice is.[3]

Egri believes that most people are interested in witnessing others being forced to reveal their true characters under the stress of conflict. It is a "fatal fascination," he says. And it's true. Uncompromising characters not only lead to the creation of strong tension, but they are the key to writing great screenplays and making great films. Uncompromising characters lead to conflict—the stuff great dramas are made of.

SPECIAL NOTES

Chinatown, released in 1974, and was nominated for nine Academy Awards, including Best Picture, Best Actor and Best Actress. Robert Towne, whose script is truly a tour de force of writing, won the Oscar for Best Original Screenplay.

In the original screenplay, Gittes and Evelyn get away at the end, but after discussions with the director and producer, changes were made. The resulting film captured the tenor of the times with the fall of Vietnam and Richard Nixon's resignation.

The third draft of the screenplay, dated October 9, 1973, is beautifully written, with attention paid to minor details which help set tone and create an authentic air. It is 145 pages long; the film is two hours and eleven minutes. The screenplay contains almost everything we see in the film. There are no changes made to the structure of the story. Except for the staging of the climax, the changes made from script to film involve line and scene deletions. There are three scenes of one or more pages cut from the screenplay. One cut scene shows Gittes discussing with his associates the ramifications of the real Mrs. Mulray showing up. Another shows him discussing Evelyn with the pilot of the seaplane that is taking him out to Catalina Island to see Cross. In the last cut scene, Gittes meets a rainmaker in the valley on his way to the avocado fields. These scenes add exposition more than action, which ultimately proved unnecessary for understanding of the story.

A number of the scenes are trimmed of their opening and closing lines. For instance, at the beginning, when Gittes is finishing up with Curly in his office, he has a speech in the screenplay which ultimately sums up the film. Curly says he's going to kill his wife for cheating on him. "They don't kill a guy for that," Curly cries. Gittes responds: "I'll tell you the unwritten law, you dumb son of a bitch, you gotta be rich to kill somebody, anybody and get away with it. You think you got that kind of dough, you think you got that kind of class?" This speech is cut from the film. In a sense, it is too on-the-nose to come this early in the film. Although it might have worked, it is unnecessary, since the film illustrates that point of view.

Endnotes:

1. Blacker, Irwin R. *The Elements of Screenwriting*. Collier Books, MacMillan Publishers, New York, 1986, p. 20.

2. Lumet, Sidney, *Making Pictures*. Knoft, New York, 1995, p. 111.

3. Egri, Lajos. *The Art of Dramatic Writing*. Simon & Schuster, New York, 1960, p. 180.

7

REVIEW

Study Film: *Quiz Show*

The previous six chapters have discussed the foundation of screenplay structure in great films. Before we go forward, let's review what we've learned so far and apply it to a film which doesn't readily lend itself to easy analysis: *Quiz Show*, written by Paul Attanasio, produced and directed by Robert Redford.

In 1995, the film was nominated for four Academy Awards, Best Picture, Best Director, Best Adapted Screenplay (based on a chapter in the book "Remembering America: A Voice From the Sixties" by Richard Goodwin), and Best Supporting Actor (Paul Scofield). It won a British Academy Award for Best Adapted Screenplay, the New York Film Critics Award for Best Film, and Golden Globe Awards for Best Director, Best Film-Drama, Best Screenplay, Best Supporting Actor (John Turturro).

Quiz Show is a modern-day *Faust*, a brilliant telling of the scandal surrounding the late 1950s TV game show *21* which ruined the lives of several men and disillusioned the American public, while the real profiteers, the network and the show's sponsors, escaped reproach. The film is a superb meditation upon corporate greed, class rivalry and the power of television.

If you haven't viewed the film lately, now is the time to do so.

THE CHARACTERS: WHAT THEY WANT AND WHAT THEY NEED

While all great films are stories about the relationships between characters, *Quiz Show* is particularly interesting because it weaves together the lives of three men who each push the action at different points in the plot. For some viewers, this creates confusion surrounding whose story it is. Is it Herb Stempel's (John Turturro)? Is it Charles Van Doren's (Ralph Fiennes)? Is it Richard Goodwin's (Rob Morrow)? Who is the true protagonist?

The story is clearly Charlie's, who is at the heart of the drama. But at different points in the film, both Stempel and Goodwin drive the action of the plot. Usually, films follow one protagonist as he tries to achieve his goal. Or, if there are multiple plot lines, then the film may follow several protagonists, all of whom are trying to achieve something. *Quiz Show* is about the convergence of three characters with conflicting wants and needs surrounding the game show *21*. As such, it allows each character to take up the thread of the same plot at different points. Since, the title of the film is *Quiz Show*, it is the show which provides the unity for the plot.

The structure of the plot puts Charlie at the center, showing his corruption, fall and, finally, his personal redemption. He is the protagonist, but Charlie doesn't really push the action as much as react to the actions taken by others—Dan Enright (David Paymer) and Richard Goodwin. Stempel compels the action in the first act as Charlie innocently arrives on the scene, dreaming of minor glory. When Charlie achieves Stempel's goal on a grander scale, by winning more money over the course of more shows, on *21*, he seems to be set. In the second act, Charlie's rise causes Stempel's wrath to increase until Stempel's actions bring Goodwin into the picture. Once Goodwin starts digging, Charlie truly has something to resist. Goodwin wants to expose the networks for betraying the public trust, but he needs Charlie to do it. With Goodwin's introduction, Charlie wants to avoid exposure and embarrassment to his family. This is his driving want.

Stempel, Goodwin, Enright, Freedman (Hank Azaria), the network chief Kintner (Allan Rich) and the show's sponsor, all have driving wants, too. Stempel really wants to get back on television, but when that becomes an impossibility, he wants revenge, in the form of bringing down Charlie. Goodwin wants to make a name for himself. He sees his investigation into television as the perfect opportunity to do this—if he succeeds in proving that game shows are fixed and the public trust in the networks is being betrayed. Enright and Freedman want to continue producing a successful show. They do not want Goodwin to discover the truth and will lie to prevent it. Kintner and the show's sponsor want to keep up appearances that both network and product are clean in the scandal. Goodwin and Stempel want to expose the hoax, while Charlie and the others want to prevent them from exposing it.

So who is the antagonist? Is it Stempel? Is it Goodwin? Each creates obstacles for Charlie. Is it Dan Enright? Enright is the real antagonist for Charlie, and this is one of the truly original constructs of the film. Most antagonists overtly oppose the protagonist, but early in *Quiz Show*, Enright wins Charlie to his side. Then, he exploits Charlie's naiveté and personal dissatisfaction to involve him in the deception. Enright causes Charlie to lose his way and to enter into a deal which betrays everything his family believes in. Enright does everything in his power to keep Charlie on the show because of his popularity and success and tries to be more of a friend than a foe. But Enright is the real antagonist because he stands for the forces of corruption, the seemingly innocent acts of dishonesty which lead us further from ourselves.

What does Charlie need? He wants to find something of his own to succeed at, to win his father's approval. Charlie's most important need, in relationship to the plot, is to clear his conscience. He finally comes to his father Mark Van Doren (Paul Scofield), to do so, which then puts him before Goodwin's subcommittee. Goodwin has a strong need, too. Despite his desire for glory, he does not want to drag Charlie and his family through the mud. He needs to hold onto to his humanity in the face of power politics. Meanwhile, Stempel needs to let go of his anger and get on with his life.

This well-conceived cast of characters, richly drawn, with strong conflicts set up between them, makes for a potent drama. The screenwriter has created wonderful, multidimensional characters whom the actors have perfectly realized in the film. We have a likable protagonist with feet of clay. We keep rooting for him to get out of this mess, maybe by doing the right thing, and wondering how he'll ever recover. We have a somewhat sympathetic antagonist, though there are plenty of other oily characters to loathe. Stempel's character is not totally repugnant, because he is shown as a man with hopes and dreams, however unrealistic they might be. Goodwin, though on a quest, is a man with a heart. Enright and Freedman have valid points of view toward their goals. This contributes to the film's overwhelming sense of truth and credibility.

Each of the three main characters faces hard, moral choices in the plot which delineates their characters. Charlie makes a choice when he answers the first winning question correctly and goes along with the deception. Then he faces another when he must decide whether or not to come clean. All he wants is something of his own, to shine for himself, but he makes a Faustian bargain to get it. He fears bringing shame upon his house, living in a family which cherishes the truth. Goodwin decides to go after the "big case." When he succeeds in bringing television to its knees, then he'll be able to write his own ticket, both politically and socially. (Don't forget that Goodwin is Jewish, too, like Stempel.) Once he's into his investigation, he makes another choice: not to involve Charlie and therefore hurt the Van Dorens. Unfortunately, events get the better of him and he cannot achieve this goal. Stempel chooses to avenge himself at any cost. He is totally irrational because he will destroy himself even though he can't see it.

The Agent for Change and the Transformation of Character

Clearly, all three of the main characters—Charlie, Stempel and Goodwin—are changed by the events of the film. The reputations of Charlie and Stempel are destroyed while Goodwin is disillusioned. Though Stempel causes the problems for Charlie, it is Goodwin's dogged pursuit of the truth that propels Charlie toward his crisis. This makes Goodwin the agent for change, because he forces Charlie to recognize the value and importance of truth. Even Stempel, at the end, seems changed by what has happened and this, too, is brought about by Goodwin's investigation.

Charlie's character arc is well drawn. He starts the film a boyish man, innocently enthusiastic yet somehow already disillusioned. A man who has yet to find himself. By the end of the film, which has shown him soar so high, he has lost his youthful ebullience but found the truth of his own character.

PRIMARY MOVEMENTS

The primary movement of Act One trades Stempel's success on *21* for Charlie's. In Act Two, the primary movement takes Charlie from his initial high at the start of his rein on the show to his abdication due to the pressures brought on by Goodwin's investigation. The primary movement of Act Three gives Goodwin his subcommittee meeting but ends with his failure to "get" TV and save Charlie.

Defining these movements allows us to see the relatively simple structure the film plot is based on. The complexity of the film comes from the deep levels of characterizations the screenwriter achieves by incorporating how the events affect each of the three main characters as well as the lives of their closest family members.

OVERALL STRUCTURE

Though Act One introduces the three main characters within the first ten minutes, it focuses on Stempel's predicament, caused when Enright tells him to lose. The main exposition introduces *21*, sets up Stempel and his problem, establishes Charlie and his family, and shows that Goodwin is unhappy at his work. In the middle of the main exposition, the sponsor calls the network to get rid of Stempel. This scene is the inciting incident. Charlie and Goodwin are both weaved into the plot line of Act One; Goodwin minimally, but Charlie more importantly when his desire brings him into the network to try out for another game show. Enright and Freedman spot their "great white hope" and try to convince Charlie to let them make him the new champion on *21*. Charlie declines to be part of the "fix" but agrees to go on the show: he wants to win, but win honestly. The Act One climax comes after Stempel takes the dive and Charlie takes the bait by responding to the question he's already answered for Enright. Charlie is the new champion. This occurs about 32 minutes into the film. It is the first step leading to Charlie's corruption and downfall and Stempel's seething resentment toward him.

Quiz Show is like *Casablanca* in that it takes the whole first act to set up the problem or basis of the film: Stempel's fall and Charlie's rise. No one rushes the development; the plot unfolds as the characters react to the situations they are in. But once the direction of the story is set—the collision of Stempel's neurotic rage with Charlie's innocent dreams—the plot stays on it. Other characters become involved, but only as a result of these two men succumbing to the power and lure of television.

Act Two grows out of Act One, with a montage juxtaposing Charlie's growing celebrity and Stempel's throbbing anger (which causes him to threaten Enright and then go to the grand jury).

These developments lead to Goodwin getting wind of the inquiry, learning of the sealed grand jury presentment (approximately 40 minutes into the film) and his interest being piqued. He arranges a trip to New York to find out what has happened (another new development). Now, Goodwin is on a quest to find the truth and this directs the rest of the film.

Goodwin looks for someone who will talk to him and, through a mutual connection, he hooks up with Charlie (48 minutes into the film). At first Charlie doesn't understand what Goodwin is doing and charms the attorney. Clearly, Goodwin respects Charlie and his family, and hopes the young instructor will be of help. When Charlie realizes what Goodwin is after, he denies any knowledge of wrongdoing and directs Goodwin to Enright. Charlie now begins to worry, anticipating how exposure of the fraud would embarrass his family. Enright dodges Goodwin, but finally, the attorney crosses paths with Stempel who reveals that Enright forced him to take a dive by promising him a spot on a panel show. Stempel also claims the show is fixed for racial purposes.

When Goodwin finally meets with Enright, the producer believably contradicts Stempel's story, casting Stempel not as fall guy but as a victim of his own neurosis. Goodwin is set to abandon his quest when he finds Stempel waiting for him at his hotel. Confronted by Enright's story, Stempel now admits he got the answers to the questions and charges that Charlie is getting them, too. This changes everything for Goodwin and serves as the midpoint of the plot (occurring about 68 minutes into the 130-minute film). Now, Goodwin wants to nail the networks even more.

From the midpoint to the end of Act Two, Goodwin continues to go after the networks but wants to avoid sending any embarrassment Charlie's way. All Goodwin wants from Charlie is the truth. But Charlie refuses to tell it to him. As Goodwin continues to look for corroboration of Stempel's story, Charlie's worry increases. Charlie tries to tell his father but can't bring himself to admit what he's done. Next, Goodwin finds Snodgrass, the artist who sent himself by registered mail a letter with the questions he was asked when a contestant on the show. Now Goodwin has the proof he needs (new development). Charlie throws the show but signs a contract with the network. Goodwin tells Enright about Snodgrass's letter, trying to convince him to testify against the network and sponsor. In the aftermath of the climax, Act Two ends with Charlie still denying to Goodwin that he received the answers, but Goodwin not believing him. Goodwin then asks Charlie not to do anything to force him to call Charlie in front of the subcommittee. Act Two ends about 92 minutes into the film.

Act Three begins with the subcommittee hearings. Stempel testifies and implicates Charlie, though few believe him. Kintner comes to Charlie and asks him to make a statement denying any wrongdoing. This leads to Goodwin having to sub-poena Charlie. Now Charlie confesses to his father who, though devastated, agrees to accompany his son to Washington. At the final climax, Charlie makes his statement, admitting his role in the fraud and destroying his reputation. But he does not im-plicate the network or sponsor in any way. Enright and Freed-man follow, testifying specifically that the network and spon-sor were not involved. Goodwin succeeds in exposing the fact that 21 was rigged but does not "get" television; Charlie loses his job, respect, his public life; Stempel comes to realize the tragedy he caused.

Five Focal Points

The underpinnings of the overall structure hinge on five focal points. The first, the inciting incident, is when the sponsor wants Stempel off the show. Now the action is off and moving as the show's producers search for their new champion. The next focal point comes at the end of the first act: Charlie is the new champ, although by winning, he has struck his Faustian bargain. The sponsor and producers have achieved their goal. However, the turn of events gives rise to new developments growing out of Stempel's anger and resentment. These developments bring in Goodwin to investigate. This leads Goodwin to Charlie, whom he likes immensely, and also to Stempel. Just when it looks as if Goodwin's investigation will come to naught, Stempel tells Goodwin he got the answers to the game show questions and charges that Charlie did, too. This strong midpoint keeps Goodwin investigating. Because of Goodwin's investigation, Charlie's life in the limelight becomes too hot. He throws the show in the second act climax but refuses to tell Goodwin the truth in the aftermath of the Act Two climax. The film now rises to the third act climax: What will Charlie do when he answers the subpoena? He admits he was part of the fraud but does not implicate the network.

We can see a strong causal relationship between these points. The thrust of the plot is set in motion at the inciting incident. The action does not cause the protagonist to act yet but it sets in motion the circumstances which will engulf him, much like *Casablanca*. By the end of Act One, Charlie has yielded to the forces of corruption, even if he can justify what he has done to himself. Charlie has made a pact with the devil to betray all that his family holds important. He has been seduced by money, fame and glory, the same as Herb Stempel.

The start of Act Two focuses on the creation of the problem by showing how Charlie's fame affects Stempel, which brings Goodwin into the picture. Goodwin's probe pressures Charlie and it finally forces Stempel to implicate himself by revealing that he got the answers on the show (at the midpoint). The thrust of the plot from the midpoint to the end of Act Two is how the mounting pressure on Charlie forces him to fold and get off the show.

In Act Three, the subcommittee hearings command center stage, dominated by the questions: Will Charlie testify? Will Goodwin succeed? Charlie does testify and admits the truth but he does not implicate the higher powers because, to his knowledge, they were not part of the fraud. In the end, Charlie clears his conscience but loses his good name; and Goodwin nails two puny television producers while the bigger network gets away.

Obstacles, Complications And Crises

All of the characters in *Quiz Show* face a variety of obstacles, complications and crises. Charlie's main obstacle is Goodwin, whom he cannot meet head on, for to do so would be to admit he has something to hide. Charlie's notoriety becomes another obstacle: all he wants is for the whole mess to go away, yet his popularity makes him too valuable to the network. His conscience represents his inner obstacles.

When Enright asks Charlie the question he's already answered, a personal crisis is created which turns into a complication for him. This complication then causes all the obstacles Charlie later faces. Also, Stempel's actions create complications for Charlie, just as Charlie's relationship with his father complicates his predicament by making it harder for him to extricate himself. Charlie's need to defer to a father figure (shown when he signs the statement denying any wrongdoing at network head Kintner's behest) becomes a complication as well.

We find Charlie in crisis any time he is put on the spot and is forced to lie to protect himself. His first crisis is personal and his last, to testify, is also personal.

The power structure—Enright, Kintner, the sponsor, and Charlie—all stand in Goodwin's way of the truth. Goodwin's affection for Charlie starts as a complication; then it becomes a personal crisis and another obstacle to his own success (when he doesn't want to call Charlie before the hearings). Stempel faces the power structure and Enright, along with his own inner demons. His crises start when he is told to lose but doesn't want to do it. Then he faces greater crises when he loses his money and can't get back on television. Another complication for Stempel's story line is when he testifies: he thinks he's going to nail Enright and Charlie but he winds up destroying himself, too.

Enright's main obstacle is, of course, Goodwin. But Stempel is one too: he starts off as a complication, a nuisance to be gotten rid of, but turns into an obstacle for Enright later in the film. Enright handles several of his crises well: the first, when he plays the doctored tape of Stempel's threats for Goodwin; later, Enright wilts under pressure from Goodwin, who is armed with proof from Snodgrass that the show was fixed.

The Plan

We see all the characters directly state what they are trying to achieve. Charlie's plan is to dodge Goodwin and his investigation. He says as much to Enright on the telephone after his first meeting with Goodwin and his actions support this. Goodwin's plan is to find out why a grand jury inquiry was sealed, then uncover what the fraud was so that he can expose television and make a name for himself. Stempel wants to bring down Enright and Charlie. He tells Enright he's going to do it and he, in fact, goes to the grand jury. Again, his actions support what he says he's going to do.

The Subplot

Quiz Show really has one plot with several sides. It shows three sides of the story by including the families of the three main characters. We see a progression of Charlie's subplot with his father. It's set in motion with Charlie's introduction in the shadow of his father. A subtle conflict between them is introduced: his father knows that Charlie is successful on the show but has yet to watch his son and doesn't grasp the amount of money involved. Once the elder Van Doren realizes the money Charlie has won, he sees his son in a new light. Van Doren now watches Charlie and gets completely caught up in the tension of the show. When the revelation hits him that Charlie has cheated on the show, he's devastated but he stands by Charlie as only a father who truly loves his son can.

The subplots for Goodwin and Stempel are sketched in less detail but no less vividly. Goodwin's family is represented by his wife (Mira Sorvino) who supports him, but who ultimately cannot understand why he won't call Charlie before the subcommittee. Stempel's family is used to soften his character, especially in the first scene at his home after winning and we see his commitment to his wife and family. His wife (Johann Carlo) is used wonderfully, for she believes in him totally, telling him not to take the dive. When she learns that he got the answers, she is shocked and hurt that he took her in, too, with all the rest of the "saps." Even so, she stands by her husband, all the while knowing the affair will end as tragically for him as it will for Charlie.

Reversals

Several reversals are used throughout the film. The first is orchestrated in Act One. Stempel has been told by Enright to lose on the "Marty" question. His wife tells him to answer the question correctly—why should he have to lose? Stempel agrees with her. However, when the moment of truth comes, Stempel does what Enright told him to do and loses.

Goodwin, learning that Stempel received the answers before each show, reverses the action of the plot. Though the audience already knows this, it still comes as a surprise that Stempel would incriminate himself this way.

In Act Three, another reversal is set up when Kintner asks Charlie to sign the statement denying any part in the allegations. Goodwin has told Charlie not to do anything that will make him call Charlie before the subcommittee. Clearly, Charlie doesn't want to sign the document and we don't see Charlie sign the statement that is drawn up by the network's legal department. But we learn through Goodwin that he did. Now Goodwin, is forced to call Charlie before the subcommittee—the one thing he did not want to do.

Revelation

The revelation of this film is in the tale of how far the good can fall. It is the revelation of characters caught up in events which overtake them, leaving them powerless to avert their destinies. In this sense, there are two moments which can be considered revelations. The first is when Charlie makes his statement before the subcommittee, admitting his part in the deception, followed by Stempel finally recognizing what he's done to a good man.

A more specific revelation comes in the scene between Goodwin and the quiz show's sponsor. In this scene, the sponsor admits everything to Goodwin, but lays out the real reason for 21's success: Audiences didn't tune in to watch an intellectual answer difficult questions but to watch the money. It is a revelation into the nature of the people supposedly betrayed by the fraud.

The Climax And Resolution

The climax has already been discussed above, in the section on overall structure. Everything that happens after Charlie's statement to the subcommittee is the resolution. An end crawl tells what happened to each of the main characters involved in the story.

THEMATIC UNITY

Quiz Show tells the story of the scandal surrounding the TV game show *21*. In doing so, it explores the topics of corporate greed, class rivalry and television's remarkable power. But at its center is a Faustian tale of how the good can fall.

If we look at the key characteristics of the protagonist and antagonist in the first act, we see several interesting details emerge. Charlie is erudite but boyish and self-deprecating. He thinks he is honest (he originally turns down Enright's offer to make him the new champ). Enright is confident and dishonest. His show is corrupt, but he rationalizes it to himself as "show business" and continues to reap professional success. He knows that people are attracted to fame and fortune. He reads Charlie like a book. And at the end of Act One, Charlie plays right into Enright's hands: he answers the question they both know he knows. Charlie can justify to himself that he knew the answer after all; it's not like he openly cheated. But he has naively traded away his personal integrity by entering into a bargain based on public deceit. Act One shows how easily one can slip into deception.

Act Two begins showing Charlie's triumphant ascent. His celebrity takes the nation and himself by storm, landing him on the cover of *Time Magazine*. Charlie embraces Enright's scheme wholeheartedly: he allows Enright and Freedman to give him the answers to the show's questions. He innocently convinces himself that he's doing no harm and accepts the money and notoriety. His fame and fortune eventually win him loving admiration from his father (who has loved him all along but in whose eyes Charlie's always felt somewhat of a failure). It is not until Charlie meets Goodwin that he starts to realize the ramifications of his actions and what is at stake if he is exposed.

At the end of Act Two, Charlie escapes Enright's clutches by throwing the show, but he is unable to elude the lure of television celebrity. He signs on with the network. This leads to his downfall when, in Act Three, he is coerced into signing the statement of innocence. This action then forces Goodwin to call Charlie before the subcommittee.

Charlie's problem is that he doesn't know who he is. He is defined as Mark Van Doren's son and Carl Van Doren's nephew, not as Charles Van Doren himself. It causes him to be somewhat disaffected, although boyishly so. This is beautifully rendered in the first act, during Charlie's initial interview with Enright when he elaborately details his personal history as a long string of artistic and scientific failures. Charlie doesn't know who he is and this leaves him open to manipulation and humiliation. Once on the show, he allows his success to define him. But his success is based on a lie and instead of fulfilling him, it only serves to further alienate him from himself and everything he and his family stand for.

All the other characters know who they are. Stempel, for instance: he willingly enters into his arrangement with Enright, selling his soul for fame and fortune. Goodwin, too, knows himself and what he stands for. Mark Van Doren, Enright, Freedman, Kintner and the sponsor all know themselves. Only Charlie is rudderless at the beginning of the film, looking for something to succeed at in order to win his father's approval.

At the end of the film, Charlie makes his statement at the hearing and admits his role in the deception. This becomes his defining moment. He tells the truth but destroys himself in the public realm in order to find himself. In the end, the film tells us that personal integrity is more important than fame and fortune.

SPECIAL NOTES

Quiz Show was in development for a number of years before making it to the big screen. Adapted by Paul Attanasio, from Richard N. Goodwin's *Remembering America*, it is specifically based on the chapter, "Investigating the Quiz Shows."

The title page of the screenplay used for comparison purposes, dated June 19, 1991, says that it is a revised draft. (It does not say which draft it is.) At 145 pages, the script contains much of what is seen on the screen. The voice of the screenplay echoes closely the tone of the film, so much so that upon first reading, one can be fooled into thinking the screenplay represents an accurate version of the film. But there are significant changes. As with the other films studied so far, the first act has been trimmed extensively. Forty-nine pages of script translate into thirty-five minutes of film. Changes are made in the locations of some scenes. Many scenes are shortened and some are reordered. The sponsor's role in the film is not included in the screenplay. His attitudes are given to the network chief Kintner.

There are many other major and minor changes, too numerous to go into individually here. What stands out is that the essential structure of both screenplay and film is the same. The inciting incident, the end of the first act, although coming many pages later, are still the same, as is the midpoint, the end of the second act and the end of the third. What is strengthened in the film are the relationships between Charlie and Goodwin; Charlie and his father; Goodwin and Stempel; and Stempel and his wife Toby. These new or retooled scenes add depth and complexity. In addition, they heighten the drama in several key places.

This film, which seems to defy standard screenwriting and film structure conventions, succeeds brilliantly by taking an innovative approach toward the protagonist and antagonist while still relying upon the fundamental principles of three-act structure to tell its story.

8

THE STRUCTURE OF SUBPLOTS

Study Film: *Tootsie*

In any great film, the subplot is not just a secondary story line which runs parallel to the main one—it supports the main plot. It cannot exist on its own but only has meaning in relationship to the whole. "Sub" stands for subordinate, therefore, the subplot is a line of action serving the main one. A great subplot cannot be separated from the main story line, but ultimately it adds to it by having a direct impact upon the main action of the entire plot.

In great films, the subplot is often the personal story and might be what audiences remember best. Think about *Witness*. For many, the relationship between Book and Rachel is what was most memorable about the film, not the details of the police melodrama. Because the subplot in most great films carries the personal story, it is also the main carrier of the theme, for, as we've seen, it is in the relationships between characters that a film's true meaning is developed.

Today, it seems as if writing an effective subplot is becoming a lost art. In the current crop of films, even successful ones such as *My Best Friend's Wedding* and *Rounders*, subplots are minuscule or nonexistent, adding little to our knowledge of the characters and even less to our interest in the plot. Still, an effective subplot is one of the great tools of construction for maintaining tension and interest in a film's second act.

A subplot is used to add dimension to the protagonist (or another main character) by showing his relationships. These relationships can produce in the audience specific feelings (such as empathy or hate) for a particular character. A subplot creates higher stakes in a film when a relationship it explores becomes at-risk in the second half of the main plot. A subplot contributes to a character's transformational arc, orchestrating changes the protagonist goes through in the course of the film. The subplot is used to set up important story details which impact the plot later. It also can confer an overall sense of reality by utilizing other settings which broaden the world of the film. Whatever its function, the subplot in a great film contributes to the main plot in a substantial way.

THE RELATIONSHIP BETWEEN
THE MAIN PLOT AND SUBPLOT

For a subplot to work well, it must be integrated with the main plot. It can't be a tangent which goes off on its own course, showing different aspects of the protagonist's life (or other significant characters' lives) but having no bearing on the main plot. It must be built around one or more of the major characters and impact the main plot in an important way, usually in the second half of the film. In the films covered so far, we see a variety of subplots used and, in some films, more than one. Let's look at them.

In *Witness*, how would you characterize the main plot and the subplot? The main plot involves Book trying to escape the crooked cops and save Samuel. The subplot, as discussed at length in Chapter Two, deals with Book and Rachel's relationship. The subplot impacts the main plot in the third act when the crooked cops track Book to the Lapp farm and attack.

In *Risky Business*, how could you characterize its main plot and subplot? After the set-up in Act One, Joel's main problem is getting his house back in order before his parents return from their trip. This means getting the Steuben Egg from Lana, later fixing the Porsche and finally buying back from Guido all the furniture. The subplot concerns Joel's education, i.e., getting into Princeton or the University of Illinois, and tracks the set- up of his interview with the Princeton alumnus, his school projects and finally converges with the main plot line on the night of the party (when Rutherford arrives at Joel's house). The subplot is resolved when Joel learns that he was accepted into Princeton.

In *Casablanca*, the main plot concerns Rick, Ilsa, the Germans and the Letters of Transit. One subplot involves Renault and the young refugees (which is more apparent in the screenplay but cut down in the film). This subplot (when Rick intercedes on the couple's behalf) converges with the main plot, showing Rick's transformation of character. Another subplot involves Ferrari wanting to hire Sam away and buy Rick's saloon (with Sam staying on); at the end, Rick sells Ferrari his saloon and raises money to get away. One subplot serves Rick's character arc while the other is used to set up important plot details to help tie up the film's end. (The Ferrari subplot is minor and could also be characterized as a set-up/pay-off tool. More about this in Chapter Fifteen.)

The Piano has two strong subplots. While the main plot deals with Ada's resistance to her new life with Stewart, the main subplot concerns her developing relationship with Baines. A secondary subplot follows the Bluebeard play. The church play adds another dimension to the story, defining the environment (struggling civilization in wild New Zealand), foreshadowing the strong emotions and heightening expectations (suspense) when Stewart introduces the axe as punishment for Ada's disobedience. (For more on the Ada/Baines subplot, see Chapter Four.)

In *Chinatown*, the main plot follows Gittes as he tries to discover who set him up and solve Mulray's murder. The relationship he develops with Evelyn forms the subplot. At the end, he tries to save her from the forces he's fighting and this raises the stakes of the story.

The subplots in *Quiz Show* are discussed at length in Chapter Seven.

Each of these subplots intersects the action of its film's main plot. Some have a stronger bearing upon the action (*Witness, Casablanca, The Piano, Chinatown*) while the others create comedic complications at the end (*Risky Business*) or show the dramatic impact of the plot's action on the characters (*Quiz Show*). As each subplot interweaves with the main plot, we are reminded of its existence as and notice its contribution of something new to the overall story and the main characters.

THE STRUCTURE OF SUBPLOTS

During a film, there are intervals which deal with the protagonist away from the main conflict. As discussed earlier, audiences tend to feel battered if conflict isn't orchestrated to rise *and* fall (see Chapters Three, Five and Six). Viewers need to be able to catch their breath once in awhile; they need time to know the characters in order to care about them. In a great film, these moments away from the main conflict deal with the characters in ways that help the audience understand the true nature of the struggle by understanding the people involved in it. The scenes off the main conflict also expand the film's universe and help establish the reality of the world in which the characters live. But if the information in a subplot isn't managed in an interesting and arresting way, these scenes or sequences feel dull and forced and the film suffers. This is when a well-structured subplot is important.

Subplots develop similarly to the main plot. The best revolve around a problem that needs to be dealt with by the characters involved. This creates initial tension: Can the characters solve or deal with the problem or not? Since the main objective of a subplot is generally to flesh out the protagonist and secondary characters by showing how they handle the situation and how their relationships develop (helping fill out the theme), their immediate problem (of relationship) is generally solved early enough to make them allies for the second half of the film.

Think of the films we've seen so far. Book and Rachel in *Witness* begin as adversaries but end as lovers, even if she doesn't leave with him at the film's close. Ada, in *The Piano*, resists Baines until he sends her away with her piano and she finally realizes what she's losing. In *Chinatown*, the real Mrs. Mulray (Evelyn) threatens to sue Gittes when they meet and yet, by the end, she entrusts him with her daughter's safety and her own.

But even as the initial problem in the subplot is dealt with, more problems may still threaten the characters' alliances in the subplot/main plot as the film progresses. Again, look at the three films mentioned above. After the midpoint in *Witness*, Book and Rachel tentatively draw closer. As they do, Eli voices his concern over how the community views Rachel's relationship with Book. In *The Piano*, Ada and Baines become lovers, but what happens? Stewart discovers them. He now tries to keep Ada a prisoner and away from Baines, posing a direct threat to their relationship. (At this point in *The Piano*, the two plots join and become one.) By the midpoint in *Chinatown*, Evelyn does an about-face and hires Gittes to find out who is responsible for her husband's death. (Gittes starts as her adversary but now he becomes her advocate.) Later, he discovers that Evelyn is holding the girl everyone is looking for and he feels misled. When he learns that Mulray died in the saltwater pond, he accuses Evelyn of killing her husband. This now forces out the truth. Once in possession of the truth, Gittes will do everything he can to save her and this becomes the action leading to the climax.

As you can see, effective subplots in great films utilize conflict, just as main plots do. Even when a subplot is used for setting up information affecting the plot later, it is more effective when conceived in terms of conflict. In *Risky Business*, many of the scenes dealing with Joel's education utilize conflict to communicate their main points. From the opening anxiety dream to an early scene showing Joel and Barry working on a school project while their buddy Glenn uses a bedroom upstairs, the use of conflict generates more interest in what's happening. In *The Piano*, the Bluebeard play dramatizes the differences between the two cultures. Look at what is set up in *Casablanca* between Rick and Ferrari: Rick doesn't like him but Ferrari still wants something from Rick. It adds to the tension of the film.

The Three-Part Nature of Subplot Structure

We can characterize the progression of a subplot similarly to that of a main plot: it has a definite beginning, middle and end. The beginning of the subplot sets up the problem it will deal with by focusing on the conflict between the characters involved in it. As the protagonist realizes the conflict and takes up this problem, new developments occur which create further problems or eventual solutions to the subplot predicament, depending upon the nature and importance of the subplot. This development constitutes the middle. In an important subplot, this conflict takes up a good portion of the second act.

A main subplot can end or climax anywhere in the second half of a film, where it usually joins the main plot. Then, its final climax plays out with the main climax of the film. But, depending on how important a subplot is to the overall effectiveness of a film, it may still have its own dénouement in the resolution. In the resolution of *Risky Business*, Joel learns he has been accepted by Princeton.

Subplots may contain any or all of the same components of the main plot: developments, complications, obstacles, reversals, crises, climaxes. Just as in a main plot, a subplot should build. It develops, showing how the characters involved with its problem clash, come together or pull further apart. Once con-

ceived, the subplot then interweaves with the main plot, usually at moments when the audience needs a break from the main
action to digest or absorb what's happening. Often, the tension
in a subplot is markedly less than that of a main plot. But there
are cases, like *Witness*, where it is the main plot which interweaves with the subplot throughout Act Two. *The Piano* develops similarly.

Although some screenwriting texts assign page numbers to
the subplot's reoccurrence in the film's overall structure, this
can make the film terribly formulaic and lead to forced plotting
instead of an organic overall design. Subplots in great films can't
be pigeonholed so easily because each one has its own purpose
and plan. Some are short, consisting of only three or four scenes
which must be effectively arranged to add their information while
still maintaining tension and contributing to the overall entertainment value of a film; others are more complex, demanding
more careful orchestration through a film's entire movement.

Often the most important subplot climaxes in Acts Two and
Three play near or concurrently with the main climaxes of these
same acts. They serve to reinforce the subplot's dramatic effect
on the main plot. An important subplot climax can also come
near or at the midpoint. Minor subplots can end in less strategically important points. Other elements, such as surprise, suspense and revelation, are also used in building effective subplots.

Most of the characters playing a role in a subplot are introduced in the first act. Rachel, Baines, Evelyn are all introduced
in Act One of their respective films. In *Casablanca*, the Bulgarian couple and Ferrari enter the film as part of the first act. In
Quiz Show, all of the characters used in the subplots are introduced in Act One. The only film which doesn't actually introduce the subplot character before his impact is felt is *Risky Business*. But Rutherford is foreshadowed when the interview is set
up at the beginning.

Complications as Subplot Starting Points
A complication is often a good starting point for a subplot because it contains inherent conflict and poses an immediate problem. Evelyn showing up and threatening to sue Gittes is a complication to Gittes' story line and it begins their subplot. (Evelyn
then becomes an obstacle for Gittes getting to the truth.) Baines
buying the piano from Stewart and wanting lessons from Ada

starts as a complication. But Baines turns into an obstacle because of what he really desires he must be overcome in order for Ada to get her beloved piano back.

As the subplot problem is dealt with, new developments occur to hold the audience's interest. In *Chinatown*, Evelyn comes on aggressively when we first meet her, threatening to sue Gittes. Her threat is a complication to Gittes' goal of the moment—to find out who set him up (and solve the mystery). He reacts to her threat by looking for Mulray, Evelyn's husband, to try and sort things out with him. This takes him first to Mulray's office, but he's not there. Gittes then goes to Evelyn's home where she tells him she will drop the suit because her husband seems to think that Gittes is an innocent man. But Gittes still wants to talk to Mulray, knowing that Mulray is the real target of whoever used him. Evelyn sends Gittes to the reservoir where he finally finds Mulray—dead. Mulray's death is a new development. It ups the stakes in both main plot and subplot and it brings Evelyn and Gittes together again. (Gittes lies to police detective Escobar to protect Evelyn, little knowing that she holds the key to the mystery. Evelyn says she will send him a check to make it look like she really did hire him.) Thus begins their complicity, his out of a chivalrous compulsion to protect the vulnerable, hers out of a desperate need to defend herself.

In *The Piano*, Stewart selling Baines the piano is a development which complicates Ada's predicament of getting it back. Another new development comes when Baines offers Ada a way to get the piano—to trade her body for it. What will she do? She agrees, but resists him emotionally (as she resists Stewart) until Baines finally becomes so miserable with himself that he gives her the piano back (another development and also a reversal). This leads to the revelation of Ada's feelings, hidden even to herself (another development).

Strong Subplots Impact Main Plots

Strong subplots usually intensify as they progress toward the point when they join the main plot line. Once the subplot impacts the main plot in the second half of the film, it is tied to that line of action and will resolve, usually around the time the main plot resolves. We see this clearly in *Witness*, *The Piano* and *Chinatown*. Each of these films has a strong subplot that plays a big role in the construction of Act Two, then dovetails into the main plot in Act Three. In *Witness*, Act Two climaxes with Book punching the local punk, thus alerting Schaeffer to his whereabouts. But there is still the personal story of Book and Rachel to deal with and this is even more powerful than the police melodrama. In realizing Book's imminent departure, the feelings he and Rachel have developed for each other come to the forefront and must be faced. The subplot climaxes when they finally express their pent-up passions by falling into each other's arms. When Act Three begins, it's not just Book who is in danger from Schaeffer and McFee, but Rachel, Samuel and Eli, too.

In *The Piano*, the Ada/Baines subplot heats up after the midpoint, when she finally realizes her feelings for him. They begin a passionate affair but Stewart discovers them. Stewart does not confront them; instead he tries to force himself upon Ada. When that doesn't work, he imprisons her in the house. Now the two plots merge and head to the second act climax, when Stewart chops off Ada's finger. The third act must conclude the story of Ada, Stewart and Baines.

In *Chinatown*, the subplot and main plot merge when Gittes confronts Evelyn and forces the truth about the girl's identity into the open. Now, Gittes' chief want is to help Evelyn and her daughter flee Noah Cross; this drives the action of Act Three.

SUBPLOTS AND CHARACTER TRANSFORMATION
In every great film, the protagonist has a goal he struggles to reach. This goal directs the construction of the main plot which shows the obstacles standing between the protagonist and his goal and what he does to overcome them—if he can. The subplot often illustrates how the protagonist grows or changes to reach a specific conclusion at the film's climax and resolution. This conceivably leads to his success (or failure) in achieving his goal, or at least in the ability to assign meaning to the task.

As in real life, struggle and frustration in the face of overwhelming obstacles can often, if one perseveres, lead to a new understanding of oneself and the conflicts one faces. A screenwriter, then, must know or have an idea regarding what the protagonist needs and how he can possibly attain it. The writer translates this need into an inner problem for the character or into a realization by the character propelled by his outer struggles and frustrations. Then, the screenwriter creates a line of action, incorporating this need, and externalizes the problem in the construction of the subplot.

In films like *Witness, Casablanca, Chinatown, The Piano* and *Quiz Show*, we see subplots which either dramatize real transformation of character (*Witness, Chinatown, The Piano*) or illustrate changes in the characters brought on by the action of the main plot (*Risky Business, Casablanca, Quiz Show*).

Chapters Four and Five have discussed in some detail theme and subplot and their relationship to character transformation. Let me add here one important difference between a main plot and main subplot (i.e., the personal side of the story). A strong subplot tends to put the emphasis on the effect the main conflict has on the protagonist instead of the effect the protagonist has on the main conflict. More often than not, great subplots deal with emotions, how they come into play and how the characters handle them. This makes the subplot a perfect vehicle to convey the protagonist's reaction to what's going on with the main conflict. Even in a film like *Risky Business*, where the subplot is mainly a complication, Joel's response to Rutherford shows how much he has been changed by the plot's action.

Tootsie

Tootsie, (written by Larry Gelbart and Murray Schisgal, from a story by Gelbart and Don McGuire, directed by Sidney Pollack) is the tale of a stubborn, unemployable actor who disguises himself as a woman to land a role on a soap opera—and finds he's a better person as a woman than he ever was as a man. Before we look at *Tootsie's* subplots, let's get an idea of the film's overall structure.

Tootsie sets up early and fast. Right under the credits, important aspects of actor Michael Dorsey's (Dustin Hoffman) life are introduced. Most significantly, these vignettes establish that Michael is "wrong" for every part he auditions for and that he is a well-respected acting coach. As the plot takes hold, we see Michael waiting tables with his roommate Jeff (Bill Murray) and the main exposition is introduced: Jeff is writing a play that Michael wants to star in. This sets up Michael's specific goal: he wants to raise $8,000 to mount the play. In general terms, he wants to act; but, specifically he wants to act in Jeff's play.

Michael and Jeff go home where Michael is surprised with a birthday party. We hear testimonials to Michael's dedication as an actor. We meet Sandy (Teri Garr), a fellow actor and friend, and see how Michael hits on women he fancies. A clear difference is shown in how he treats his women friends (Sandy) and how he treats women he's sexually interested in. Michael leaves to walk a depressed Sandy home and learns about her upcoming audition. He helps her get ready for it, running lines, clearly understanding the male/female dynamic of the scene. He agrees to lend her moral support at her audition the next day. But at the audition, Sandy is denied even a chance to read for the part. Indignant, Michael tries to get her a reading; he knows one of the soap's actors. When Michael tries to contact his friend, he discovers the actor has left the show to star in a revival of "The Iceman Cometh." Shocked because he thought he was being considered for that part, Michael leaves Sandy high and dry and runs to his agent's (Sydney Pollack) office. Here (approximately 18 minutes into the film), Michael learns that no one will hire him because he's too difficult to work with: he's an arrogant, unemployable actor. This is the crux of his problem and the film's inciting incident. He is an actor who lives for acting who can't get a job because he argues and fights over every line.

So Michael dons women's clothes and gets himself a reading for Sandy's part. The first act climax comes when Michael, as Dorothy, lands the role that Sandy couldn't even read for. Now Michael can act—but not as himself.

Act Two deals with all the situations, developments and complications which result from Michael masquerading as Dorothy. These are explored in the subplots but the broad movements of the second act focus on the effect Dorothy has on Michael's life. While Michael would argue and fight, Dorothy is more politically savvy: she listens but then does what she wants and justifies it later, with generally good results. By the midpoint, Dorothy is a major success on the show, making the cover of every magazine imaginable. Everybody in the country is taken with her, even Michael. But from the midpoint on, Michael's life grows more complicated. He's fallen in love with his co-star Julie (Jessica Lange). Maintaining his double life while dodging his male suitors exacts a toll. Then, the producers pick up his option—he'll be on the show for another year. By the climax of the second act (about 95 minutes into the film), Michael desperately wants off the show and back to his life but his agent tells him there is no way to break the contract.

The third act is very brief. After Julie tells Dorothy they can't associate anymore, Michael must find a way to get his life back.

He takes advantage of a live airing of the show to unmask—or "unwig"—himself, thereby revealing to all who he is. Here, at the climax, Julie rejects Michael for deceiving her. The rest of the film resolves the main subplots, ending with Michael convincing Julie that they should give each other a try.

Tootsie—The Subplots
The main plot of *Tootsie* deals with an actor finding work in a woman's role on a daytime soap. The subplots show the effect that masquerading as a woman has on Michael as well as his effect on those around him. But just as importantly, the subplots influence the main plot. *Tootsie* tracks five subplots, three of them fairly substantial. They are:
   1) The Dorothy/Julie subplot;
   2) The Michael/Sandy subplot;
   3) The Dorothy/Les subplot;
   4) The Dorothy/Van Horn subplot;
   5) The Julie/Ron subplot.
The first two subplots have clear, strong progressions, with definite beginnings, middles and ends. Let's look at them first.

The Dorothy/Julie Subplot
This subplot is the most important since it carries the theme of the film, dealing with friendship and love. There is no small amount of irony that Michael and Julie's boyfriend Ron (Dabney Coleman) use similar lines to explain their relationships with women (Ron/Julie, Michael/Sandy). Michael, by being Dorothy and watching how Ron treats Julie, sees the male-female relationship from the other side and it changes him. As he says to Julie at the end, he becomes a better man as a woman.

The Dorothy/Julie subplot helps add dimension to the main plot by giving us the motivations for Michael's actions in the main plot. This subplot also raises the stakes when we start caring about the relationship developed between Dorothy and Julie, wanting it somehow to survive.

The Dorothy/Julie subplot set-up starts at Dorothy's audition, when Dorothy and Julie meet and we see that Michael is immediately taken with her. Its inciting incident occurs when Julie asks Dorothy to come for dinner and run lines. Michael thinks of this as their "first date" and brings Julie flowers. It results in the two of them hitting it off. Now their friendship begins and the subplot develops.

Julie begins to rely on Dorothy, both professionally and personally. Dorothy coaches Julie in her acting and encourages her to stand up for herself with Ron. Ron is not thrilled with Julie's developing friendship with Dorothy and is, in fact, threatened by her/him, which creates tension in their subplot. Julie invites Dorothy home for the Easter holiday. In the country, Dorothy/Michael clearly falls in love with Julie. Michael's main obstacle standing between Julie and him is Dorothy. Meanwhile, Julie, taking Dorothy's advice about Ron, is determined to break up with him and asks Dorothy to baby-sit and provide moral support. This leads, in the break-up's aftermath, to Dorothy's attempt to kiss Julie, the subplot's "second act" climax.

As a result, Julie refuses to see Dorothy anymore. The subplot's "third act" climaxes with the main plot, when Michael unmasks Dorothy and reveals himself and when Julie reacts by punching him and leaving. The subplot resolution comes when Michael convinces Julie that the hard part is over—they're already friends—and they head off together.

The Michael/Sandy Subplot

This subplot runs counterpoint in many ways to the Dorothy/Julie subplot. The set-up of the Michael/Sandy subplot is in the first act, when it establishes a long-term, ongoing friendship between the two. Where the tension in the Dorothy/Julie subplot (for the first half of the film) is beneath the surface, coming from the fact that the audience knows Michael is attracted to her, conflict in the Michael/Sandy subplot churns and boils over once Michael gets the part of Dorothy, spilling over into farce at times. The climax of this subplot's "first act" is when Michael sleeps with Sandy. It changes the nature of their friendship and puts it in jeopardy.

The "second act" of the Michael/Sandy subplot shows how Sandy's insecurities take hold and how Michael contributes to them. He stands Sandy up, he lies to her. Though he's lying to protect her, he's still lying to her, even when she confronts him about his behavior. The subplot's "second act" climax occurs when Michael tells Sandy he's in love with another woman and she ends their friendship. Their subplot resolves when we see Jeff's play has opened, starring Sandy and Michael.

The end of this subplot (or its "third act") simply resolves things for Michael and Sandy because the main climax in a sense, also climaxes Michael and Sandy's subplot (for she now realizes what has been going on).

In each of these two main subplots, we see a strong set-up, development and climax; these elements clearly focus the plot lines. The separate climaxes also serve to turn the subplots in new directions and keep the audience guessing about each one's final outcome.

The Dorothy/Les Subplot

This subplot has its set-up just before the midpoint, when Les (Charles Durning) meets Dorothy at the autograph signing. The inciting incident really takes place in the Dorothy/Julie subplot, when Julie invites Dorothy home, stating her Dad is Dorothy's number one fan. Julie invites Dorothy home as much for her father as for herself. The subplot's "first act" climax has Les clearly falling for Dorothy.

The next section of the subplot shows Les courting Dorothy, taking her dancing and for drinks. This line of action climaxes when Les proposes and gives Dorothy a ring. The main climax, where Michael reveals himself, again serves as the climax of this subplot, because it shows why Les and Dorothy can't be a couple. The Dorothy/Les subplot resolves when Michael brings the ring back and Les forgives him.

The Dorothy/Van Horn Subplot

This subplot's set-up comes when Dorothy is warned about the lecherous Van Horn, the actor who plays the lecherous Dr. Brewster on the soap opera. Dorothy changes their first scene together and slaps him. This serves to challenge Van Horn, and is the subplot's inciting incident. The "first act" climax comes when Van Horn kisses Dorothy anyway.

The subplot develops, showing Van Horn's admiration and affection for Dorothy become total desire. He wants her. The subplot's second act climax occurs when Jeff arrives home and rescues Dorothy from Van Horn's advances. The subplot climaxes with the main climax when Dorothy reveals herself to be Michael.

The Julie/Ron Subplot

Though Julie and Ron are glimpsed together, the set-up of this subplot really comes in the first dinner scene between Dorothy and Julie when Dorothy asks pointedly about Ron. This establishes the nature of Julie's relationship with Ron and how Dorothy views it. As Dorothy and Julie's friendship blooms, Ron becomes threatened. We see the condescending way Ron treats Julie, Dorothy, and women in general. This subplot climaxes when Julie breaks up with Ron as a result of her friendship with Dorothy.

All of these subplots have clear lines of action, with their own developments and climaxes, yet some of them intersect or intertwine at points with others. This creates a strong interrelationship between the plot lines, and helps strengthen the overall cohesion and unity of the screenplay, making it feel like a seamless tapestry of characters and events—the sure sign of a screenplay meticulously laid out.

SPECIAL NOTES

In 1982 *Tootsie* took the nation by storm. It was nominated for nine Academy Awards, including Best Picture, Best Actor, Best Director, Best Original Screenplay, and Best Supporting Actress for which Jessica Lange won. Dustin Hoffman won a British Academy Award for his virtuoso lead performance in 1983, and the writers, Larry Gelbart, Murray Schisgal and Don McGuire took home the Writers Guild of America Award for Best Original Screenplay, 1982.

The credits for the screenplay stand as: Screenplay, Larry Gelbart and Murray Schisgal, from a story by Larry Gelbart and Don McGuire. An uncredited polish was done by Elaine May.

In the screenplay dated March 8, 1982, by Larry Gelbart, all the major beats of the film are here, though there are a few changes: several scene deletions, some line changes. But most of the comedy is here in this draft.

The beginning vignettes are written, but the film adds to them. An opening scene introducing Michael's ex at the restaurant is cut, as is his reference to not wanting to remember it's his birthday. The beginning is a little smoother in the film, but it's all essentially in the script. Later, a few scenes which are changed have to do with emphasizing how the role of Dorothy takes Michael over. The scene in which Michael becomes enamored with Sandy's dress, which leads to him undressing and then to them making love, is more thematic and direct in the film. In the screenplay, Michael sees Sandy's underwear as she twirls with happiness over getting the part in Jeff's play. He wants to get a better look at the fit, and this leads to Sandy mistaking his intentions instead of Michael having to cover up his actions.

In the second half of the script, during the Easter Holiday sequence, this draft has Ron come up late and wow everyone with all his skills, from cooking to milking cows. The speech Ron delivers to Dorothy just before Julie breaks up with him in the film comes here at the end of this sequence. This important speech is saved from the cut scene, and then used at just the right moment later on.

A scene with Jeff discovering Michael's contract has been picked up and being a little resentful about it is cut. Julie's son in the screenplay is changed to a daughter in the film. More is made of Dorothy's baby-sitting in the film. In the screenplay, the child sleeps, and there is a nasty scene with Ron when he and Julie return.

Overall, it is mostly fine-tuning which takes place, shading and shaping the characters and situations to get just a little more comedy and subtext in the film. But this draft of the screenplay is a terrific example of comedic writing at its best.

STRUCTURE AND THE ENSEMBLE FILM

Study Films: *Diner, Parenthood,*
The Best Years of Our Lives, Grand Hotel

Great films come in all shapes and sizes. They can be about a single person trying to accomplish a specific goal or about several people with their own special wants and needs. The ensemble, or multi-plot, film follows a number of different protagonists as they each attempt to reach their goals or solve their problems. Many filmmakers attempt this type of film; many fail. But when an ensemble film succeeds, it can be sublimely satisfying because the audience generally feels it has had a real look at life.

The multiple plot film is as old as the feature film itself. The first feature-length film, *Birth of a Nation*, was made in 1915 by D. W. Griffith. The next year Griffith made *Intolerance*, an interwoven, four-story, three-hour epic about bigotry and prejudice throughout history. Since then, ensemble films have become a staple of filmmakers. From *Grand Hotel* and *Dinner at Eight* in the '30s through *Metropolitan* and *Short Cuts* in the '90s, writers and directors continue to explore their worlds through the tapestry of interwoven stories and character relationships allowed by the ensemble film.

In this chapter, we expand the number of study films. Our principal reference films are *Diner*, written and directed by Barry Levinson; *Parenthood*, written by Lowell Ganz and Babaloo Mandel, directed by Ron Howard; *The Best Years of Our Lives*, based on a story by MacKinlay Kantor, screenplay by Robert Sherwood, directed by William Wyler; and *Grand Hotel*, based on the Vicki Baum novel, screenplay adapted by W. A. Drake, directed by Edmund Goulding. Other films are used to explain variations on the basic structural organization of material in ensemble pieces, and are worth viewing, too.

Ensemble films are essentially subplots which must be connected without the benefit of a main plot holding them together. These "mini-plots" have their own individual protagonists, conflicts and resolutions, but they are not strong enough to carry the momentum of an entire film; they have simpler story lines (though not necessarily less dramatic). Separately, these mini-plots don't need as much development as a single plot to drive a film because intercutting among them diverts the audience. Still, a core must be created to take the place of the main plot and to bring the mini-plots into an overall relationship.

The difficulties in creating an ensemble film are numerous. Problems include: how to focus the story and keep audience attention; how to shift from one plot line to another; and how to create a synthesis which holds all the plot lines together. There are no hard and fast rules for the construction of an ensemble film. One film may find the unifying agent in a setting (*Nashville*) while another may find it in an object (*The Yellow Rolls-Royce*). But the key ingredient in all great ensemble films is dramatic unity—the synthesis of thematic ideas and plot movement—which enables the screenwriter and filmmaker to integrate the lines of action and construct the framework for the film's plot.

DRAMATIC UNITY

As described in Chapter Six, the ancient Greeks defined the parameters of Greek tragedy in the "three unities"—the unity of time, place and action. This meant that a play unfolded in one locale, during the course of one day, with a single protagonist pushing the action to its climax. Obviously, theater and film no longer restrict play and screenplay construction this way. The fluidity of film, in particular, allows artists, screenwriters and filmmakers, to explore their worlds to the limits of their imaginations: the story can move through numerous locales, it can travel back and forth in time and follow several lines of action to depict whatever it demands. But in order to take advantage of these special properties of film, a filmmaker must have some way to focus the material and manage the information so that even as he breaks with the more conventional story telling techniques (a sole protagonist, linear narrative structure), he winds up with an intelligible, unified whole.

Typical plot design for most films focuses on a single protagonist pursuing a goal; this provides the fundamental plot unity (unity of action: the first act establishes the protagonist's goal, the final climax shows whether he achieves it or not). In an ensemble film a number of characters share the spotlight, each with his or her own story to tell. But standard plot design tends to be insufficient for constructing a framework which will hold the various stories together. Unless a film centers upon a group of characters with a common goal—*The Seven Samurai, The Great Escape, Independence Day, Armageddon*—finding unity in centralized action for all the characters can be difficult, because such unified action usually contradicts the very nature of the ensemble story. Usually, an ensemble film is a tapestry of intertwining stories, each with its own definite action. The key to a good ensemble film is how seamlessly the plot lines weave together and intersect and how they pay off at the end.

To create a seamless intertwining of plot lines, a filmmaker needs three things:

1) A clear issue or theme for the characters;
2) A context in which the characters relate;
3) An event which frames the story.

What is the Story About?

Most great ensemble films are based on clear issues the characters must face which then combine to form a unified theme. Ensemble films use these issues to create a common denominator between the characters and their problems for the audience, whether the issues concern war veterans coping with coming home or young men making the transition to adulthood. For example, in *The Best Years of Our Lives*, the three main characters are returning WWII veterans facing readjustment to civilian life; *Diner* deals with a group of immature young men confronting adult responsibilities; *Parenthood* examines the difficulties of parenting in the modern age. By the end of an ensemble film, a deeper theme usually emerges as the characters cope with these problems in their own ways. A great ensemble film is one in which diverse character paths to different outcomes work together to develop the theme.

The collective issue which the characters face is what focuses the film and helps the viewers understand the material's overall meaning. Even in a film like *Grand Hotel*, which deals with a broad spectrum of characters with particular problems, there is one overriding goal—the search for happiness. At the end of the film, the disparate character outcomes show us who finds happiness and who does not.

All great ensemble films, as with all great movies, reveal their themes in the main climax and resolution. *The Best Years of Our Lives* tells us that only love can heal the wounds of war. In *Diner*, we learn that the process of growing up is painful and confusing but must be embraced to move forward in life. *Parenthood* tells us we must accept life's downs and ups, for it is never perfect, no matter how hard we try to make it so. In *Grand Hotel*, we learn that we must seize the day and live it because no one knows what life will bring.

In addition, the themes are often realized in a fuller, truer sense than in films driven by a single protagonist. For example, many ensemble films end without tying up every plot line positively. Since some plot lines conclude ambiguously and others unhappily, this view of life seems more authentic than the standard Hollywood fare with its "happily ever after" endings. Consider the conclusion of *Diner*; on the happier note, Eddie (Steve Guttenberg) marries Elyse and Boogie (Mickey Rourke) brings his dream girl to the wedding. But then, Billy (Tim Daly) never resolves his situation with Barbara while Fenwick (Kevin Bacon) doesn't deal with his problems at all. Shrevie (Daniel Stern) and Beth (Ellen Barkin) move on in their marriage, but they do not confront the differences between them. This ending more accurately reflects the world we live in, where some things work out and others do not. We see the same thing in other ensembles, such as *Grand Hotel, Nashville, Short Cuts*, the French films *Children of Paradise* and *Grand Illusion*: some plot lines end happily and others tragically, which is essentially a description of life.

Not all ensemble films use a central issue to create the primary focus for the plot and the basis for a theme. For example, *Nashville* and *Short Cuts* both follow numerous characters with separate problems and goals. Each film intercuts between separate plot lines, yet the characters do not really face similar issues and their lives touch only tangentially. Instead, these films weave together their characters and plot lines in the service of the theme. *Nashville* comments upon the corrupting influence of commercialism on American society while *Short Cuts* deals with the difficulties human beings have communicating with one another.

However, a universal theme or single issue is not enough to integrate an ensemble film. While Griffith's *Intolerance* is unified by theme and is an amazing work, it is more a historical curiosity than an example of timeless storytelling. The most enduring ensemble films have solid structures (even as some stretch to three hours or more in length) based on their integration of theme and action. But the action must play out in a believable context, allowing the characters to logically interact as they pursue their own individual goals.

Story Context

Story context is another way of saying "unity of place," but without restricting the backdrop (as the ancient Greeks did) to one locale. Ensemble films work best when characters cross each other's plot lines and play supporting roles in other characters' stories. The easiest, most believable way to effect this is to utilize a setting where all the characters can logically meet. The action of *Grand Hotel* takes place in the Berlin hotel during a 24-hour period; *Diner* brings the group of friends together in Baltimore for Eddie's wedding during Christmas week, 1959; the present-day *Parenthood* takes place in an unnamed city which is home to three out of the four siblings; *The Best Years of Our Lives* is set in Boone City (middle America), 1945, home to the three returning WWII vets.

The context for a story does not have to be a place, though often, it is. Context can be created by an object (the car in *The Yellow Rolls-Royce*, an overcoat in *Tales of Manhattan*, or the twenty dollar bill in *Twenty Bucks*). Context can be formed by relationships or work, even if those involved are separated by vast distances during the course of a film (*Hannah and Her Sisters*, *The Right Stuff*). What the story context creates is a believable set of circumstances for the characters which keeps them interacting with each other until the climax and resolution of the plot.

Event Frame

In order to manage your material and construct an effective plot for an ensemble film, all the protagonists must have clear wants and needs driving their actions—just as in standard plot design. These wants and needs direct the construction of the characters' mini-plots so that the action in each rises and falls while holding the audience's interest. And, just as in most films in which a single protagonist pushes the plot, the action in an ensemble film generally leads to an event which incorporates the main climax or resolution. With a single protagonist, it is easier to see where a film is heading, in the sense that most films have a protagonist who is trying to reach a goal. This is Aristotle's "unity of action" rule. Because the protagonist meets with conflict, we know he must face the forces standing in his way (usually the antagonist), in a final confrontation (the main crisis and climax). Even as we anticipate the final clash in great films, their endings surprise us because we cannot predict what will happen or where it will occur. When the climax comes, the result feels true to the characters involved in the story.

In an ensemble film, with its multiple protagonists, viewers find it harder to anticipate where the end will take them. Each protagonist must push the action of his mini-plot through confrontation to climax. Even if one character seems slightly more important than the others, the audience can't expect the main climax to always involve him. (This character will need a main climax to his story, but it may not take place at the very end of the film.) This unpredictability is sometimes what is most surprising and inspiring about a great ensemble film. (Think about what a surprise the Baron's death is in *Grand Hotel*.)

Aristotle's unity of action, however, applies to ensemble films in which the multiple protagonists share a mutual goal or problem. *The Seven Samurai, The Great Escape, Independence Day, Armageddon* all use centralized conflicts which unite the characters in a common purpose. The problem—to defend the village (*The Seven Samurai, The Magnificent Seven*) or to save the world (*Independence Day, Armageddon*)—causes the characters to respond with a course of action that ends at an event (the main climax) in which the opposing forces finally meet to resolve the conflict of the plot.

In ensemble films which do not employ a mutual goal as a unifying agent, some other plan must be devised to structure the plot. Therefore, many ensemble films create an overall impression of unity of action by organizing the material within a story frame. A story frame anchors the plot to an event that will play out by the end of the film. The audience does not necessarily expect it, but when it does take place, the event brings the film to a satisfying close. In a film with one unified goal—to defend the village or save the world—accomplishing that mission frames the development of the plot through to the climax. But in an ensemble film in which the characters have different goals, a story frame can focus the action on a point which will draw the characters together by the film's end. Doubt may arise as to whether or not the event will occur, and doubt should arise to build suspense, but however the event is used, this climax functions as a focal point for both characters and audience as the film narrows in scope and reaches its end.

Depending upon the type of film, the event at the end can be major or minor in dramatic importance. An event can be climactic or arrive in the resolution, bringing the major characters together at the end to give a sense of wholeness. Whatever the event is, it must be foreshadowed, and, for most films, the earlier the better.

In *Diner*, the framing event is Eddie's wedding. We learn about it four minutes into the first act, even though the action casts doubt upon its ultimate outcome with the introduction of Eddie's football quiz. *The Best Years of Our Lives* frames the story with a wedding, too. Seven minutes into the film, we learn that Homer (Harold Russell) has a girl at home waiting to marry him. But Homer is coming home from the war with prosthetic hooks instead of hands and he's not sure his fiancee still wants him. The film ends with him marrying Wilma (Cathy O'Donnell) which also provides the setting for the climax of the story involving Fred (Dana Andrews) and Peggy (Teresa Wright) thereby, resolving its plot line.

Parenthood ends with a birth which brings almost all the characters together, but this event is not foreshadowed in the first act. However, the idea is introduced in the first part of the second act when Susan (Harley Kozak) tells husband Nathan (Rick Moranis) that she wants another baby and he responds by saying no. The idea is picked up again near the end of the second act when Helen's (Dianne Wiest) daughter Julie (Martha Plimpton) announces that she's going to have a baby. It is reinforced at the end of act two when Karen (Mary Steenburgen) tells her husband Gil (Steve Martin), who has just quit his job, that she is pregnant. The film ends after the climax: the family is gathered at the hospital for the birth of a baby—but from the film's direction we don't know which woman is having it. We think it's going to be Karen. But, before we know for sure, we see that Susan is pregnant; then we see Karen holding her new-born so we think it's Julie. But then we see her with her child. The new mother turns out to be Helen, who has married her son's biology teacher. The film ends with all the families gathered, celebrating the new arrival. They have weathered their crises and reaffirmed the notion of "family" by extending it.

Grand Hotel frames its story with a birth, too. The opening shows four of the five main characters on the telephone establishing their various problems. The first caller, Senf, (Jean Hersholt) the head porter and a minor character, is trying to find out if his wife has had her baby. (Throughout the film, Senf is asked about his wife. The answer is always the same: She hasn't had the child yet and he's worried.) As the phone calls continue, we learn that Mr. Kringelein (Lionel Barrymore) is dying; General Director Preysing (Wallace Berry), a businessman, must close a deal or his plant will go bust; a secretary explains that her boss, dancer Grusinskaya (Greta Garbo), will not dance that night; Baron von Geiger (John Barrymore) must come up with some money and will steal to get it. As the film resolves and ends, with the main characters leaving the hotel the next day, Senf the porter finally hears that his baby has arrived and his wife is doing fine.

We see from our four study films that story frames often translate into questions about one or more of the main characters. In *Diner*, the story frame questions whether Eddie will marry Elyse. In *Parenthood*, the story frame asks if Susan can convince Nathan to have a second child, then builds from there. *Grand Hotel* uses the porter's predicament, asking what will happen to his wife during this difficult birth. *The Best Years of Our Lives* sets up the question, Will Homer's girl still want him? One way or another, these questions are answered at the end of the films.

The ambitious film *Short Cuts*, which interweaves the mini-plots of 24 different characters, most connected by the thinnest of threads, also frames its story thematically. *Short Cuts* starts with one of California's ecological problems—a medfly infestation. A newscaster, who becomes a character in the film comments on the problem right at the start. A helicopter pilot who sprays the Malathion insecticide is introduced early and becomes a character, too. The final climax brings the film to another natural disaster—an earthquake. Again, a newscaster is used (although not the one from the beginning); he interviews the helicopter pilot from the start of the film who puts the temblor into his airborne perspective. The film closes with a kind of symmetry established by the bookending of these similar actions.

A story frame gives an ensemble film a sense of completeness. By setting up early the reason why all the characters will gather at the end (or by introducing the idea which the climax or resolution returns to), the framing event feels organic to the structure rather than forced or farfetched. We return to the question raised in the first act (or early in the second) about the characters involved and complete the course started, like returning to the main theme of a symphony at the end to complete it. Answering at the end the questions asked at the beginning helps create a sense of balance in the work.

THE ACT TWO AND THREE CLIMAXES

All of these films have strong climaxes for the major plot lines. In ensemble films, the strongest climax often comes at the end of Act Two instead of Act Three. In *Diner*, Boogie's plot line is the most dramatic; he's in trouble with a bookie who wants his money. Coping with this problem takes up the majority of the action in Boogie's mini-plot (and in Act Two of the film), as he involves his friends in various schemes to raise money. Ninety minutes into the 105-minute film, Boogie's plot line climaxes when he goes to face the bookie and meet his fate. (Twenty minutes earlier, the bookie's henchman had worked Boogie over, threatening him with more harm if Boogie doesn't get the cash.) The audience now expects the worst because Boogie's schemes to raise the cash have failed. When he meets the bookie's henchman, Boogie learns that his debt has been paid by family friend and fellow diner patron Bagel (Michael Tucker). The violence promised earlier is still delivered when Boogie decks his adversary and pronounces them even. (This action functions as the second act climax.) Boogie then agrees to work for Bagel to pay his debt, taking some measure of responsibility for his life. This action resolves Boogie's mini-plot. The film then picks up Eddie's plot line which leads to the film's main climax: 99 minutes into the film, Eddie decides the wedding will take place. The actions during the wedding tie up the plot lines and resolve the film for all the main characters.

In *Parenthood*, Act Two climaxes when Gil, having quit his job because he didn't get the partnership, comes home to learn that his wife is pregnant. The last thing he wants is more pressure and responsibility; he is particularly frustrated when Karen suggests he eat crow and ask for his job back because of the pregnancy. This is a dramatic high point and it occurs 86 minutes into the 124-minute film. Throughout Act Three, Gil and Karen are at odds with each other. Act Three climaxes at his daughter's play. With his youngest son destroying the set on stage, Gil has an epiphany, but it is not in the form of a dramatic encounter. With the chaos all around him, he realizes that life is a roller coaster and he has to accept it. Instead of becoming uptight over the disaster inflicted at his son's hands, he must laugh and accept life's surprises.

In *Grand Hotel*, the second act climaxes 93 minutes into the 116-minute film, when Preysing kills the Baron. This is the dramatic high point. The third act deals with how the death affects the other characters at the hotel. The final climax comes at the 108-minute mark, when Mr. Kringelein asks Miss Flaemmchen (Joan Crawford) to leave with him and she agrees to go. The rest of the film shows what happens to the others and resolves the film.

The Best Years of Our Lives, at a nearly three-hour length (170 minutes), structures its plot with two strong climaxes. At the 2:28 minute mark, Act Two movingly climaxes when Wilma gently confronts Homer about their situation. Her parents want her to leave town to get over him, but she doesn't want to go. Homer doesn't want her to be tied down—she has too kind a heart. But Wilma persists, and so Homer shows her what life would be like with him, what she would have to deal with. He shows her his amputated stubs and his helplessness without the aid of his prosthetic hooks. Wilma responds by reaffirming her love for him. Their coming together ends the second act.

What's so strong about *The Best Years of Our Lives* is the drama which unfolds in the third act, when the story picks up Fred's plot line. While many ensemble films use short third acts to tie up tamer story lines, this film's last act intensifies as it covers Fred's story. Just before the close of Act Two, Fred has lost his job defending Homer. Now, he can't get another one and his wife has filed for divorce. With nothing left to hold him in Boone City, Fred returns to the local Air Transport Command (the film begins in another ATC), to catch a plane out of town. While he waits, he walks through a field of planes all headed for the junkyard. Fred finds a bomber like the one he flew during the war and climbs inside it. In a stunning visual sequence, the emotional turmoil of Fred's character is revealed without him uttering a word. His emotional moment is interrupted by a contractor who Fred mistakes for the junkman. Now he learns that the planes aren't being junked; instead, they will be used to make prefabricated homes. Fred jumps at the opportunity and lands a job, the one thing he wants and needs to hang onto his self-respect. This climaxes Fred's main plot line and it occurs two hours and forty minutes into the film. The plot picks up Homer's wedding which brings the three men and their families together. As Homer and Wilma take their vows, Fred and Peggy tensely acknowledge each other. But before the newlyweds have finished, Fred and Peggy salvage their relationship (at the 2:48 minute mark), thus ending the film on a high point.

PLOT SEQUENCES

Chapter Eleven deals with sequence structure in greater depth, but here let me point out a common mistake made by many screenwriters attempting to write an ensemble screenplay. When structuring the plot, writers often feel the urge to intercut the various mini-plots too frequently. The first scene starts with character A, the second scene goes with character B, the third with character C, and then back to character A again, and so on. This can be very confusing to the a reader, as well as to the viewer. After the initial tension of keeping the separate plots straight wears off, the audience starts to feel frustrated if a story line they can follow does not develop.

Ensemble plot construction needs to group scenes into sequences during key periods in order to manage the story information and to maintain momentum for the audience. As discussed in Chapter Six, the plot must be constructed of scenes with cause-and-effect relationships to convey to the audience the action and meaning of the story. This is just as true for an ensemble film. Plot lines must build (develop and escalate) to maintain tension. But constant intercutting of the mini-plots will undermine the tension of an escalating line of action. The screenwriter must understand his story's most dramatic points and their purpose to orchestrate that material into scenes which build and develop the plot.

Think what *Diner* would be like if the sequence of scenes showing Boogie's first date with Carol Heathrow at the movie theater was intercut with the scene of Eddie and the other friends at the diner. Cutting away to a milder mini-plot would seriously undercut the tension and suspense over whether or not Carol will "go for his pecker" and would thus frustrate the audience.

Cutting to a particular mini-plot just as it starts to build to a key point enables the screenwriter to escalate the tension while creating a cohesive and understandable scene progression. The story continuity pulls viewers along, allowing them to become more deeply involved in the specific mini-plot as well as the entire story. However, intercutting many mini-plots as they become more dramatic distracts and frustrates audiences. Just as we finally understand the significance of what's going on, we are pulled away to another plot line which may not be as dramatic as the one we are involved in, resulting in a letdown.

There are, of course, exceptions. *Nashville* maintains tension and momentum while it intercuts among the 22 characters for most of its 159 minutes. But at significant moments in the film, a scene will involve many of the characters we're following; or, several consecutive scenes will develop one mini-plot to a crucial realization or climax, thus allowing it to make its dramatic point and enabling the audience to grasp the threads of the story.

Transitioning Between the Mini-Plots

Shifting between the mini-plots of an ensemble film can be accomplished in a variety of ways, depending upon the style and nature of the film. Transitions can be verbally based. In *Parenthood*, Gil ends his discussion with Karen about his son Kevin's problems by mentioning his sister's kid. "Now there's a kid with problems," he says, and the film cuts to Helen's plot line and her son Gary.

Ensemble films often move from one mini-plot to another merely by shifting the focus from one set of characters to another. In *Diner*, several of the guys meet Billy at the station and bring him back to the diner, establishing their relationships. When they part, the film stays on Billy as he goes to Eddie's house, thus focusing on their friendship.

Another strategy for shifting plot lines is to have characters pass each other as one scene ends and another begins. In *Grand Hotel*, Preysing notices Flaemmchen's legs while she's in his hotel room working for him. He flirts with her a little, but then a note arrives saying his big deal is off. Distracted, he contemplates what this means while she leaves to go meet the Baron. Outside on Preysing's balcony, the Baron passes and the film shifts its focus by following him.

Mostly, however, plot lines shift from one to another as sequences finish and the need to reintroduce others arises. There are no hard and fast rules; one must develop a rhythm to the writing that makes these transitions feel well-suited to the work while keeping the pace of the film moving.

THE FILMS

Throughout this chapter, the four study films have been discussed in relation to the main points and concepts for constructing an ensemble film. Let's take a brief look at each film's framework to understand how it supports the entire structure.

Diner

The story frame for *Diner* is Eddie's impending wedding. One could surmise that the main climax of each act should have something to do with Eddie's marital situation; if this film solely concerned Eddie and his problem, this would be true. But Eddie's story is just one of several, and it is not the most dramatic. That distinction belongs to Boogie's story, which winds up involving all of the characters in its plot.

If we study *Diner*, its basic structure sets up like this: Ten minutes in, we learn that Boogie has placed a $2,000 bet on a basketball game that he is sure he will win. This is not a dramatic inciting incident because the initial bet has taken place off-screen. But in any mini-plot, like a subplot, the problem must be framed within the context of the whole action. Once all the characters are set, the first act climaxes when Boogie learns he has lost the bet. This sets up Boogie's want for the film—to get the money to cover his debt. This happens 38 minutes into the film. Though this seems a little late for a first act climax, it does not feel late in the film because the time is divided between two building (developing and escalating) plot lines: Boogie's and Eddie's. Seamlessly intertwined within these two plots are the introductions of the three other mini-plots belonging to Billy, Shrevie and Fenwick.

As screen time divides between the two main plots lines of the first act, Boogie keeps the action focused and moving forward with his betting (i.e., he bets that dream girl Carol Heathrow will "go for his pecker" on their first date). We wonder—at a basic level—if he will win or lose and, what will happen; this keeps us involved with the plot. The action of Eddie's plot is focused on his naiveté and his neurotic commitment to his football quiz as determining factor in whether or not he'll marry Elyse. These elements also reveal his want—which is to know if getting married is the right thing. As we watch him, we wonder how far he will take this. Is he really serious? And this keeps us involved; we want to see how it turns out.

As the second act begins, Boogie bets he can bed Carol on their next date; this bet becomes the spine of Act Two. Everyone gets in on it. Now the action begins to intercut between the other plot lines. However, continuity in many of these scenes hinges upon the guys trying to help Boogie come up with money to pay his debt, or wanting to see how his bet turns out. Their characters are drawn and contrasted as they deal with their own problems while trying to help Boogie with his. The midpoint occurs (70 minutes into the film) when the bookie's henchman works Boogie over. Now the stakes go up.

Seventy minutes into a film may seem late for a midpoint, especially since *Diner* is only 105 minutes long. But let's consider this action the midpoint of Act Two, between the opening of the second act (when Boogie bets he can bed Carol Heathrow) and climaxing with his discovery that Bagel has paid his debt. We then see the attack on Boogie shaping into a strong midpoint, falling about 28 minutes into the 52-minute second act.

After this point, the action rides on Boogie's plot line even as it is intercut with Eddie's. Right after Boogie gets worked over, he learns that Carol has the flu. He's sunk, until he spies Beth and comes up with his sleazy plan to substitute her for Carol. Though we cut away to Eddie's plot line and the football quiz (which Elyse fails resulting in Eddie calling off the wedding) we return to Boogie's story when Shrevie decides to tag along with Fenwick to "validate" the bet. Suspense builds until Boogie realizes he can't use Beth this way and confesses to her. We cut away again, this time to Eddie and Billy at the strip joint, discussing their problems with women. But then we're back to Boogie as he heads off to the diner to deal with his problem. The act climaxes when he learns that Bagel has paid his debt.

Act Three focuses on Eddie and what he will do. In the film's final fifteen minutes, Eddie realizes that he is afraid he'll have to give up his friends after he marries. Billy reassures him that their friendship "won't change, only if we let it." After the piano sequence with the stripper, Eddie decides he will get married after all, (this occurs 97 minutes into the film). The film climaxes once we actually reach the wedding (99 minutes in), and resolves by showing each of the characters with their dates and with each other.

Boogie's and Eddie's stories relate to each of the other mini-plots in some way. For example, Billy's mini-plot relates to Eddie's. It starts in the first act when the guys meet Billy at the station, and builds as he goes over to surprise Eddie. Conflict arises when we meet Barbara (Katheryn Dowling) at the news station and we see that she's not happy to see him. Billy's mini-plot picks up steam in the first half of the second act when he learns that Barbara is pregnant. This is the mini-plot's new development. Billy wants to marry Barbara but she says their one night together was a mistake. During the course of the second act, Billy discusses Barbara with Eddie and the two characters are contrasted in their views of women. Billy wrestles with this problem for the rest of the film: Can he convince Barbara to marry him?

Fenwick's plot line, which opens the film, involves all the characters. It is interjected sparsely after the opening and during the first hour of the film, but Fenwick's presence is always felt. His drinking and disaffection are set up early and they build once he offers to help Boogie by asking his brother for money (about an hour into the film). Once we see Fenwick with his brother and discover his family's views of him, we see that his problem is his alienation from everybody but his friends at the diner. After his brother refuses to help him, Fenwick ends up drunk in the manger of a church nativity scene. Shrevie, Eddie and Billy try to get him away before he gets in trouble, but his anger and hostility explode and they are all arrested. While the others are bailed out by their fathers, Fenwick's family leaves him in jail for the night. This is pretty much the climax of Fenwick's mini-plot. After this point, he is used in Boogie's plot line (when he and Shrevie go to verify the bet), but he is the device to follow the action that involves others (Boogie, Shrevie and Beth).

Shrevie's mini-plot also involves all the characters at some point, but because of Beth, his story is most tied to Boogie's. His problem is that he feels estranged from his wife, like they have nothing in common anymore. His indifference toward Beth is set up early, at the dance, when they talk about Eddie and Elyse, and again later, at the theater. He never fully lets her into his world and so they remain at a distance. Toward the end of the first act, when Eddie asks Shrevie if he's happy with his marriage, we see Shrevie's confusion. In the second act, Shrevie confronts Beth about his record collection. This fight, after which Boogie arrives to borrow money, lays the groundwork for Boogie's later plan with Beth. Shrevie is used in Fenwick's mini-plot (he grabs Billy and Eddie out of the theater to rescue Fenwick from the manger). Then, Shrevie is used in Boogie's plot when he tags along with Fenwick to verify the bet. Shrevie's plot line resolves at the wedding, when he surprises Beth with vacation plans for the Catskills. Nothing has really changed between Shrevie and Beth—they will just go on—but they have, in effect, tried to goose their marriage with another honeymoon to restore the excitement they once had.

Parenthood

The structure of *Parenthood* is slightly less complicated than that found in *Diner*. Gil's plot line is the spine of the story. He starts the film with his fantasy, telling us he swore he'd be the "perfect parent," and he climaxes it with his realization that no matter how hard you try, there will always be problems to cope with.

The basic structure of *Parenthood* sets up like this: Six minutes into the film, Karen lays the groundwork for Gil's problem by mentioning their upcoming meeting with the school principal who is concerned over their son Kevin's school performance. After the other characters are introduced and set up (Helen, Susan, Larry [Tom Hulce] and their father Frank [Jason Robards]), Gil and Karen meet with the principal; they learn that Kevin has emotional problems and the principal believes they should place him in a special education class. Gil rejects the principal's recommendations, but it's clear he blames himself for his son's shortcomings. At the film's 32-minute mark, the first act climaxes when Gil learns that his chances of becoming a partner at his firm are in jeopardy because he's too much of a family man. His boss lays down a challenge: Gil has one month to prove himself a company man. The issue here, job vs. home, is an aspect of the problems one may encounter when trying to be the perfect parent.

In the first act, each mini-plot poses the characters in the middle of their own family predicaments: Divorcee Helen has problems with daughter Julie and son Gary (Leaf Phoenix). After an argument, Julie moves out to join her boyfriend Tod (Keanu Reeves); Susan wants to go to Mexico with Nathan, but he doesn't want to leave their daughter behind; the family prodigal, Larry returns and moves in with his parents, bringing along his bi-racial son Cool; meanwhile, the family's patriarch, Frank, welcomes Larry with open arms, which is contrasted to the obvious disappointment he exhibits for his other son, Gil.

Act Two interweaves Gil's mini-plot with those of his siblings Helen, Susan and Larry. As this act gets underway, Gil struggles with the pressures of being a "company man" and the perfect father; Frank begins to suspect that Larry is in some kind of trouble; Julie is returned home by the police; Helen must deal with the fact that her daughter is married to Tod; and Nathan discovers that Susan doesn't want to wait until their daughter is five before having another child. A mix-up at the midpoint, when a stripper arrives to entertain at his son's birthday party instead of Cowboy Dan provides Gil with the opportunity to shine as the perfect Dad and save his son's celebration

In the second half of Act Two, the plot lines intensify. While Tod helps Helen's son Gary through his crisis, he and Julie have their ups and downs; their relationship comes to a head when Helen returns from a date with her son's biology teacher and learns that Julie is pregnant. In the meantime, Larry tries to sell his father's beloved classic car for the cash he needs to pay off the gambling debt to mobsters. Then, Susan decides to leave Nathan. And Gil can't keep denying his son's emotional problems. The act ends when Gil does not getting the partnership he worked so hard to win; in frustration, he quits his job. He comes home to learn that Karen is pregnant and she tells him that he should ask for his job back. They fight, unable to resolve the issues between them.

In Act Three, each mini-plot builds to its climax and resolution. Frank, recognizing that Gil is a good parent, asks his advice on what to do about Larry. Kevin finally catches a fly ball and gains some measure of self-respect, making Gil proud. Larry will receive help from Frank, but only on Frank's terms. (Larry seems to accept it, but he finagles an escape plan which Frank knowingly allows.) Nathan wins Susan back. Helen helps Julie accept Tod's professional choices. The act climaxes when Gil survives the panic attack brought on by his youngest son's destructive behavior at his daughter's play during which he realizes that life truly is a roller coaster. The film resolves with all the families gathered for the birth, having weathered their crises and reaffirming the notion of family.

The Best Years of Our Lives

Unlike *Diner* and *Parenthood,* in which the protagonists are friends or family, *The Best Years of Our Lives* brings together three main characters who do not know each other and interweaves their stories of readjustment to life after war into one unified whole. This film uses a wedding to frame the film, foreshadowed seven minutes in, when the men share a plane ride home to Boone City and talk about their lives. In the first nine minutes, we find out about the girl waiting for Homer, Al's (Fredric March) fear of being "rehabilitated," and Fred's desire for a good job (he's not going back to the soda fountain!) and to see his wife. (These problems serve as separate inciting incidents for each mini-plot.)

The men share a cab ride and we see each one's homecoming. Homer's family has trouble trying to pretend his hooks aren't there, and he can't even wrap his arms around his girl, Wilma, an act that clearly defines his alienation. Al is welcomed home by his daughter Peggy and son Rob (Charles Halton) before finding comfort in the arms of Millie (Myrna Loy), his loving and supportive wife. Fred arrives at his father's (Roman Bohnen) place and is surprised to learn that his wife Marie (Virginia Mayo) has taken her own apartment. The first act climaxes at the 23-minute mark.

Act One ends with all the characters back home. Now the question is: What will happen to them? Two of the protagonists, Homer and Fred, have clear problems. For Homer, it is how he will ever readjust and accept what's happened to him. Fred's problem is to find his wife.

Act Two begins by focusing on Al. It quickly becomes clear how restless he is at home after four years overseas. He finds it difficult to talk to his wife, finally insisting they go out to celebrate. Now his alienation is exposed. He can't really relate to her; all he wants to do is get drunk. Coming home is scary, as he said on the plane ride home. Al's problem further defines the issue affecting the three main characters: how will they adjust?

Act Two interweaves the characters' mini-plots as each one attempts to deal with his own problems while crossing the others' paths. Homer's mini-plot shows the tension between him, his family and Wilma. As Al's mini-plot develops, we learn that his problem is more an alienation from work than from home. How will he go back to being a cautious banker when his war experience has taught him that risks sometimes have to be taken? Meanwhile, Fred can't get a job so he goes back to work at the soda fountain, losing his wife's respect as well as his own. But Fred's problems with Marie have nothing to do with his employment: she married Fred because of his Captain's uniform and he married the beautiful woman because she was crazy for it. In other words, they have nothing in common.

The real heart of this story is the relationship that develops between Fred and Peggy in Act Two. It is what keeps Fred involved in Al's plot line, and vice versa. Homer's plot line involving his relationship with Wilma is really a separate tangent, but continues to cross paths with Fred and Al through the bar his uncle (Hoagy Carmichael) runs.

In the first half of Act Two, Peggy meets Fred while out celebrating with her parents. When Fred can't get into his wife's apartment, Millie and Peggy take him to their home; then, Peggy glimpses Fred's painful memories when he has a nightmare. Clearly, she is attracted to him, but he is a married man.

At the film's midpoint (1:32), Fred goes back to work at the soda fountain where Peggy runs into him. They agree to meet for lunch and hit it off; afterwards, he kisses her. This sets Peggy on a course of action (to break up Fred's marriage). But her father intercedes, asking Fred to break it off: he doesn't want his daughter involved in a painful "backstreet" romance. Fred's life further disintegrates when he defends Homer at the soda fountain and loses his job for it. This is Fred's Act Two climax. Leaving, he tells Homer not to lose Wilma, to go to her. As we follow Homer, the main Act Two climax occurs when he finally confronts his problem—his fear that she will reject him. Instead, she embraces him and their problems are resolved.

The three mini-plots climax and resolve at different points, staggered through the second half of Acts Two and Three. Al's plot line is the first to climax and resolve (about 20 minutes after the midpoint), when he is honored by his bank and is asked to give a speech. Al makes a speech which defines his role as new Vice President of Small Loans. He says he won't play it safe, he can't. He's got to gamble with his company because he'll be "gambling on the future" of this country. Homer's mini-plot climaxes at the end of Act Two (at the 2:24 mark). Act Three picks up with Fred's story: He can't get a job, his wife wants a divorce and he decides to leave town. As discussed above, this leads him to his Act Three climax (at 2:40) and to the main climax of the film (at the airfield, where he lands his construction job). The film resolves at Homer's wedding, which serves to bring Fred and Peggy together.

Grand Hotel

Like *The Best Years of Our Lives*, *Grand Hotel* opens on a group of strangers and weaves their lives together. The first act of *Grand Hotel* sets up very quickly, in 24 minutes. Five problems are introduced with great economy in the first five minutes as the characters talk on the telephone: Kringelein is dying; Preysing's business venture is in danger of failing which would cause his ruin; the ballerina Grusinskaya (Greta Garbo) will not dance at her performance; the Baron needs money and reveals he will steal it. Senf, the porter, is the only minor character in the opening, although his problem (awaiting news of his wife and child) is used to frame the film. At the 11-minute mark, the fifth main character, Miss Flaemmchen, arrives to work for Preysing, but while waiting for him, she meets the Baron in the hallway. This is the key to her involvement in the plot. The first act ends when the insecure Grusinskaya reluctantly leaves the hotel to dance at her recital.

When Act Two begins, the Baron reveals to the chauffeur (who is hounding him about the money he owes), that he intends to steal Grusinskaya's pearls; this will square him with everyone. As the other relationships develop, a number of different conflicts are introduced. It turns out that Kringelein worked for Preysing's firm and he thinks the General Director is a tyrant. Preysing, who has announced to a business associate that he is an honest family man, begins to get ideas about Miss Flaemmchen (however, bad news about his business deal arrives before he can act upon them). The Baron gets into Grusinskaya's room and grabs the pearls, but he can't get out because Preysing is on his balcony. This forces him to hide in the dancer's room until she returns, broken from her recital. The Baron stops her from suicide and the two spend the night together. By morning, they're in love; he confesses his failures to Grusinskaya, swearing he'll get money to leave with her the next morning. This is the film's midpoint (58 minutes in).

The Baron's need for money directs the plot construction of the second half of *Grand Hotel*. Though the plot lines for Kringelein, Flaemmchen's and Preysing are developed, all of them now are intertwining with the Baron's, either directly or indirectly. Because of her love for the Baron, Grusinskaya now has the inspiration to dance. The Baron treats Kringelein kindly and tries to help him; as a result, Flaemmchen befriends the old man, too. (This draws both the Baron and Kringelein into Preysing's purview, due to the businessman's interest in Flaemmchen.)

Conflict escalates between the three men as Preysing's arrogance collides with the Baron's kindness toward Kringelein. But with the Baron in love with someone else, Flaemmchen agrees to Preysing's proposition to accompany him on a business trip, even though she despises him (because she, too, needs money).

When the Baron loses the little money he had in a poker game, he steals Kringelein's wallet, but realizes he can't keep it. Instead, he goes after Preysing's wallet, but is caught. When the Baron tries to leave before the authorities come, an enraged Preysing kills him. The Baron's murder climaxes the second act (at 1:34 into the film).

Act Three deals with the effects of the Baron's murder. Preysing tries to get Flaemmchen and Kringelein to lie for him, but they won't and he is arrested. Grusinskaya's entourage keeps the news of the Baron's death from her; she leaves the hotel thinking he will meet her at the train station. The film climaxes when Flaemmchen agrees to go with Kringelein, promising they will find a doctor to cure the ailing man. As they leave the hotel, Senf learns that his wife has had her baby. Meanwhile, new guests arrive, and the world continues to pass through the Grand Hotel.

SPECIAL NOTES

Diner was the sleeper hit of 1982 and marked screenwriter Barry Levinson's directorial debut. Produced by Mark Johnson, Levinson's semi-autobiographical film was nominated for an Academy Award for Best Original Screenplay. Along with *Rainman* (written by Barry Morrow and Ron Bass), *Diner* ranks with the best of Levinson's directorial works.

The screenplay used for comparison is not dated. It is 104 pages long with "A" and "B" pages throughout, indicating revisions. Its structure remains intact in the film, with a couple of scenes cut, most notably a sequence where several of the characters go to a Baltimore Colts game. There are minor changes.

The screenplay opens on Fenwick breaking windows. Modell (Paul Reiser) sees him, walks up the stairs to the dance and finds Boogie. The film opens with title cards telling us we're in Baltimore, 1959, and it's Christmas Night. Then Modell comes up the stairs to the dance and finds Boogie. Boogie heads to the basement where he finds Fenwick breaking windows. The film picks up the screenplay at this point. Another minor change involves Billy: in the screenplay, he arrives at the airport; in the film, the boys pick him up at the train station.

Many scenes have been trimmed. For example, "The Gripper" scenes are more developed in the script; they have been edited down in the film. Consequently, the first act break occurs on page 49 of the screenplay, while it takes place at the 38-minute mark in the film. In the screenplay, when Boogie learns that Bagel paid his debt, it feels more like the climax of the entire story. (This comes on page 93 of the 104-page screenplay; in the film, it comes at the 90-minute mark, with 15 minutes of film left.) In the film, the action of Eddie and Billy plays more definitively, clearly building to Eddie's decision to proceed with the wedding (as climax) and the actual wedding (as resolution).

Most of the dialogue is in the screenplay, but some scenes allow the actors to embellish and ad lib, enriching the already wonderful camaraderie between the characters that was established in the script. Lines are added in the film to increase the character shadings. One notable addition comes at the police station when we learn that Fenwick's father is going to let him spend the night in jail while the other fathers have bailed out their sons. Another addition which slightly alters our view of Shrevie comes at the end of his speech to Eddie about marriage. The screenplay makes Shrevie more pessimistic about his marriage, but in the film he comes off more confused with the addition of his last line, "But it's good, nice." There are other slight changes, such as Billy taking Eddie to a Bergman instead of a Fellini film.

The conclusion of the film is more polished than the screenplay, adding scenes which nicely end each of the major characters' plot lines. In the screenplay, Fenwick and Boogie are given short moments to end on; Billy has a longer episode (plus a moment when he gets to confront his last high school tormentor, which is cut from the film); Shrevie is left out. In the film, a scene with Shrevie and Beth is added. In the script, Boogie's short scene with Ann Chisholm is combined with Fenwick's lines to his date. The film separates these beats. Billy's dialogue and action with Barbara are edited down from the script to simply a dance with no dialogue. In the screenplay he and Barbara seem to resolve things positively; this contrasts nicely the upbeat ending and gives the film a more realistic tone. The film adds the ending monologue by Modell which beautifully closes the story.

Produced by Brian Graizer, *Parenthood* was released in the summer of 1989 and was an immediate hit. Screenwriters Lowell Ganz and Babaloo Mandel created a story with director Ron Howard (who shares story credit with them) and fashioned a screenplay that, while tightly structured, still manages to capture the spontaneous flow of family life.

The seventh draft of the screenplay, dated December 19, 1988, is 127 pages (including a number of "A" and "B" pages with revisions dating from January and February, 1989). It was called "Untitled Comedy" until someone penciled it out and wrote in above it, "Parenthood." In many ways, that is the most significant change to the screenplay, which contains the scenes in the film plus a number more. The screenplay is not significantly changed, except for some scene deletions, scene editing and character shadings.

In the screenplay, Gil's mother Marilyn has a larger role, and Grandma has a few more scenes. There is more of Gil at work, so we have a better idea what he does, but the film edits these work scenes to a minimum (or cuts them altogether); they are not missed. In the screenplay, some of the scenes are longer; some scenes are more focused. Karen is more of a druggie in the screenplay; in the film, Gil makes reference to it as part of her past. Kevin's character is slightly more hostile in the screenplay; in the film, he comes across more troubled and insecure than angry.

The structure of the film is laid out in the script while the cutting and trimming of many scenes makes the film move faster. Approximately ten pages are cut out of the first act. In the screenplay, Gil confronts his boss on page 43 (not including the 4 "A" and "B" pages added), corresponding to the 33-minute mark of the film. The midpoint problem with Cowboy Dan comes 73 pages into the script; in the film, it starts less than an hour in. Gil learns that Karen is pregnant at the end of the second act; in the screenplay this comes at page 103 while in the film, it comes at the 86-minute mark. The climax is essentially the same, but more is made of the resolution at the hospital by visually extending the suspense over whose baby it is and showing the family's connection.

The Best Years of Our Lives, produced by Samuel Goldwyn, took home seven Academy Awards in 1946, including Best Picture, Best Director, Best Screenplay, Best Actor and Best Supporting Actor. In 1947, the film and its director, William Wyler, were honored by the Golden Globes, The New York Film Critics Awards and the British Academy of Film. This film, written by Robert Sherwood, is credited with changing the style of Hollywood filmmaking in the years to come.

The screenplay, dated April 9, 1946, is 220 pages long. It contains revised pages through July 16, 1946. It is fully written, elaborately describing scenes, action, the feelings of the characters. Its structure is the same as the film, establishing each of the three characters and their problems. But, there are changes. Many involve cutting transitions between scenes, trimming scenes of ending dialogue, changing and shortening some needed transitions. A few scenes have been cut completely. But the most forceful moments are there, though they appear at different locations in the film. (In the screenplay, when Al comes home, Millie is in the dining room setting the table; in the film, she is in the kitchen and the two meet in the hallway for a long embrace.)

The most significant change is at the end when Fred is at the airfield. In the screenplay, during this sequence, his father reads the citation while Fred walks through the discarded airplanes. When Fred climbs into the bomber, we hear the voices haunting him and see in flashback part of what he experienced when he was wounded. In the film, this is all cut. Instead, the moment relies on Dana Andrews acting, William Wyler's direction and Hugo Friedhofer's music to communicate the action and meaning.

Grand Hotel was producer Irving Thalberg's idea. He decided to take a big star like Wallace Berry (who could carry a film on his own), and put him in a film with other big stars, Greta Garbo, the Barrymore brothers, Joan Crawford. The result was Hollywood's first all-star melodrama. *Grand Hotel*, based on the Vicki Baum novel, screenplay by W. A. Drake and directed by Edmund Goulding, was a big hit. It received just one Academy Award nomination, but it won—for Best Picture. If you can get past the staginess of the direction and some of the performances, the film is a testament to how strong a role structure plays in keeping a film timeless. The screenplay of *Grand Hotel* could not be located for a comparison of the film to the script.

10

STRUCTURE AND THE NONLINEAR PLOT

Study Films: *Citizen Kane, Rashomon, The Conformist, Annie Hall, Reservoir Dogs*

Great films fracture our expectations. They take us into different worlds and expose situations so fraught with conflict that we find it difficult to anticipate what will happen next. For most films, a strong rising conflict—which creates intense jeopardy for the hero and his immediate circle—generates maximum suspense and helps keep the audience transfixed on the images flickering before them.

But not all films work this way, as we have seen from the last chapter on ensemble films. The nonlinear film also defies the conventional rules of plot construction because it breaks apart the standard notion that the plot's scenes must proceed in chronological order, from the opening exposition to the conflict's climax and resolution. A nonlinear structure deconstructs a complicated event, situation, character or a combination of these elements by reordering the time sequence and creating a new composition for dramatic (or comedic) purposes. This new arrangement of events makes the telling of the story more surprising, compelling and unpredictable than if it was told in a straight, linear fashion.

Don't confuse the nonlinear film with one that utilizes flashbacks. A number of films open on a situation in the present and flash back to the story. Then, at the end, they return to the opening situation (*Saving Private Ryan, Little Big Man*). Or, they may open with the culmination of the conflict then flash back to the origins of the conflict, proceeding in sequential time up to the point where the film began (*Sunset Boulevard, Carlito's Way*).

This method creates initial tension that will grab our attention and make us wonder what brought on this action or what it means. Other films use a major flashback in the middle of the plot (*Casablanca*). These are not nonlinear films, but rather, they use flashback strategies to create context and tension, or to deliver exposition in their plots—the main plots of these films still proceed in a chronological order.

Traditionally, a nonlinear structure puts the emphasis on character even as it develops a complicated plot. Nonlinear plots are usually a strategy for describing a character without the constraints imposed by a linear, goal-oriented structure. The filmmakers may want to focus on a character's whole life instead of on one segment. Or, the character may have a nonmaterial goal or spiritual need compelling him to act (a need which may not easily translate into a concrete, goal-oriented action, but nevertheless is the basis for a strong thematic unity). In either case, unity of action is too limiting to use as the plot device; instead, thematic unity through character revelation becomes the driving force.

Films such as *Reservoir Dogs*, *Pulp Fiction* and *The Usual Suspects* forego an emphasis on character and use a nonlinear plot to unravel a complicated event or set of circumstances; in *Pulp Fiction* and *The Usual Suspects*, plots twists and action take precedence over characterizations. Segments proceed linearly, although they may be interrupted and commented upon (*The Usual Suspects*) or they may overlap and intersect (*Pulp Fiction*). These films may seem boldly original upon first viewing, but without the strength of compelling character relationships or focused characterizations at their centers, their plots grow increasingly transparent and hollow upon further viewings.

A well-written nonlinear film exposes a character or a situation from a number of different vantage points; the use of more than one vantage point to construct the plot allows characters and their motivations, both conscious and unconscious, to be explored in greater depth. In the same way, different perspectives expand a situation, often developing their origins and ending until the film's full meaning comes into focus. These multilayered portrayals of character or situation in great nonlinear films strengthen the theme and significance, and are eminently watchable in repeated viewings.

In this chapter, our study films are: *Citizen Kane*, written by Herman J. Mankiewicz and Orson Welles, directed by Welles;

Rashomon, written my Shinobu Hashimoto and Akira Kurosawa, based on two stories by Ryunosuke Atkutagawa, directed by Kurosawa; *The Conformist,* written by Bernardo Bertolucci and Alberto Moravia, based on Moravia's novel and directed by Bertolucci; *Annie Hall,* written by Woody Allen and Marshall Brickman, directed by Allen; and *Reservoir Dogs,* written and directed by Quentin Tarantino.

Several other films are mentioned and worth looking at in this distinct category. *Two for the Road,* written by Frederic Raphael and directed by Stanley Donen, though dated by its impossibly hip Sixties sensibility and unlikable protagonist, has an unparalleled structure for crossing time boundaries which, by the film's end, achieves a resonance rarely seen today. Other flawed, though interesting, nonlinear films include: *Isadora,* written by Melvin Bragg and Clive Exton, directed by Karel Reisz; *The Last Temptation of Christ,* adapted by Paul Schrader from Nikos Kazantzakis' novel, directed by Martin Scorsese; *The Usual Suspects,* written by Christopher McQuarrie and directed by Bryan Singer; and Quentin Tarantino's *Pulp Fiction.*

Nonlinear films are as varied in their approach to structure as ensemble films are—perhaps more so because they often differ in their purpose as much as in their structural considerations. Whether they focus on exposing a character (*Citizen Kane, The Conformist, Annie Hall*) or an event (*Rashomon, Reservoir Dogs*), their approaches can be radically different. Just as with ensemble films, there are no set rules for constructing a nonlinear plot. But the key ingredient in all great nonlinear films is still dramatic unity—the synthesis of thematic ideas and plot movement—which enables the screenwriter and filmmaker to integrate viewpoints and construct the framework for the film's plot.

DRAMATIC UNITY

As discussed in the last chapter, dramatic unity focuses the management of information that filmmakers wish to cover in a film. A nonlinear structure is no different. Great nonlinear films achieve clarity by creating relationships between various time segments which, taken together as a whole, form a specific meaning. Make no mistake, a nonlinear structure does not mean that audiences will understand a film in a new and different way. Audiences still understand by making cause-and-effect connections between the scenes in order to assign meaning. Information must be conveyed in a clear and intelligible manner, which means that each beat or segment of information must relate to what comes before and what follows, even as the scene transcends a chronological order of time.

Dramatic unity in great nonlinear films is achieved by the intersection of two key ingredients:
1) a controlling theme or idea;
2) a framing action.

The Controlling Theme or Idea

Theme defines what a film experience is about; it determines the choice of incidents and events which make up the plot. In a nonlinear film, in which action does not unify or direct the plot construction, theme takes on an even greater importance. The more diverse and out of sequence the incidents, the more the theme is needed to hold these various segments together. At the end, when they are added up in the mind of the viewer, each scene and sequence should contribute to the ultimate discovery of what the film is about.

The theme of *Citizen Kane* deals with the impossibility of finding love if one does not learn how to give it. Charles Foster Kane (Orson Welles) needs to be loved, and he actively searches for love, yet he does not know how to return it. Numerous sequences tell the story of his life, centering around his lonely death in his mansion, "Xanadu." Major sequences include Kane becoming the world's biggest collector, being taken from his family as a child, punishing the man who took him away, marrying and becoming disenchanted with marriage, seeking public office and losing it, finding a mistress and driving her away. All of these sequences depict his failed attempts to find love; all end tragically because Kane can't love in return.

The Conformist deals with the nullification of feeling and how it betrays and destroys the soul. The protagonist Marcello Clerici (Jean-Louis Trintignant), is shown in various episodes seeking conformity, the reasons why he seeks it and the damage it causes to his soul.

Annie Hall is about the difficulties of maintaining a modern relationship and how our own neuroses conspire against us in our search for happiness. As soon as Alvy (Woody Allen) finds Annie (Diane Keaton)—who makes him happy—then he tries to change her, making her unhappy. Alvy's neurotic fears collude to keep him from finding happiness and satisfaction.

Citizen Kane, The Conformist and *Annie Hall* each explore the complex psychology of a character. Through desire, obsession, contradiction, ambivalence and conflict, a believable human paradox is crafted. These films affect us because the characters are less heroic and more true-to-life.

In *Rashomon*, sequential action takes on a greater role, but the film can only be understood if one looks at the theme. *Rashomon* deals with the obliterating consequences to the human psyche when an "objective" truth cannot be substantiated; only compassion can restore our faith and make sense of the human experience.

Reservoir Dogs depends less upon a definitive theme than on a controlling idea. The film dissects a bungled jewelry store heist as the survivors try to figure out what went wrong. Ultimately, the theme tells us that trust is impossible among those who break the rules of society.

When the point of a nonlinear film is the exploration of character, theme often relates to the protagonist's inner need and emotional state. The organization of out-of-order sequences may illustrate the connection between the character's actions and his need, but this connection must be shown through directed action. We see this clearly in *Citizen Kane*—sequences reflect Kane's grasping for the love of the people or for Susan (motivations) but then they show his inability to give love as he destroys these relationships. In *The Conformist*, Marcello needs to confront his self-loathing, understand how it was caused by his experiences and assert his individuality; unable to understand himself, he ends up a hollow man at the mercy of his compulsions. Alvy in *Annie Hall* also needs to accept himself to be able to accept others. Unlike Marcello, Alvy reaches a level of self-understanding, though it is not enough to change his personality; therefore, his relationship with Annie is doomed.

The Framing Action

Like an ensemble film which relies upon an event frame to help unify its plot structure, all great nonlinear films use some level of action to frame the plot. This framing action creates a continuity in the plot and establishes a context in which to tell the story. It also creates continuity by focusing on a specific action or task to be accomplished. As the separate episodes shatter normal (sequential) time by intercutting past, present and future episodes to illuminate different aspects of the story, the framing action produces a unified flow in a specific plot progression to which viewers can orient themselves. Whenever the film cuts back to the present task, the audience understands where the characters are in relation to that task and the plot. In this way, a context is established.

For example, in *Citizen Kane*, the reporter Thompson (William Alland) is assigned the task of finding out what "Rosebud" means. This is his want and the reason he meets the various characters and hears their recollections of Kane. Thompson provides the link between the separate episodes in the plot as he pursues his goal.

The nonlinear plot is grounded in a specific set of circumstances by the story task and context; these form the dramatic reason for the examination of the other elements in the film. In *The Conformist*, Marcello's pursuit of his former professor Quadri (Enzo Tarascio) is the framing action that links together separate segments—from as far back as his childhood to as recently as the previous night. During his quest, he reflects on his life; we enter his stream of consciousness provoked by his ordeal. In *Rashomon*, three men sit under the Rashomon gate in the pouring rain and try to make sense of the separate stories in which each participant admits to killing the husband (Masayuki Mori). *Reservoir Dogs* focuses on the situation in the warehouse when the heist survivors try to determine who set them up at the jewelry store.

Of our study films, only *Annie Hall* does not seem to have an ongoing current problem for the characters to deal with. Instead the film opens on Alvy, standing before the camera as if performing a stand-up routine before an audience. He jokes about life, how meaningless it all is and how it's over way too quickly. But then he gets to the point: Annie has left him and things just haven't been the same. The film spends five minutes showing us a few funny scenes delineating Alvy as a child and adult, then it cuts into a scene with Annie where we see the relationship is already in trouble. The film unfolds as if it is a visualization of a long comic monologue about male/female relationships. In this way, Alvy's relationship with Annie becomes the frame of the film: Alvy's pursuit of Annie is the action which directs the plot's construction.

The framing action is stronger if there are obstacles and complications which prevent the protagonist from completing the "present" task. In *Citizen Kane,* Thompson has no idea what "Rosebud" means and neither does anyone else. In *The Conformist,* Marcello's problem is that he admires Professor Quadri and loves Quadri's wife Anna (Dominique Sanda). Marcello wants to save her from the assassins but does not know how. In *Rashomon,* the confusing and contradictory stories form barriers for the men as they try to comprehend what really happened. In *Annie Hall,* Alvy's main obstacles to a successful relationship with Annie are his own neuroses. In *Reservoir Dogs,* the men's attitudes, fears and Mr. Orange's (Tim Roth) stomach wound are obstacles or complications which the characters must deal with in the course of the framing action.

In a nonlinear film, a framing action helps strengthen overall dramatic unity the same way that action unifies most linear films. It allows the audience to focus on a specific course leading toward a distinct goal—and the audience hopes for success or failure depending upon the nature of the mission. The more dramatic the framing action of the film, the higher the tension and the more deeply involved the audience will be.

PLOT SEQUENCES

Like great ensemble and linear films, the best nonlinear films construct sequences which advance the plot; they develop their plots with sequences to sustain a sense of continuity and to build momentum. Rarely do nonlinear films cut from a scene in one time period to another unless each time period has been firmly established, and then, this is generally done only late in the film to achieve a specific emotional effect (*Two for the Road*). Constant intercutting undermines and destroys tension in an escalating line of conflict. (These plot sequences, better known as scene or action sequences, are discussed in Chapter Nine and, at greater length in Chapter Eleven.) Let's look at a few aspects of plot sequences which are specific to the nonlinear film.

Sequences can be thought of as episodes constructed within time frames so as to develop character and theme through action. Because action and conflict are used in each sequence, tension is created, making the information presented more involving. Sequences are mini-plots, complete with beginnings, middles and ends (set-up, development and climax). Think of the sequence in *Citizen Kane,* when Thatcher (George Coulouris) comes to take young Kane (Buddy Swan) from his family. The sequence opens on young Kane sledding while his parents finalize the terms of the boy's departure (set-up). Thatcher wants to get the papers signed and be on his way; Kane's father (Harry Shannon) doesn't want his son to go (conflict); Kane's mother (Agnes Moorehead) is determined to send her son off, but is deeply troubled by it (inner conflict). Once the papers are signed, the adults go outside to inform Kane that he must go and live with Thatcher. The boy does not want to go and hits Thatcher with the sled. His father says that what the boy needs is a good beating while his mother explains this is the reason she's sending him away (climax). The resolution of the sequence shows Charles spending Christmas with Thatcher and receiving a new sled, but the gift giving is coldly impersonal. The action and conflict produced in this sequence offer a more involving segment than if we simply watch Thatcher pick up young Kane and take him away. The parental conflict illustrated in this group of scenes reveals motivations and contributes to our understanding of Kane's character later in the film.

Each sequence generally has its own protagonist who may or may not be the film's main protagonist. During the sequence, this character pushes the action toward an outer goal or inner objective. In the sequence above, Kane's mother pushes the action of the sequence with her desire to get Kane out of the clutches of her ill-tempered husband. Later, in the sequence leading to Kane's wife Emily (Ruth Warrick) discovering his mistress Susan (Dorothy Comingore), Emily pushes the action.

In *Rashomon*, we clearly see that each sequence is dominated by the character telling the story, either bandit (Toshiro Mifune), wife (Machiko Kyo) or husband.

In *Annie Hall*, the first half of Act Two is made up of several sequences. Annie pushes the action in the first segment (when she tries to get Alvy to notice her); once Alvy asks her for a date, he pushes the action (by trying to get to know her).

In *Reservoir Dogs*, we see numerous sequences with separate protagonists. Mr. White (Harvey Keitel), Mr. Pink (Steve Buscemi), Mr. Orange (Tim Roth) and Mr. Blonde (Michael Madsen) each push the action at different points: Pink is the protagonist of the sequence which shows his escape; White pushes the action in several sequences (he gets Mr. Orange back to the warehouse and tries to soothe him, he meets Joe [Lawrence Tierney] and comes on the job in his flashback); Blonde also pushes the action in several sequences, most prominently during the torture segment, but also when he comes to Joe looking for a job; Orange pushes the action of the sequences which shows how he got the job and as he prepares for the robbery.

A sequence's true objective may not be entirely apparent during all of the scenes but it should become evident by the end of the sequence. In *The Conformist*, a sequence near the beginning focuses on Marcello's family life. It exists to reveal character but it needs action to keep from being static. The sequence starts on Marcello, with his fiancée Giulia (Stefania Sandrelli) and her mother who talks about a letter they have received which states that Marcello's father is in a mental institution. Marcello admits it, but denies his father's affliction is hereditary, as implied in the letter, and offers to have medical tests to prove it. This provides the exposition for the scenes which follow. In the next scene, Marcello goes to his mother (Milly), a drug addict who admits to having an affair with her Japanese chauffeur while disapproving of Marcello's middle-class fiancée (development). Marcello picks her up for their weekly visit to his father (sequence objective). While his mother gets ready, Marcello instructs his companion, Manganiello (Gastone Moschin) to beat up and get rid of the chauffeur (result of the development) who provides his mother with morphine and then "has his way with her." Marcello and his mother then drive to the mental hospital, where the father (Giuseppe Addobbati) is in a straitjacket and somewhat incoherent. But Marcello asks his father about a specific incident and learns that, during his military work years before, his father tortured and killed others. The scene suggests that it was his military duty that drove Marcello's father mad. Later, we understand that this same affliction befalls Marcello.

In this film, information is conveyed dramatically. Exposition about his father comes from Marcello's fiancée and her mother. Next, Marcello's goal is to arrive at his family home to take his mother to see his father; in the process, he becomes upset with his mother and has her chauffeur beaten and taken from her (character development). At the hospital, he visits with his father (his apparent goal) but his real goal is to find out about his father's horrific past. The sequence maintains a sense of direction while surprising us by where it finally ends.

Time Transitions

There are no hard and fast rules for creating the transitions which move the plot back and forth in time; it is an art. Each story is different and has its own requirements. But like ensemble films cutting too quickly between the mini-plots and creating confusion, in nonlinear films, intercutting back and forth in time too frequently will frustrate the audience. Viewers need to familiarize themselves with the significance of the incidents they are watching. (*Jacob's Ladder* is an example of a film that disappointed and baffled audiences because viewers were not allowed to get their bearings in the plot and therefore could not understand the story as it developed.)

Generally, nonlinear films build sequences in different time frames which allow the audience to ground themselves in the concrete actions of the characters. Remember, it is through action that a character truly defines himself. As discussed above, the framing action helps the audience understand what the film is about on a simple level—in terms of action and goal. Nonlinear films rarely intercut one scene in one time frame with another scene in a different time frame and still another in a later time frame unless the audience is completely oriented to all the time periods being explored. Quick intercutting between time periods at the beginning may generate initial curiosity, but it will soon turn curiosity into frustration if filmmakers do not ground the story in a driving action, enabling the audience to make sense of these scenes soon after the film begins. At the beginning of *Two for the Road*, scenes from different time periods overlap, but only during the transitions with the cars. It is a little confusing at first, but after awhile, these quick cuts actually help the audience understand how time transitions will be made in the film. Near the end of the film, short scenes from different time periods are cut together to create a type of montage, like snapshots, of the couple's life seen on the road. This montage serves as a great metaphor for the trials and tribulations of marriage, which, of course, never end.

Flashbacks

Flashbacks are used in linear as well as nonlinear films. A flashback is the presentation of an earlier incident or episode that pertains to the story. Usually, it concerns a major character's past experience and relates to his motivations by exposing the reasons for his behavior. In the best films which utilize this technique, the flashback shows viewers information instead of telling it to them in an expository speech while relying on conflict to make the scene (or scenes) more compelling.

In a great film, a flashback is not conceived merely as a device to communicate exposition to the audience, but it is an integral part of a film's structure used to convey information to the characters. This means that the flashback scene (or group of scenes) is conceived as part of the whole composition; its placement is woven into the plot to deepen our understanding of the characters and the situation at a specific point in the film. In *Casablanca*, a flashback starts near the beginning of Act Two. Its purpose is to dramatize Ilsa's relationship to Rick so that we understand what she means to him and why he is so devastated by her appearance. Dramatically, there is no other way to get this information across. Rick would never cry on someone's shoulder and tell them what happened; he is the type of man who would deny his feelings before he would admit to them. Today, one might argue that his flashback really isn't necessary to the plot's construction; the audience would understand Rick's feelings of abandonment by his behavior and when he argues with Ilsa at the bazaar (the midpoint), revealing the exposition about Paris. However, the flashback comes at a dramatically potent moment in the film—the beginning of Act Two. It is woven into the plot as a result of Rick's drinking (the motivation for the flashback) and shows the audience his memory of Paris—from his sheer happiness to his bitter disappointment. The dramatization of his situation makes a stronger impact on the audience—we see what happened, we don't just hear about it. The flashback also increases his antagonism toward Ilsa when she arrives at his saloon later that night. As a result of his memory, his hatred drives her from him before he can get the explanation he desperately needs to get on with his life.

Casablanca uses an extended flashback sequence, running about 10 minutes. But flashbacks can be a short scene or a longer segment, depending upon the unique structural requirements of each film. *Midnight Cowboy* uses flashbacks at several points in its structure. Early in the film, scenes of Joe Buck's (Jon Voight) unhappy childhood are presented in flashback; later, another flashback reveals a brutal incident which presumably motivated him to leave his hometown. All these flashbacks are fully developed scenes which dramatically convey information and increase our understanding of Joe Buck and his situation. *Ordinary People* uses flashbacks as memory fragments in the first half of the film when Conrad (Timothy Hutton) dreams/remembers the boating accident. The same image is used at several more points in the plot, building tension, until the end of the second act when Conrad, with his psychiatrist, relives the boating accident and his brother's death in a full flashback.

Using flashbacks to manipulate time is one of the more challenging aspects of filmmaking. Flashbacks can be specific incidents which are played as if they are happening right now, but they can also be exploited in various ways. In *Annie Hall*, Alvy and Annie show up in their flashbacks, commenting on the memories and making the scenes more humorous. But often, flashbacks feel forced and tacked on, especially when they are merely used to give exposition. Instead of contributing to the momentum of a film, the flashbacks slow it. If this technique is going to be used, flashbacks should add to the overall structure, tone and pacing of a film.

Nonlinear films are made up of flashbacks and many also use flash forwards. These films use more than two time frames, intercutting action over various time periods. But films like *The Usual Suspects* and *The English Patient*, which use only two time frames with scenes proceeding in a chronological order in each one, are essentially linear films. A framing story is set up and then the flashback story—which is the center of the film—starts. Time is not truly reordered as in *Citizen Kane*, *Rashomon*, *The Conformist*, *Annie Hall* or *Reservoir Dogs*. Instead, the framing story provides the reason for the telling of the main story which proceeds in flashback.

FOCUSING THE ACT BREAKS

Just as in linear films, material in nonlinear films must be focused into segments or acts if its meaning is to be clearly understood. (Many nonlinear films use a present-time situation as an anchor for the acts, but there are no set rules.) Material should be shaped to provide information—in the most dramatic and interesting fashion—through action, conflict, crisis and climax while servicing the theme. The best way to understand the structure of a nonlinear film is to first understand it conceptually. What do the acts accomplish individually? In the best nonlinear

SECRETS OF SCREENPLAY STRUCTURE

films, we can see clear primary movements directing the organization of the material in the acts and segments.

Citizen Kane

Citizen Kane uses its framing action to very clearly delineate the acts. Structurally, Thompson's assignment and his interviews are strategically placed at the inciting incident (13 minutes into the film), at the beginning and end of Acts Two and Three, and at the midpoint. The first act introduces the public figure of Kane (through the newsreel), but emphasizes his rise and fall through the Thatcher papers. Thatcher's autobiography illustrates how Kane found fortune when he lost his parents; how he took out his anger on Thatcher by using his newspapers to attack his ex-guardian's enterprises; and finally how he lost control of his newspaper empire to Thatcher after the Crash of 1929. At the end of Act One, Kane is still a paradox but we have a clue as to why he became that way. Act Two deals with the rise of his newspaper empire, the creation of his public persona and his political self-destruction. Act Three shows Kane's personal self-destruction as he destroys his last chance at a relationship by driving Susan away.

At the end of each act, the reporter, Thompson, concludes his research or interviews, still unable to discover the meaning of "Rosebud." The first act ends with Thompson leaving the Thatcher Library (29 minutes). The second act includes the interviews of Bernstein and Leland (Erskine Sanford, Joseph Cotton respectively). Bernstein's interview ends just before the midpoint (when Kane marries the niece of the President of the United States, foreshadowing his hope to become the President). Leland's interview picks up with Kane's marriage to Emily and shows the distance that develops between husband and wife over nine years. Leland punctuates his account at the midpoint (55 minutes into the film), talking to Thompson again as he switches from Kane's personal life to his public ambitions and how he ruined them. The second half of Act Two reveals the self-destructive behavior hinted at earlier by depicting the reckless way Kane ran his newspapers, and including segments dealing with Kane's affair with Susan, his political loss and the destruction of his friendship with Leland over Susan's singing career (second act climax, 83 minutes).

At the start of Act Three, Susan agrees to talk to Thompson. Her story overlaps Leland's, showing her embarrassing singing career and Kane's decline at Xanadu. Act Three climaxes when Susan leaves Kane (106 minutes). The interview ends and Thompson returns to Xanadu to play out the aftermath of Susan's exit. We hear about her departure in the interview with Raymond (Paul Stewart), when he describes how Kane wrecked Susan's room (109 minutes). In the resolution, only the audience is privy to the insight into Kane's character that Thompson so futility sought—we are shown the sled with the brand name "Rosebud" as it burns in the furnace (116 minutes).

Rashomon

Rashomon intercuts between three separate time periods—the "current" predicament, the time frame of the incident itself (with its aftermath and the capture of the bandit) and the interviews at the prison courtyard afterward. The current predicament, showing the men sitting out the rain at the Rashomon gate and trying to understand the incident, serves as the foundation for the film. At the beginning of each act, the narrative returns to these men, who are still unable to understand which of the individuals involved in the incident is lying and why. The acts are organized around the accounts told.

The first act sets the scene by giving an overview, primarily using the bandit's version of the incident since it includes the entire scenario. The bandit's capture is the inciting incident, which sets the film on course. This act climaxes when the bandit kills the woman's husband in a fair fight (his version of the "truth," 33 minutes into the film). The action of Act One ends at the bandit's interview in the police courtyard. Then it returns to the three men at the Rashomon gate—and Act Two begins.

This act is organized into two distinct halves; the first half cuts into the woman's version of the events (after the rape) as she tells the police in the courtyard, contradicting the bandit's account. She indicates she must have stabbed her husband in the chest when she fainted (47 minutes). At the midpoint, the men reveal that the dead man told his story through a medium; this version takes up the last half of the second act, climaxing when the husband (through a medium) claims to have killed himself (60 minutes). The second act ends at the prison courtyard.

Act Three again starts with the men in the rain. The woodsman (Takashi Shimura) now admits that he saw what happened after the rape. His version contradicts the three earlier accounts and portrays all the characters in a disagreeable light. This act does not climax after the bandit kills the husband (in an unheroic sword fight)—the murder is anticlimactic by this point. Instead, the action returns to the three men and the discovery of the crying baby. This leads to physical conflict between the men, and then, to the climax. The commoner (Kichijiro Ueda) forces into the open the fact that the woodcutter must have stolen the husband's dagger. The woodcutter is, thus, a liar and so may not be telling the truth at all.

The commoner runs off, leaving the child in the arms of the priest (Minoru Chiaki) and the woodcutter clearly ashamed. The woodcutter tries to take the child from the priest but the priest responds harshly. He has lost complete faith in man and suspiciously regards the woodcutter's motives. The woodcutter humbly explains that because he has six children already, one more will not matter. The woodcutter's action restores the priest's (and our) faith in man. (Act Three climax and resolution, 82 minutes.)

The Conformist

The Conformist is not as rigorous in its reliance upon a current situation being used to frame the action at the beginning of an act or to end one; instead, the acts are organized around the idea of betrayal. The first act is concerned with how Marcello gets into his current situation and reveals his minor betrayals—of mother, woman and self. It begins by showing that Professor Quadri has left his home and Anna has gone with him. Marcello gets his gun and follows with Manganiello. Marcello somehow wants to stop Anna from being hurt. The drive provides the context for the story, making the narrative seem as if Marcello is reflecting upon the events which lead him to this point in his life. He is originally asked only to spy on his old philosophy professor and he readily agrees (inciting incident, six minutes into the film). The first act shows his efforts to conform to the prevailing order, then climaxes in the flashback, when Marcello's original instructions to spy on the professor are changed: Marcello is now ordered to kill Professor Quadri (38 minutes). The first act cuts back and forth in time, at one point including a flashback within a flashback. Using the frame of the present dilemma helps illustrate Marcello's conflict over the situation.

The second act develops Marcello's assassination plans for Professor Quadri while he falls in love with Anna. (Betrayal plays an even larger role in the action—will he betray Anna and her husband?) The act proceeds fairly linearly, as it shows how Marcello goes about insinuating himself among his former professor and colleagues, how he uses his wife Guilia and falls in love with Anna (midpoint, 60 minutes into the film). In the second half of Act Two, Marcello's colleague, Manganiello, knows that Marcello is having second thoughts. Marcello tries to reach Anna and warn her against going on retreat with her husband while she tries to make him promise not to hurt them. The professor's plans indicate that Anna will follow him later. The second act ends when Anna tells Marcello that she is leaving with her husband the next morning and Marcello is unable to convince her not to go (83 minutes).

Act Three returns to the current situation in the framing action; it plays out linearly as the assassins close in and finally kill both Quadri and Anna and Marcello watches but refuses to acknowledge her (93 minutes). (We see he has betrayed Anna and himself.) In a lengthy resolution, the film cuts ahead in time—to the end of the war and Mussolini's resignation to show that Marcello will never change: he turns on his friend and tries to blame the old homosexual who raped him as a child for the professor's murder.

In the second and third acts, linear action unifies the plot and builds momentum. The action of the second act brings us up to speed with the opening of the first act and then proceeds to the final climax and resolution. The thematic ideas dealing with self-betrayal strengthen the unity of the first act and contribute to an integrated whole. The style of the beginning allows the filmmakers to jump ahead in time to the war's end in the resolution without the film suffering or feeling disjointed.

Annie Hall

Annie Hall uses Alvy's relationships to organize its material into a coherent structure. The first act emphasizes Alvy's character in terms of his difficult relationships with women. When the audience first meets Annie, they see that the relationship is on shaky ground. Through flashbacks, we glimpse the failed marriages of Alvy and his first and second wives. The first act ends on an argument between Alvy and his second wife Robin (Janet Margolin). Act Two starts just before Alvy meets Annie and deals with their relationship through to their second breakup. The third act shows the effect of their separation on Alvy: he can't live without her and asks her to marry him. She refuses and they go their separate ways.

Like *The Conformist*, the second and third acts of *Annie Hall* are primarily linear, dealing with Alvy and Annie's relationship from its inception to its destruction. This creates momentum and continuity. The style established in the first act allows the time leaps in the resolution to feel natural and organic.

Reservoir Dogs

In *Reservoir Dogs*, the survivors of a heist gone wrong try to figure out who set them up. This frames the plot. The reordering of time is purely the storyteller's construct; it is designed to make the plot more interesting, not to examine the characters more closely. (The author does not attempt to make the break up of time seem like the characters are reflecting on their lives.) Conceptually, the material in the acts is organized around the situation and the idea of trust. The first act establishes that there is a rat in the group and the characters have to figure out whom to believe. The second act focuses on how the situation developed, revealing Mr. Blonde's character and how he became involved. Act Three shows how Orange became a part of the team then returns to the situation in the warehouse, ultimately proving that none of the men can trust each other.

After the lengthy introduction of the characters involved in the robbery (a seven-minute scene), the first act sets up the situation by showing the criminals running for their lives after the bungled robbery. Mr. Orange is shot in the stomach; Mr. White feels responsible; Mr. Pink arrives at the warehouse, sure there's a rat in their midst (inciting incident, 14 minutes). Pink knows that none of them can afford to trust anyone. He wants to leave the warehouse but White is too consumed with guilt and worry over Orange, and anger towards Mr. Blonde, to ponder this. The first act climaxes when Blonde arrives and breaks up a fight between White and Pink (32 minutes into the film).

Act Two begins by refocusing on the predicament at hand, discovering who the rat is and the guys trying to get away. When Blonde won't cooperate, White turns his anger on him. Pink settles them down and Blonde reveals he has a hostage: a cop. The audaciousness of this act sets up Blonde's flashback showing how he came on the scene. At the end of Blonde's flashback (the midpoint, 47 minutes into the film), Eddie (Christopher Penn) arrives. Blonde continues to push the action to the climax of Act Two when Orange regains consciousness and shoots him before he can set the cop (Kirk Baltz) on fire (59 minutes). As the second act ends, we learn that Orange is a cop and the rat (62 minutes into the film).

Act Three begins with Orange's flashback which takes up 23 minutes of the act. We see how Orange worked to gain confidence of Joe and White, only to betray them. In the context of Orange's story, more of the robbery plan is shown. We also see how Orange got shot and how in return, he shoots and kills a woman. The Act Three climax begins at the standoff over Orange and ends when White shoots Orange for betraying him (93 minutes).

Reservoir Dogs clearly uses the framing action to focus and climax each act. The framing action contributes to building a smooth plot flow as the conflict escalates and advances toward the final climax. The flashback segments are constructed linearly, contributing to the film's momentum. They are also used to heighten the drama, by providing exposition in the context of the bad situation, and by adding humor to relieve the unrelenting tension.

Surprise

One of the prerequisites of a great film is the element of surprise that grows out of the plot as it evolves. The first act generally sets in motion a course of action which heads in one direction; suddenly, as the act closes, it veers off in a new direction which then refocuses the plot on a specific course and problem for the remainder of the film. In *Witness*, the first act appears to set up a story about a good cop hunting down a bad cop. The first act climax reverses the story and it instead becomes a story about a bad cop hunting a good cop. *Risky Business* seems to be about a guy losing his virginity; instead it turns into a story about a guy chasing a girl and getting a lesson in how the world works.

A great film creates a first act which is as interesting as it is surprising before finally announcing the true topic for Acts Two and Three. Nonlinear films seem to contradict this notion. In all our study films, the problem of the film is announced within the first 10 to 15 minutes and does not evolve or change. In *Citizen Kane*, the plot builds upon the search for the meaning of

"Rosebud." *Rashomon* asks what really happened that afternoon. *The Conformist* sets up Marcello's desire to save Anna from harm. *Annie Hall* establishes Alvy's relationship with Annie and how troubled it is. *Reservoir Dogs* asks, "Who's the rat?"

A nonlinear film uses its structure to surprise the audience and create tension, which comes from our inability to predict with certainty where the film will go. Because a nonlinear film breaks with our assumptions about how plots unfold in sequential time, we are never sure where the next scene will go. This creates surprise and builds tension.

Often, the first act in a nonlinear film is the most diverse in the material it covers. In *Citizen Kane*, *The Conformist* and *Annie Hall*, the first act spans a large amount of time and encompasses a wide range of events as it develops the main character with respect to the plot problem. This makes us wonder more about the character and what he will do than how he will accomplish his specific goals.

Rashomon and *Reservoir Dogs*, while placing emphasis on the action of the plot and its meaning more than on specific characterizations, still deconstruct time in order for us to understand the characters involved in the plot problem and to better grasp the incident in terms of the personalities involved.

SPECIAL NOTES

Orson Welles burst onto the Hollywood landscape with *Citizen Kane*, his first film. It received eight Academy Award nominations and won for Best Original Screenplay. Although critically lauded, the film was a financial disappointment in its time. Many books have been written about the production of the film, the feuding between RKO (the film's producer and distributor) and William Randolph Hearst, and the bad blood between Welles and his collaborator, Herman J. Mankiewicz. The little I'd like to add concerns a comparison between original screenplay and film.

The shooting and continuity scripts for *Citizen Kane* are both contained in *THE CITIZEN KANE BOOK, Raising Kane* by Pauline Kael, Limelight Editions, New York. The shooting script is the actual screenplay for the film; a continuity script is a list of shots with the dialogue which try to provide an accurate written description of the film.

The shooting script of *Citizen Kane*, dated July 16, 1940, is nearly the same as the film, but there are at least two significant alterations beyond line and speech trimming, scene deletions and name changes of minor characters. The most important change comes at the end of the first act. In the screenplay, the Thatcher sequence ends after Kane tells his ex-guardian that, at the rate of losing a million dollars a year, it will take 60 years before he has to close the paper down. The following scene in the screenplay shows Thompson leaving the library. In the film, a scene is added showing Thatcher taking control of Kane's newspaper empire after the stock market crash of 1929. This scene fills out the first act, giving an overview to Kane's life by focusing on the beginning and end of his financial empire.

Another difference from screenplay to film is the construction of the sequence on the *Inquirer*'s celebration after hiring the best newspapermen in the business. In the screenplay, the festivities are punctuated with Kane trying to convince Leland to cover the war in Cuba and Leland resisting. Kane tries to soften his old friend by taking him to a brothel. There, Kane relents and gives in to Leland, promising him that he can write whatever he wants about the war in Cuba, even if it's not the point of view of the *Inquirer*. In the film, the brothel scene is dropped. The conflict of the scene centers around Leland's disillusionment with Kane's enterprise. At the opening of this scene, the screenplay has an exchange between Leland and Bernstein over the politics of the new employees. The film uses this exchange at the end, providing the reason why Leland has been so disgruntled throughout the evening and making it the main point of the scene. The film focuses on the festivities but uses Leland as a counterpoint because he worries that Kane's stands will be corrupted by the new blood arriving at the paper. (This is his first realization Kane may not believe in anything.)

Most of the other changes are minor, consisting mostly of line cuts and name changes. Many scenes lose their first and last lines when transferred from page to film. In Act Three, the sequence in the Everglades adds the jazz band. In the film, Kane's political opponent is named Gettys; in the screenplay, he's called Rogers. In the screenplay, a character in the original newspaper office is named Mike; in the film it's changed to Solly.

Kane's campaign speech is rewritten for the film; in the screenplay it is bland and lacks humor. An important exchange in the screenplay between Kane and Leland (in which Leland lays out Kane's selfishness) is cut from the film. The film relies on Kane's actions and Leland's insights to Thompson at the end of his interview to communicate this angle of the story.

One short scene in Act Three is cut, in which Raymond reads a statement about Kane's separation from Susan and then is alerted to trouble at the mansion. Then, Raymond arrives to find Kane destroying Susan's room. In the film, Raymond begins his story to Thompson with Susan leaving, then returns to Kane who is unable to leave Susan's room. Kane goes back inside and fumbles with the latch of an open suitcase, becomes infuriated, and then destroys her room in anger. In the screenplay, he comes out and instructs Raymond to lock the door, then says "rosebud." But in the film, Kane mutters "rosebud" in the room, then staggers out and walks silently past the staff. The development of the film's action plays with much more strength, showing Kane more in the grip of his unconscious demons and less demonic than in the script. These changes strengthen the structure and subtext of *Citizen Kane*.

Rashomon hit the international scene in 1950 at the Venice (Italy) Film Festival where it took home the Grand Prize. In 1951, *Rashomon* won an Academy Award for Best Foreign Language Film and introduced Akira Kurosawa and Japanese cinema to the world. *Rashomon*'s critical reception, however, was not unanimously favorable. Some found the point of the story too perplexing while others found it obscure. But many found the film strangely fascinating, oddly entertaining and powerfully affecting. Today, it remains a favorite of museums, revival houses and universities.

The continuity script for *Rashomon* is contained in *RASHOMON*, Akira Kurosawa, director, Donald Richie, editor; Rutgers Films in Print, Rutgers University Press, New Brunswick, CT and London, England. An original screenplay was not available for consultation.

The Conformist was released in 1971, and became a critical and box-office success. Based on a novel by Alberto Moravia, Bertolucci collaborated with the author to create an impressive screenplay which jumped around in time without the benefit of narration or storytellers to keep the narrative and structure grounded. The script was nominated for an Academy Award, Based on Material from Another Medium; it was also nominated for Best Foreign-Language Film at the Golden Globes; and the National Society of Film Critics voted Bertolucci Best Director of the year.

An original screenplay for *The Conformist* was unavailable.

Annie Hall, one of the most highly regarded comedies ever made, was Woody Allen's breakthrough film. It is the film in which the zaniness of his early comedies gave way to a more sober tone while remaining cloaked in humor. The film won Academy Awards for Best Picture, Best Actress, Best Screenplay and Best Director; Awards from the Directors Guild for best direction and the Writers Guild for Best Original Screenplay; a Golden Globe for Diane Keaton, and it topped the National Society of Film Critics Awards with Best Actress, Best Film and Best Screenplay. Besides all this, *Annie Hall* was a substantial box-office success.

The screenplay for *Annie Hall* is contained in *Four Films of Woody Allen*, Random House, New York, 1982. Though not published in true screenplay format, the screenplay is an accurate description of what plays on the screen. As such, there are no discrepancies between the script and the film.

Reservoir Dogs, released in 1992, was an auspicious debut film from Quentin Tarantino, a former video store clerk. Assuredly written and directed, it presaged the success that Tarantino achieved with his second film, *Pulp Fiction*, released two years later. Though based on the Hong Kong action picture *City on Fire*, directed by Ringo Lam, Tarantino turned the linear structure of that film on its head and created his own. *City on Fire* deals with a Hong Kong undercover cop infiltrating a gang of thieves and participating in a jewelry store heist which goes wrong. Its story includes subplots dealing with police politics and the undercover cop's romantic difficulties. Tarantino, instead, focused on the aftermath and, without showing the actual robbery, he deconstructs the incident to give insight into why the robbery had to go wrong. In doing so, he created a taut melodrama.

The screenplay used for comparison is dated October 22, 1990. It is 100 pages, with no A or B pages. The essential structure of the screenplay is the same as the film, with two major differences beyond scene and line editing: the screenplay does not contain a Mr. White flashback but it does include a considerably longer Mr. Orange flashback. This longer Mr. Orange flashback (which is titled "MR. ORANGE & MR. WHITE") shows Orange in his official police capacity discovering White's criminal past; White's activities indicate he is a professional killer. This is completely dropped from the film. In the screenplay, more attention is paid to exposition on who the police are after—Joe Cabot. In the film, once Orange tells the captured policeman who the true target is, any further mention of Joe would be superfluous. Several other scenes from the Orange section of the screenplay are dropped from the film, all providing exposition which is essentially unnecessary or redundant. Instead, the film focuses on the surviving members of the gang and on their immediate problems: Orange's stomach wound, determining whether the warehouse is safe and discovering the rat.

Most of the scenes are trimmed in the film, starting with the opening diner scene which loses a page and a half. This scene in the screenplay opens with the discussion of Madonna's "Like a Virgin," but it is trimmed in the second half. In the film, Mr. Pink reveals he does not tip; in the script it is Mr. White who is the tightwad. Scenes throughout are trimmed and a couple are cut entirely from the second half, most notably, the scene dealing with Orange's discovery of White's violent past. The end of the film is more ambiguous than in the screenplay. The film makes it feel almost as if Pink is the only character who gets away. The screenplay makes it clear that he is caught as he leaves the warehouse.

There are other minor changes, dealing with the choreography of the final Mexican standoff and the policeman's name. (In the script, his name is Jeffrey, in the film it's Marvin.) All in all, the screenplay offers the same structure as the film. The additions and deletions in the film advance the momentum and serve well Tarantino's version of the story.

11

BUILDING MOMENTUM: STRUCTURING SCENE AND ACTION SEQUENCES

Study Film: *The Last of the Mohicans*

Great films have a driving force, a thrust in the movement of the action. This driving force, or momentum, builds as the plot approaches its climax, escalating the tension and compelling the audience to wait in anticipation for the final outcome. Momentum literally means the force or speed of movement, the energy of motion. This is an equally good definition for dramatic momentum—the energy from the movement of the plot that captures the audience's attention.

Great films achieve momentum with strong cause and effect scene relationships, powerful rising conflict and foreshadowing the main protagonist/antagonist struggle. Chapter Six discusses these principles of action at length. Here, we refine these ideas into another tool for creating the plot and building momentum: the plot sequence.

A plot sequence is a group of scenes structured around the confrontation of an obstacle, complication or problem. Characters have to deal with this problem and produce a plan of action to do it. Plot sequences vary in length, structure and focus. A plot sequence can encompass the events leading up to the problem as well the results of confronting it. Or, it can start with the problem itself and build through to a solution—which may or may not be successful.

A scene sequence is a miniature plot. It has a beginning, middle and end in the form of its own set-up (inciting incident), development, confrontation and climax. The scenes build sequentially, without interruption from subplots or character scenes, and move in clear cause and effect relationships until the sequence reaches its climax. The sequence usually has its own protagonist pushing the action. This protagonist is not always the main protagonist of the film. If the sequence involves violent confrontation, we call it an action sequence. Alternatively, a sequence can develop the plot movement by showing characters trying to solve a specific problem. Sequences increase narrative momentum in two ways: they show a definite progression toward a goal that seems in jeopardy until the sequence climax; and, they increase overall suspense in the film by introducing this new jeopardy.

ACTION SEQUENCES

The clearest form of scene sequence is the action sequence. Action sequences utilize obstacles and crises. Remember, a crisis is a period of time in the plot when the protagonist confronts an obstacle and the outcome seems uncertain. In action sequences, the obstacle generally presents a direct threat to the protagonist and his goal. These sequences use physical action and violent confrontation in their construction. The clearest example of an action sequence from our study films so far can be seen in *Witness*. At the start of the Act Three, Schaeffer, McFee and Fergie attack the Lapp farm. This action sequence runs about 15 minutes, all the way through to the film's climax.

Witness's action sequence establishes Schaeffer and his cohorts' arrival at the start of Act Three. They reach the farm house, but Eli hollers out to warn Book before Schaeffer can stop him (the inciting incident of the sequence). Book takes action (a plan). He sends Samuel to Hochleitner's farm and heads for his sister's car. But the engine won't engage (obstacle). The sound of the engine cranking attracts Fergie (crisis). Book lures Fergie into the grain silo and successfully entraps him (development). But Book still has McFee and Schaeffer to contend with (more obstacles). Fergie's shotgun blasts draw McFee. While McFee hunts for Book and Fergie, he calls Schaeffer. Schaeffer leaves Rachel and Eli alone in the kitchen to see what's happening, and Eli comforts Rachel. Book gets back to the silo and digs for Fergie's gun (obstacle); McFee follows, hunting him. Back in the kitchen Rachel is hysterical with worry—until she and Eli spot Samuel in the house. Schaeffer calls Rachel and Eli outside, but before they go, Eli communicates to Samuel to ring the farm bell. With

McFee on his trail, Book gets Fergie's gun and backs out of the silo just as McFee arrives. Book shoots and kills the corrupt cop. Samuel now rings the bell (development). Schaeffer sends Eli to stop Samuel and puts his gun to Rachel's head (yet another crisis), forcing Book to put his gun down. From across the fields, running, answering the Amish call for help, come members of the community to see what is wrong (development). Schaeffer tries to take Book away, gun to Book's head, intimating that he will kill whoever tries to stop him, but Book has had enough. He stands up to Schaeffer, asking if he is going to kill all these men and Samuel, too. How many is he going to kill? Schaeffer sees he is licked and puts his gun down, solving the problem set in motion at the beginning of the action sequence and, in this case, the whole film.

We see in this sequence that the action sets up with the arrival of the men at the Lapp farm, then has its own inciting incident in Eli's hollering to warn Book. Book's first objective is to escape, but when that fails his only chance is to turn the tables on his pursuers. He meets with a series of obstacles and complications which he must overcome to save Samuel and himself. The sequence has two mini-climaxes—Fergie and McFee's deaths. The main climax comes when Book forces Schaeffer to put his gun down.

The choreography of the action is clear cause and effect, based on Schaeffer and his men's pursuit of Book. From the start, the odds are stacked against him: three armed men against one unarmed man. The action set in motion poses a challenge to Book, asking whether he can survive it or not. The action also has a certain amount of originality in its construction of a shoot-out—using the grain silo to stop an adversary—and the sequence builds excitement and suspense. Not only is Book's life at stake, but the lives of other characters we care about, too.

Casablanca also uses an action sequence to lead to its climax. The action is not as overt as in *Witness* with its cat-and-mouse chase, but it builds through confrontations to a violent showdown with Major Strasser at the airport.

Another strong example of an action sequence is in *Chinatown*. Gittes arrives at the avocado fields and encounters the angry farmers who think he was sent to poison their wells. This clearly uses physical action and violent confrontation. Once Gittes knows he is in trouble, he tries to escape, but is cut off at every avenue. Once caught, he is physically beaten until he passes out. The sequence ends when Evelyn comes to pick him up and a new sequence begins.

Action films like the *Lethal Weapon* series, the *Die Hard* series and *Armageddon*, depend upon action sequences throughout their plots in car chases, shoot-outs and other daring feats. But other genres rely on them as well: War films (*Saving Private Ryan*), westerns (*Dances with Wolves*), dramas (*Witness, Lawrence of Arabia*), even love stories (*The African Queen*).

A great action sequence is original, exciting and suspenseful. Often unexpected physical obstructions that get in the way of both the protagonist and antagonist complicate the action. Emotions or moral dilemmas create complications, too. Look at *The Piano*. At the end of Act Two, Ada sends Flora to deliver a message scratched into the piano key to Baines. Flora's conflicting emotions motivate her to disobey her mother for the first time in the film and send her to Stewart instead. This leads to Stewart physically confronting Ada and chopping off her finger.

SCENE SEQUENCES

Scene sequences are similar to action sequences but do not usually involve violent confrontation. Generally, they do not put the protagonist in direct conflict with the antagonist. But there is still a problem that must be faced. The scenes are structured in cause and effect relationships, showing the protagonist of the sequence trying to accomplish something. They are also structured around the meeting of an obstacle, complication or problem that the character has to deal with in the course of the plot. Then, the scene sequence shows how the character deals with it.

An example of an expertly crafted scene sequence is in *Diner* when Boogie bets he can get Carol Heathrow to "go for his pecker" at the movies. The sequence begins in the theater with the film *Summer Place* rolling. Boogie sits next to Carol sharing a box of popcorn. A few seats over are Fenwick and Eddie. Boogie unzips his pants and opens the bottom of the popcorn box to stick his penis inside the box. Fenwick sees and when he catches Boogie's eyes, shakes his head and mouths, "Bet's off. Not fair." Boogie nods, "Yes." As the film continues, Carol reaches into the popcorn box and suddenly screams. She bolts from her seat and races up the aisle with Boogie going after her. Boogie catches up with Carol in the girls' bathroom where he succeeds in settling her down a little. The scene proceeds in the lobby where

Boogie concocts a story, turning a bad joke into flattery. The two return to the theater to watch the end of the movie.

The set-up for this sequence is established several scenes before it actually starts: at the diner when Boogie takes bets on Carol from the boys. The sequence then establishes they are in the theater waiting. The inciting incident is Boogie's action of slipping his penis into the popcorn box. The response comes from Fenwick who tries to call off the bet. Suspense builds as Carol unknowingly keeps dipping her hand into the popcorn box. When is she going to make contact? Finally, she screams and runs off, Boogie following: Her response and the climax. The sequence resolves when Boogie follows and convinces her what happened was an accident and makes it all sound flattering to her. The sequence ends when they return to watch the end of the film.

Every film discussed so far contains scene sequences. Another example in *Diner* happens when Fenwick and Shrevie go to verify Boogie's last bet, when Boogie has Beth masquerade as Carol. *Risky Business* has a wonderful scene sequence surrounding the Porsche rolling into the lake. This sequence is different from the two mentioned in *Diner* that proceed in almost continuous time. In *Risky Business*, the sequence starts when Lana invites Joel to go for ice cream. At the lake, they lean against the car where she proposes her plan to get their friends together to make some money. Joel rejects it. She grabs her sweater from inside the car, accidentally shifting it out of gear and locking the doors. Their conversation then turns serious, to exposition regarding Lana. Before long, she becomes defensive and hostile. She leaves, and when Joel follows, the car starts rolling (the inciting incident). He can't stop it and into Lake Michigan it goes. Now Joel has a problem. We pick him up at the Porsche dealership (development), then at the nurse's office where he comes up against the granite-faced nurse who refuses to write him an unexcused absence (obstacle). Joel winds up with a two-week suspension (effect), trashing his whole academic career. Joel borrows a bike and takes off (development), ending up at Lana's where he agrees to her plan (scene sequence climax and the climax of Act Two).

This scene sequence, though not plotted in continuous time as the two mentioned in *Diner*, still proceeds sequentially on the topic of the conflict. The scenes are related through cause and effect relationships. The conflict revolves around how Joel will be able to raise the money to repair the Porsche and not get into more trouble at school. He fails in trying to save his high school career, only making it worse for himself. The last portion of the sequence shows him trying to get to Lana to see if she can help.

The Cowboy Dan sequence in *Parenthood* shows how Gil deals with the problem of the wrong entertainer showing up for his son's birthday party. In *Quiz Show*, Goodwin knocks on doors, trying to find someone to talk to him—a short sequence that ends with him meeting Charlie. *The Best Years of Our Lives* uses scene sequences throughout the film. The most memorable is the sequence with Fred at the airfield (see Chapters Nine and Fourteen for a full discussion). Another sequence develops Homer's family relationships. He turns on his own sister and her friends, then refuses to deal with Wilma about their relationship.

Tootsie makes use of many scene sequences to construct its plot and achieve a strong momentum. The first time we see Michael in women's clothes marks the beginning of a scene sequence that leads to him getting the part on the soap. Dorothy's first day on the set is the start of another scene sequence that ends when Van Horn kisses her (him). Another sequence builds when Julie invites Dorothy home for the holiday and when Julie asks Dorothy to baby-sit and provide moral support for her break up with Ron.

Scene sequences enlarge the scope of the main conflict as well as contribute to a film's momentum and suspense by actively playing out how the characters deal with problems. The end of a scene sequence sometimes leads to the character taking new actions, though not in every case. Often scene sequences serve to complete an entertaining section of the plot that helps the audience empathize with the character.

The Last of the Mohicans

The most recent interpretation of James Fenimore Cooper's novel was released in 1992, screenplay written by Michael Mann and Christopher Crowe, based on Philip Dunne's 1936 screenplay and the book. Michael Mann also directed and co-produced with Hunt Lowry. Set during the French and English war in the American Colonies, this version focuses on the transforming relationship between Hawkeye (Daniel Day-Lewis) and Cora (Madeline Stowe) as they attempt to escape the vengeful Magua (Wes Studi).

The film opens in 1757, the height of the conflict between the French and the English over land on the American continent. We meet Hawkeye (called Nathaniel throughout the film), his Mohican brother Uncas (Eric Schweig) and his Mohican father Chingachgook (Russell Means) as they hunt together as a perfect team. Further exposition on the English and French conflict is given when this trio arrives at the Cameron farm. Hawkeye and his family want no part of the conflict, seeing it as a political battle that has nothing to do with them.

Major Duncan Heyward (Steven Waddington) arrives at British Headquarters in Albany in time to hear General Webb (Mac Andrews) concede terms to the Colonial Militia. Heyward can barely contain his disgust. He meets Magua who is to guide Heyward and two women to Fort Henry the next day, then finds Cora Munro, the woman he wishes to marry. Cora thinks of Heyward as a friend, but he convinces her to at consider his marriage proposal.

Heyward, Cora and Cora's sister Alice (Jodhi May) begin their trek to Ft. Henry, led by Magua, where Cora and Alice's father, Colonel Munro (Maurice Roeves), is waiting. Magua betrays the group, leading a Huron war party against the soldiers and almost kills Cora before Hawkeye, Uncas and Chingachgook arrive and drive them off (the inciting incident). Hawkeye, Uncas and Chingachgook agree to take Heyward, Cora and Alice to Ft. Henry. En route, they discover the Cameron cabin burned and their friends killed. Cora and the others do not understand why Hawkeye, Uncas and Chingachgook will not bury the dead, though she realizes that Hawkeye knew them well. Later, as they rest, Cora apologizes, knowing Hawkeye acted for her benefit. Another war party approaches (crisis), then retreats, realizing they are in a burial ground (Act One climax). By the end of the scene (and Act One), Cora has surprised Hawkeye by revealing how stirred and excited she is by the beauty and savagery of the land.

Act Two begins with the party finding Ft. Henry under siege (new development). They are able to cross the river and enter the fort. Exposition tells us that Munro is out-gunned and his couriers never reached General Webb. Hawkeye reveals that a war party attacked the Cameron cabin, meaning men from the Militia's families are in danger and should be released to defend them. Munro hesitates to give the order. At the French encampment,

Magua reports to General Montcalm (Patrice Chereau), saying he will kill Munro as well as Munro's children, but he does not tell why.

Hawkeye finds Cora bandaging wounded Uncas and makes clear his interest in her. She clearly feels the same. Colonials try to convince Munro to release them on Hawkeye's word, but Heyward will not support Hawkeye. Heyward lies about the Cameron cabin, seeing it as his duty to keep the men here to fight for the crown. Though indebted to Hawkeye for the safety of his children, Munro threatens to have him locked up and hanged for sedition if he encourages men to leave. Hawkeye does just that. Cora turns on Heyward, saying she will never surrender her own judgment and marry him. She finds Hawkeye and they hold each other. The next morning, Hawkeye is arrested for encouraging other men to return home (midpoint and new development).

Cora defends Hawkeye, but Heyward continues to lie to Munro. Hawkeye tells Cora to stay close to her father for that is how she will survive when the fort falls. He promises to find her. The French siege continues until finally a truce allows Montcalm to convince Munro to surrender and leave on agreeable terms. This ends Montcalm's need for Magua who is enraged that he no longer has the French support in his desire for revenge. Magua reveals the reasons for his hatred of Munro. He holds Munro responsible for the deaths of his children and ruining his life.

The British leave Ft. Henry and walk straight into Magua's ambush. In the chaos, Hawkeye is freed and, with his brother and father, runs to find Cora and escape. Magua finds Munro and kills him. Hawkeye's group find canoes by the river. They steal these and meet Heyward on the river, all pulling hard to get away from the war party behind them. They pass through rapids, ditch the canoes and hide in canyons beneath the falls, hoping that Magua will miss them. Magua does not. With his powder wet and outnumbered, Hawkeye knows their only chance for survival is if he escapes and later comes looking for Cora. With Heyward calling him a coward, Hawkeye, Uncas and Chingachgook leap into the falls and escape as Magua arrives and takes them prisoner (Act Two climax).

Act Three begins with Hawkeye and his family climbing out of the river and trekking up the mountain after Magua. Magua takes his three prisoners to Sachem (Mike Phillips) and offers them as gifts—Heyward to be sold to the French and the women to be burned. Hawkeye, however, takes away Magua's moment when he enters the village unarmed and walks through a gauntlet of blows delivered to stop him. He reaches the group and asks Heyward to translate into French for him. Hawkeye tells Sachem that Magua has misled him. He and Magua go back and forth with their versions, until Sachem finally stops them and settles matters by giving Alice to Magua as his wife, freeing Heyward and killing Cora in return for Magua's children. Hawkeye now offers his life for Cora's, but Heyward changes the translation, offering his own. Heyward is tied to a stake and burned while Cora and Hawkeye are freed. Hawkeye shoots and kills Heyward in the flames, then takes off with Cora and Chingachgook. They follow Uncas who is chasing Magua and Alice. On the mountain, Uncas confronts Magua's party, killing several warriors before meeting Magua. The two men fight, but Magua is stronger and kills Uncas. Rather than follow Magua, Alice steps off the cliff and falls to her death. Chingachgook now arrives and challenges Magua. Filled with a father's fury, he kills Magua and the rest of Magua's party disperses (final climax). The film resolves on the top of a mountain with Hawkeye, Cora and Chingachgook offering a prayer for Uncas.

The Last of the Mohicans is a love story set against an action backdrop and belongs to the two lovers, Hawkeye and Cora. Hawkeye is clearly the protagonist, a man who does not want to get involved in the conflict, but is forced to by feelings he develops for Cora. He does not change through the conflict, except for falling in love, but his character serves to influence and transform Cora and Heyward. Through his relationship with Cora, she is liberated from her world's ideas of supreme authority.

The theme deals with individual freedom vs. sovereign authority. Hawkeye is already committed to the idea of individual freedom at the opening: he refuses to get involved in the English and French conflict. But meeting Cora forces him to get involved. Hawkeye will fight but only for reasons he considers important, not the impersonal reasons forced upon him by a foreign power. Through her relationship with him, Cora sees how supreme power can be abused, and rejects Heyward and her father.

This film is constructed with five main action sequences and one important scene sequence. The film begins with a short action sequence, three minutes long, showing Hawkeye, Uncas and Chingachgook hunting, in unison to bring down an elk. The second action sequence is a four minute segment, starting in the woods with Magua leading an ambush against Cora and Alice. The inciting incident of the attack is Magua's betrayal. The obstacles build when the Hurons attack. The action develops with the arrival of Hawkeye, Uncas and Chingachgook. Hawkeye sees Magua try to kill Cora and drives Magua and his followers off (climax). The sequence resolves when Hawkeye offers to take Cora's group to Fort Henry.

The first action sequence presents a problem (hunting the elk) which we understand only in the final moments when the elk appears. The sequence climax thus presents the problem and solution. But the men are clearly moving, running toward something unseen until the climax of the action. We see in the second sequence a clear development of the action and conflict through to a climax that ends the sequence. It serves to define the problem by showing Magua sighting Cora, showing his specific intent to kill her.

The third action sequence begins with the fort under siege at the beginning of the second act. The inciting incident is the discovery of the siege, because it complicates their arrival. The problem is now how to get inside the fort. They find boats (a development) and use these to usher the women across, arriving amid cannon-fire and rifle shots (climax). This three minute sequence is less intense than the first two, but still develops a small plot line that leads them from one place to their goal—to enter the fort and unite Cora and Alice's with their father.

The fourth action sequence runs 12 minutes and details Magua's attack against the British as they leave Fort Henry. This action sequence can be looked at from two points of view: Magua's, and Cora and Hawkeye's. Magua's goal is to catch and kill Munro and family. Hawkeye and Cora's is to escape. The inciting incident is the first Huron warrior attacking them in the valley. The development is the fighting. Hawkeye must free himself and get to Cora. That takes us to the middle, moving through the obstacles of warriors and soldiers fighting to get to her. Magua fights to get to Munro, successfully brings him down and then goes in for the kill (climax). Hawkeye makes it to Cora, then off the battlefield to the river where they find Huron canoes (development). They escape on the river, pursued by Magua's party, meeting up with Heyward and a soldier escaping. They team up and race through rapids (more obstacles) and finally ditch the boats to head inside caves. They wait, but Magua finds them—leading Hawkeye and his brothers to escape into the falls so that he can come for her later (climax).

The last sequence is Hawkeye's chase after Magua and Alice. The inciting incident is actually in the scene sequence that ends just before, when Sachem gives Alice to Magua. That scene sequence ends with Heyward giving his life for Cora. The next action sequence picks up Uncas giving chase up the mountain after Magua. His goal is to save Alice. Uncas overcomes the initial obstacles, killing several warriors, then confronts Magua (the main obstacle). Magua kills Uncas (climax). Alice jumps off the cliff (development), the Chingachgook kills Magua (the final climax).

The scene sequence starts with Magua's arrival at Sachem's village at the beginning of Act Three. He offers his three prisoners for recognition and prestige in the tribe. The sequence develops with Hawkeye's arrival through the gauntlet to plead for Cora, Alice and Heyward's lives. The conflict develops between these two men, verbally, until Sachim offers a solution. But the solution demands Cora's life (development). Hawkeye offers his own life, but Heyward translates it as his (another development). Cora is freed with Hawkeye while Heyward is dragged off to the fire to be burned to death. Hawkeye gets Cora out of the village, Heyward's screams echoing behind them. Hawkeye takes his rifle, shoots and puts Heyward out of his misery to end the sequence (climax).

SPECIAL NOTES

The Last of the Mohicans was released in 1992 and received mixed critical reviews. The public, however, reached a different conclusion, driving domestic box office grosses to $72 million. The story had been told before, but writer/director Michael Mann brought a new sensibility to it, creating a film that was both old-fashioned and current. Mann credited Philip Dunne, writer of the 1936 filmed version of *Mohicans*, because, Mann said, the original writer should be honored. The 1936 version of *The Last of the Mohicans* is, Mann says, the first film he remembers seeing.

The screenplay used for comparison is dated 7/31/90, and contains numerous revisions, up 9/28/91. It numbers 117 pages, but with the numerous A and B pages the actual count is 179 (the film runs only 114 minutes); many of the script pages are very short. The screenplay is extremely detailed, indicating many of the camera angles, reverse and reaction shots, thus increasing its length.

Structurally the script and film are almost identical. There are a number of scene deletions from screenplay to film, usually of scenes adding more exposition about the war. Many scenes that survive are trimmed extensively, stripped of unneeded exposition.

The order of two important scenes is changed. In the screenplay, Cora emphatically refuses Heyward after they arrive at the fort. The next scene shows Heyward lying and contradicting Hawkeye about what they saw at the Cameron cabin to support Munro. In the film, these two scenes are transposed, Heyward contradicting Hawkeye comes first, followed by Cora refusing him. In the screenplay, it reads that Heyward contradicts Hawkeye out of spite. In the film, Heyward is acting out of his sense of duty to Crown and not to the truth. This is what Cora rejects—Heyward's blind obedience to the Crown—and the theme is thus strengthened.

12

OPENINGS AND THE MAIN EXPOSITION

Study Film: *Jerry Maguire*

The opening of a great film arouses our curiosity. It unlocks a door and invites us to enter a new world. A great opening draws us into this world, using the language of film—images and sounds—to evoke feelings in the audience while carrying the story's mood to them. A great opening asks more questions than it answers. It takes us to this new place and makes us wonder, "What are we doing here? Where are we going? What's going to happen?" And by making us ask these questions, it forces us to leave our own world behind and join the film's.

The best opening is visual, using the images we see on screen to incite our interest. The important information, or main exposition, is skillfully conveyed, utilizing action to grab our attention and obscure from us its purely expository nature. (Action here does not necessarily mean car chases or shoot-outs.) The action of an opening sequence is designed to catch our interest and hold it as it conveys exposition important to our understanding of the story that follows.

The first shot of *Witness* begins on a field of wheat blowing in the wind. Gradually, a group of people dressed in 19th Century fashion appear. We see more shots of these people, horse drawn buggies and so on. As the group heads down a road toward a farmhouse, a title superimposed over the screen appears: "Pennsylvania, 1984." The contradiction between images and title raises a basic question in the viewer's mind—what is going on here? When the audience starts making sense of what it sees, the viewer participates in the film and becomes more deeply involved in it. A great opening grabs the audience and the great story that follows doesn't let the viewers go.

THE MAIN EXPOSITION

Before an opening can be written, a screenwriter must have an idea of the main exposition of his film. In Chapter Two, we defined the main exposition as the initial information the audience needs in order to understand the story that unfolds. The main exposition makes clear that which is not self-explanatory. It concerns setting, the main characters, their central relationships, the tone and the main conflict. However, everything needed by the audience to understand the basis for a film is rarely packed into one opening scene. The information usually unfolds over the course of several scenes in the opening 15 minutes or so; sometimes, this exposition is not complete until the end of the first act.

To understand what the screenplay's main expostion is, the writer needs to know three things:

1) What does the protagonist want?
2) Why does he want it?
3) What is the main conflict?

What the protagonist wants determines direction of the plot. Why he wants it refers to who the character is and what is motivating him. The main conflict defines the protagonists opposition as he pursues his goal. The answers to these questions help identify what specific exposition is needed to get the screenplay rolling.

Once these answers are clear in the writer's mind, he must devise a line of action to convey the information to the audience and lead them into the film. This plan comprises the opening scenes, which must draw the viewers into the story and give them enough information to understand the significance of what they are watching.

There are a variety of methods to manage the main exposition; great films usually rely on a combination of them.

Narration

Voice-over narration is an obvious way to handle much of the main expoisition in a film, but getting it right can be tricky. Often it comes across as unnatural and forced. Is the narrator a character we will meet in the film or is he just a voice to communicate specific facts? Narration works when it contributes to the film's tone and style and is not used just to expedite the exposition. When narration works, it strikes just the right chord.

The narrator in *Casablanca* uses a style common to news-reels of the day. He quickly sums up the state of the world in the middle of war and establishes the backdrop—the city of Casablanca in French Morocco. The newsreel style contributes a measure of authenticity to the situation, but once the story engages, the film never returns to narration. Even though narration is not used again, the hard-boiled style of the film makes it easy to accept.

Risky Business and *The Piano* use narration to begin their stories, too, having the protagonist begin each tale. In *Risky Business*, Joel narrates a dream he has been having that gets to the heart of his character—he's incredibly worried that his mediocre high school career has screwed up his future. *The Piano* lets Ada tell us that what we're hearing isn't her speaking voice, but her "mind's voice." She goes on to say that she hasn't spoken since she was six and that her father has married her off to a man she has never met. At the end of each film, Joel and Ada return to narrate the close of their stories.

All three of these opening narrations share one characteristic: All present situations rife with conflict. Casablanca is teeming with refugees who are trying to escape the world war raging around them; Joel is having anxiety dreams, Ada hasn't spoken since she was young and her father has married her off to a man she doesn't know. These narrators are not trying to tell us that the sky is blue and roses are red: they are establishing situations of conflict. This is what forces us to pay attention.

Narration is usually one component of the main exposition. After the narration sets the initial scene, other factors must be communicated in different ways.

Graphic Presentation

As the narrator sets the scene in *Casablanca*, visuals accompany the spoken information: on screen we see a globe and then a map showing us where the film takes place. Animation is used to show the direction the refugees take to stream across Europe and to reach Casablanca. Superimposed over this map are shots of people traveling to escape the war. The graphic illustrates the refugee problem so we understand the background of the film.

This style of exposition may seem dated by today's standards, but consider the opening of *Star Wars*. "Long, long ago, in a galaxy far away..." begins the story crawl. As it continues by receding into space, it spells out the story of the ongoing battle and it tells us about the Death Star. This roll establishes a significant portion of the main exposition, while setting the film's tone by letting us know that *Star Wars* is a fantasy.

Using a graphic or written presentation to open a film should be carefully considered. It must be right for the material and consistent with the tone the writer wishes to set.

Visual Dramatization

Witness uses a visual dramatization to convey the first part of its exposition. As we follow the scenes into the story, they expose us to the Amish community as the people converge at the Lapp farm. The funeral introduces us to the young widow, Rachel and her son Samuel.

The credit sequence in *Quiz Show* (which occurs immediately after the scene in the car showroom that introduces us to Goodwin), visually clues us in on what the film is about. It gives us the series of preparatory steps for the game show *21*, taking the questions from bank vault to television studio in Rockefeller Center. This journey is intercut with scenes of America getting ready to watch the number one television show—*21*! The sequence visually sets up the context for the story; it also shows us how far the producers will go to protect their hoax.

A visual dramatization communicates important details of the main exposition through images on screen. Rarely can a feature film set up all of its main exposition this way, but a visual dramatization can be an effective portion of it.

The Main Exposition in Dialogue

In many films, scenes with dialogue are used to convey all or part of the main exposition. *Grand Hotel* exclusively uses dialogue to impart its main exposition. The film opens on the hotel switchboard, then cuts to the head porter in a phone booth who is calling to find out if his wife has given birth; in the next booth, Kringelein reveals he has quit his job and is going to die; in Preysing's telephone call, we learn of his corporate merger plans and how he may be ruined; the next caller, Grusinskaya's maid, tells us that the ballerina will not dance that night; the last person introduced on the phone, the Baron, lets us in on his plan to settle his debts through thievery. By the end of this sequence, which runs about five minutes, we have met all but one of the main characters; we know their problems and we are oriented to the action of each character's plot line.

In *Casablanca*, important exposition comes directly after the narration. A police official posts a bulletin on the murder of two German couriers who were carrying important documents. The official instructs all suspicious characters to be rounded up.

In *Chinatown*, dialogue becomes the tool of the main exposition when the fake Mrs. Mulray arrives to hire Gittes to find proof of her "husband's" extramarital affair. The dialogue sets out the facts of the case as Gittes interviews her.

The key to writing effective exposition in dialogue is to make the information and/or the action conveying it dramatic. If characters merely discuss information on screen, the effect is not exciting (and the audience will not be interested in it or the story). Tension must be created to grip viewers and hold their attention. In *Grand Hotel*, the characters all face problems that are life-changing if not life-threatening; in *Casablanca*, the exposition involves murder and stolen documents; in *Chinatown*, conflict is created when Gittes tries to discourage his new client from hiring him.

The Main Exposition's Relationship to the Main Climax

Once the main exposition is complete, a problem is presented to the protagonist. As discussed in Chapters Six and Nine, the protagonist's action in trying to solve this problem provides the basis for the film's structural unity. If the protagonist solves this problem too soon, and veers off in a new direction, audiences feel disoriented and misled. Unless the plot returns to deal with a new issue created by the solution of the original problem (but is still related to it), viewers will see the film as disjointed and muddled. (Imagine if, in *Jaws*, the fishermen really had bagged the Great White at the midpoint, and suddenly a giant squid attacked the beachgoers. You'd think you were watching two separate movies; credibility would be destroyed.)

In great films, the problem set up at the beginning has a direct relationship to the main climax. This relationship maintains unity between the parts: the problem presented at the beginning of the film is the one that is solved or answered at the end. In the last act of *Witness*, Book finally confronts the rogue cops who were responsible for the train station murder that occured in the film's first ten minutes. At the end of *Risky Business*, Joel is accepted into Princeton and he has lost his naiveté, the character problem set up early in the first act. In the first two minutes of *Casablanca*, everyone wants the Letters of Transit; they finally reach Ilsa and Laszlo at film's end. In *Quiz Show*, the hoax established in the first act is exposed at the end. The main exposition in *The Piano* makes us wonder if this damaged woman, Ada, can live without her piano; at the end, we learn that she can. The first act of *Tootsie* establishes Michael's charade and makes us wonder if he can maintain it; the climax shows us he can't.

Ensemble films can alter this concept slightly by climaxing the strongest plot line at the end of the second act, as in *Diner*. But even if this is the case, the third act still must return to its story frame in order to unify the plot. In nonlinear films, the question raised at the start is resolved in the climax. Look at *Citizen Kane*: what does the word "Rosebud" mean? Look at *Rashomon*: what really happened? Look at *Reservoir Dogs*: what went wrong?

It doesn't matter whether the main exposition is essentially complete in the first five minutes of the film (*Grand Hotel*) or takes most of the first act to develop fully (*Risky Business, Casablanca, The Piano*). What does matter is that once the main exposition raises the central question or issue, it must be answered or dealt with before the end of the film.

Exposition in General

Exposition, particularly in dialogue, continues without interruption until the climax of the movie because writers must reveal further aspects of the characters and plot as they develop. This information often illuminates the back story or new developments. It is introduced as needed, or when the viewer requires the information in order to understand what will happen next.

Screenwriters, when working on the main exposition, often think in terms of the following points:

1) What is essential to be revealed at the start?
2) What can be held back?
3) What can be implied?

Holding back or implying certain information can help to maintain tension for the audience; it causes viewers to anticipate what will happen next. If a writer reveals too much information too soon, the audience becomes annoyed and apathetic. For example, if, in *Casablanca*, the audience finds out at the start why Ilsa left Rick in Paris, the story would have short-circuited and their subsequent scenes would have lacked much of their tension.

Problems can arise when the screenwriter has key pieces of information which must be established in the plot but he mistimes their placement. Writers often establish or foreshadow these key points early in the plot without determining if they are absolutely necessary to understanding the story at that point. If the information is not acted upon within a certain amount of time, the impact is lost on the audience; or, dispensing too much new important information at the same time can make the story hard to follow. It's a good idea to wait until the audience really needs the information before giving it. Or, if it is planted early, the writer should emphasize and develop it at the point that it is most vital to explaining the story.

OPENING SCENES—WHERE TO BEGIN?

Great films begin as close as possible to the introduction of the main conflict; they do not spend 15 or 20 minutes setting up the protagonist and other main characters. Filmmakers know that it doesn't matter if the protagonist if sympathetic to the audience in the opening minutes of the film—it is enough that he is interesting. The protagonist is not what grabs the audience and starts the story—it is his problem.

In *Witness*, the main conflict is between Book and the rogue cops. Eleven minutes into the film, the murder takes place and the problem is set.

In *Risky Business*, the main conflict engages (16 minutes in) when Miles calls the hooker.

In *Casablanca*, the main conflict is raging within Rick's soul, but is personified by the Nazis invading Casablanca and the world and demanding a reaction from him. As the war is established in the opening, the main conflict boils down to a battle between good and evil.

In *The Piano*, 14 minutes into the film, Stewart leaves Ada's piano behind, thereby drawing and the battle lines.

In *Chinatown*, it takes four minutes for the fake Mrs. Mulray to enter the scene, hooking Gittes into main conflict.

In *Quiz Show*, at the 7-minute mark the sponsor calls and complains about Stempel. Five minutes later, Kinter tells Enright that Stempel has to go.

From the moment *Tootsie* starts, Michael Dorsey's conflict is clear: he can't get an acting job.

The rest of the study films show us exactly the same thing: conflict is established quickly. Even in the films which take an entire first act to define the plot's main conflict, such as *Risky Business* or *Diner*, an aspect of the main conflict is engaged early to set the plot on its course.

Once the writer has determined the key moment when the conflict starts, he must pick a point to begin the film in relation to this moment. This is typically the inciting incident (the moment the main conflict engages), but not in all cases. Some films require additional time to set up before the protagonist meets the main conflict and truly decides upon his course of action, as in *Risky Business* and *Casablanca*. But if the opening few minutes lack conflict, viewers start wondering why they are there.

Below are examples of starting points to consider.

Point of Crisis or Decision

Many great films find a crisis or introduce a decision the character faces (one that will set him on his path toward the inciting incident) which is then used as the starting point. Often, these crises or decisions are dramatic and life-changing.

Witness begins with people arriving for the funeral; the film opens just after a death. *Risky Busines* begins with Joel's anxiety dream. *Casablanca* begins with the world at war. *The Piano* begins with Ada preparing to leave Scotland, for a marriage to a stranger halfway across the world. *Tootsie* begins with Michael's rejections. *The Best Years of Our Lives* begins with men returning home from war. *Citizen Kane* starts with Kane's death. These are all upsetting or life-changing situations for the characters involved.

Great films can begin a few scenes before this crisis or decision, in the midst of a crisis or just after it. *Witness* starts on the blowing wheat, then moves toward the funeral to establish the community, then on to Rachel and Samuel. *The Piano* begins at Ada's home in Scotland as she finishes packing and tells us of the reason for her impending journey. In *The Best Years of Our Lives*, the main conflict deals with each man trying to readjust to civilian life; the film begins with them on their way home. *Risky Business* and *Tootsie* begin at the crisis: Joel is in the dream, Michael is being rejected for a part. *Grand Hotel* begins with four of the main characters already in crisis and explaining it on the telephone.

Starting close to a crisis or decision sets up expectation in the minds of the audience. They know something is going to happen and that something is about to change.

The Problem

Great films often begin by establishing the problem right at the start. *Casablanca* sets up the the refugee problem, the war, the hunt for the murderer of the German couriers and the search for the Letters of Transit—all before the introduction of the protagonist. *Citizen Kane* also starts with the problem of the film—the man dies with "rosebud" on his lips and the question of the plot is, what does this mean?

Starting with the problem immediately sets up conflict and tension. It is a way to pull the audience into the film and get them asking "what is going to happen next?" The exact problem is not important. The problem represents a dramatic change in the film's world, and any significant change demands a response.

A Change in the Environment

Opening a film with a change in the environment is similar to opening with the problem because both options set up the problem. But a change in the environment can more simply set up a dramatic situation that will catch our interest. *Witness* begins with people coming to the funeral of Rachel's husband. His death represents an important change in the world of Rachel and her son's.

A change in the environment also sets up expectation in the audience as viewers wonder how this shift will affect the protagonist once he joins the story. This type of change can influence the protagonist directly or indirectly. A change can be represented by a war, a natural disaster, the arrival of someone new, a death in the family.

The Protagonist

Many films open with the introduction of the protagonist. As in real life, first meetings make strong impressions, so great films do not waste time with incidental material about their important characters. Great filmmakers know exactly how they want to present the character to the audience. They know if they want the audience to laugh at the protagonist or pity him, take him seriously or write him off. They know if they want the audience to identify with him or objectify him.

Chinatown begins in Gittes' office as he hands over the photographs of a wife and her lover to his client Curly. We see immediately how Gittes handles the situation, picking a cheap Scotch instead of a more expensive brand. While his words are aimed at comforting the sobbing man, Gittes' whole attitude seems somewhat patronizing. This is a detective who has seen it all.

Diner begins with Modell walking up the stairs. He has no dialogue as he moves through the dance. He finds Boogie and tells him something the audience does not hear, causing Boogie to leave. In the basement, Boogie finds Fenwick breaking windows. Boogie talks to Fenwick and stops him from causing anymore vandalism. Though Boogie looks the part of the dandy, he comes across as a good guy while Fenwick is immediately established as troubled.

The opening narration in *The Piano* establishes Ada's embittered voice. *Quiz Show*'s opening introduces Goodwin's appreciation of the finer things which he feels are out of his reach.

The moment the audience meets the protagonist is the start of his character arc. Ada begins as bitter and defensive; Gittes begins as jaded; Michael, in *Tootsie*, is set up as a great actor, but also as egotistical and difficult to get along with. By the end of their respective films, each of these characters changes from this starting point.

The Opening and The Theme

Many films use the opening to emphasize their themes or aspects of them. *Risky Business* uses Joel's dream at the start to foreshadow elements of the theme: anxiety over his future place in the world. *Quiz Show*'s first scene gets to the heart of consumer America. *Parenthood* begins in Gil's memory/fantasy and establishes his dream of being a great father.

Viewers do not need to be hit over the head with the theme, but they need hints, or pieces of it, which they can put together as the plot develops. If the elements of the theme are woven into the structure early, the audience will grasp the film's true intent sooner.

Scene Considerations

Several elements go into making an effective opening. (In terms of scene construction, there are specific considerations for the opening that can be highlighted here, but Chapter Sixteen covers the actual writing of scenes in more depth.) In many great films, the first scene raises a question about what will happen next in the film. In *Witness*, we wonder what will happen to this young widow and her son? In *The Piano*, we wonder about Ada and her daughter, given their situation. The opening scenes of *Tootsie* make us ask if Michael will ever give up. And in *Casablanca*, how will the war affect the people we'll meet in the story?

Good opening scenes have components of conflict and/or action to draw us in. Just think of every opening discussed so far, except *Quiz Show*. Action (movement) and/or conflict play important roles in all them. In *The Best Years of Our Lives*, Fred can't catch a plane home at the civilian airport, but learns he might be able to get a plane at the Army Air Transport Center. Conflict, even subtle, makes a viewer pay closer attention to what is happening on screen.

Foreshadowing conflict can also be an effective way to draw the audience into a film. *Citizen Kane* begins on a gate with a sign that reads, "No Trespassing." The sign foreshadows conflict; it tells us we should not be here. Every aspect of Ada's beginning in *The Piano* signals trouble ahead. The opening scenes overflow with foreboding: She does not speak, her father has married her off to a stranger far away, she is taking a big piano on a perilous journey across the sea.

Never underestimate the power of excitement and titillation when constructing the opening scene. In the opening of *Chinatown*, the grainy black-and-white photographs of two lovers caught in the act serve to capture the audience's attention immediately. There is nothing wrong with exploiting people's instinctive reactions to create a more compelling film.

Tense, exciting action catches our attention and pulls the viewer into the following scenes. Look at the beginning of *Raiders of the Lost Ark* or *Jaws*, the *Lethal Weapon* series or any of the *James Bond* films. All use exciting action sequences to take the audience's breath away and leave them asking for more.

Jerry Maguire

Written and directed by Cameron Crowe and produced by Crowe, James L. Brooks, Laurence Mark and Richard Sakai, *Jerry Maguire* tells the story of a successful sports agent who has a crisis of conscience and acts upon it. The action costs him his job, clients, fiancée and his self-image. But as he is forced to do exactly what his conscience tells him to do. To connect with other people—he discovers his true self and finds love and meaning in his work.

The opening of *Jerry Maguire* does something truly unique: in 11 minutes of opening narration, Jerry (Tom Cruise) tells us a story that would take a typical Hollywood film two-thirds of the plot to complete. This 11-minute bit is used as the film's starting point. Before we consider it in detail, let's look at the basic structure of the film.

The first act sets up Jerry's world: he's a super-agent to top athletes but he is personally dissatisfied with his job. In a sense, he realizes that his conflict is between living his life or letting his job live it for him. In trying to address his inner conflict, he writes a "Mission Statement" for the company, but it is really for himself (inciting incident). This is what Jerry needs to do, not simply what his company ought to do. The Mission Statement persuades a company employee Dorothy Boyd (Reneè Zellweger), that Jerry is different from the other sharks, but it has also convinced management that Jerry has gone soft and must go. The act ends when he is fired and is able to hold on to only one client —Rod Tidwell (Cuba Gooding Jr.), probably his most difficult—but he vows a comeback. The only person who supports him is Dorothy.

Act Two breaks down into two main sections, although not equally divided. The first section shows Jerry coping with his new situation; he saves his career initially by holding on to the NFL's number one draft pick, only to lose it all when the draft pick signs with his old agency. This takes up about the first 20 minutes of the second act. Jerry has dropped down to rock bottom: no clients (except Rod), no girlfriend, no self-respect.

The rest of Act Two shows Jerry's struggle to climb back up into his professional world. But he can't do it until he fulfills his Mission Statement: he must create real personal relationships, not superficial ones, with Rod and Dorothy, in order to truly succeed in life. He learns how to deal with Rod (he must be completely honest), but he has a more difficult time with Dorothy. (he must not only be honest, but he must also develop his feelings). By the end of Act Two, he has failed and so he loses her.

Act Three focuses on the result of Jerry honestly trying to help Rod succeed. Because Jerry has finally reached Rod, Rod is able to win the love of his fans, something he has wanted to achieve but which has eluded him because of the chip he had on his shoulder. In watching Rod's success, Jerry feels the emptiness of his own life and realizes what Dorothy means to him. In the climax, he returns to Dorothy, winning her back. The resolution shows Rod getting his new, multimillon dollar contract and ends with a scene of Jerry, Dorothy and Ray—a family.

The opening of *Jerry Maguire* has a direct relationship to the main climax. The Mission Statement, which serves as the film's inciting incident, lays out Jerry's want— to personally connect with others in his business. But this runs counter to the competitive nature of his business (which creates a ruthless pursuit of the dollar). At the end, Jerry achieves professional and personal success, by meeting Dorothy on her terms and by getting for Rod the monetary recognition he desires.

The main exposition (at seven minutes into the film) is given in the narration and emphasized with visuals. It not only gets right to the heart of the conflict (when Jerry tells us, "I hated myself" and he proceeds to write his Mission Statement), but begins near a crisis as well (at the 6-minute mark, when he has his breakdown). As the narration ends (at approximately 11 minutes), we overhear two agents whispering that they give Jerry about a week before he's fired. This foreshadows the outer aspect of the main conflict. In the next 10 minutes, before he is fired (at 21 minutes), the film sets Jerry's character.

The main exposition also foreshadows the theme. Jerry is so wrapped up in his business persona that he has forgotten who he is. The Mission Statement asks that he become the very best version of himself. If he can take less and care more, for the clients and himself, life will mean more, be more fulfilling and success will follow. His Mission Statement tells him what he has to do to be alive. The real story in *Jerry Maguire* is not about business success, although Jerry finds that it at the end, but rather on achieving success in personal relationships which bestows the most meaning on one's outward success.

SPECIAL NOTES

Jerry Maguire was released at the end of 1996, and played through the summer of 1997. The film was nominated for five Academy awards, including Best Picture, Best Actor (Tom Cruise), Best Original Screenplay Written Directly for the Screen (Cameron Crowe) and Best Editing. Cuba Gooding, Jr., won an Academy Award for Best Supporting Actor, the picture's only Oscar. In spite of being ignored at the Oscars, *Jerry Magure* won a Golden Globe for Tom Cruise; was nominated for a Directors Guild of America

Award and nominated for a Writers Guild of America Award; it made many Top Ten lists and was a box-office triumph.

At a certain level, the structure of *Jerry Maguire* is simple: Boy meets girl, boy loses girl, boy gets girl. It's the simplest and oldest of Hollywood formulas. What *Jerry Maguire* does with that old formula that so many other films fail to do is give it an original spin to make it fresh.

The screenplay used for comparison is not dated and contains no revised pages. It is 131 pages long. It is written in a very personal style; Crowe knows that he'll be directing it. A few of his scenes are written, knowing that dialogue will be ad-libbed later, as in the scenes with Laurel's (Bonnie Hunt) Women's Group or in the bachelor film.

Although the essential screenplay structure is laid out in this draft, there are numerous changes. Many of the scenes are trimmed or cut, especially in the first half of the film. In a few places, the sequence of scenes is reordered in the film. In this draft, Dickie Fox appears only once, during the opening narration, instead of throughout, as in the film. The most important changes from screenplay to film involve pacing, focus and back story.

The screenplay spends more time developing other characters, even incidental ones, and creating transitions, especially in the first 70 pages. On page 70, Jerry arrives at Dorothy's house after losing the number one NFL draft pick, Cush (Jerry O'Connell), and breaking up with Avery (Kelly Preston). In the film, this occurs after 55 minutes; approximately fifteen pages of script have been cut. Crowe accomplishes this in the film by staying on his two leads, Jerry and Dorothy. For example, on page 9 of the screenplay (minute 11 in the film), Jerry is on the plane, sitting in First Class with a young woman executive. The written scene begins with the woman passenger talking to Jerry about doubts she's having with her boyfriend. Approximately two and a half pages of this scene are spent on her problem; in the film, all of this is cut out. The scene starts with Jerry telling his proposal story; then, the film cuts to Dorothy in the Coach Section with her son. Jerry meets Dorothy on page 16; in the film, their meeting comes at minute 13.

The bachelor party is significantly different in the screenplay, using Jerry's friend Dooler (Eric Stoltz) to develop Jerry's problem at work. In the script, Dooler stresses that no one is laughing at the gag film and says something must be wrong. The screenplay also underscores the fact that everyone at the party is avoiding Jerry. In the script, by the time Jerry returns to work, he is totally paranoid. In the film, these scenes focus on Jerry's other problem, his lack of intimacy with women.

Bob Sugar (Jay Mohr) fires Jerry on page 26; in the film it happens at minute 21. In the script, by the time Jerry and Dorothy leave SMI and the first act ends in the parking lot, we are on page 40. In the film, the scene in the parking lot (when Dorothy asks about medical) is placed into the elevator scene (when they are interrupted by the deaf couple). The line, "You complete me," is in the screenplay, but in the film it is used to end the first act (at 31 minutes into the film). Nine pages are cut out of act one, as the film zeroes in on Jerry and Dorothy.

From this point on, most of the scenes in the film are in the screenplay but many of these are edited. All the scenes in the screenplay that shift the focus onto other characters (such as Avery) and away from Jerry and Dorothy are cut. Transitions, especially in the next 30 pages, are trimmed drastically or cut. In the film, we enter scenes directly, already in progress, without any buildup (as in the script) and many end sooner in the film. In the screenplay, a scene with Rod, which essentially repeats information we already know about him, is cut; another, with Rod and Cush in conflict, is cut; and the progression of Rod's relationship with Jerry is slightly altered to greater effect in the film. In the screenplay, Jerry's father and brother are included at the wedding; in the film they aren't used. In the script, Jerry and Dorothy are at the birth of Rod and Marcee's (Regina King) baby; but the scene is cut in the film. All the changes in the film result in a stronger and more focused driving action.

The second half of the film takes advantage of the visuals suggested in the screenplay; in addition, the film takes time with the emotional moments of the story. For example, more is made visually of the wedding—seeing Jerry and Dorothy at separate moments, each realizing the marriage may be a big mistake. A montage is added of Jerry going to Rod's games, essentially avoiding Dorothy toward the end of Act Two. All this strengthens the storytelling viscerally, allowing the audience to feel the events of the film along with the characters.

There are a few pieces of background information included in the screenplay, but which are left out of the film: In the screenplay, a speech Jerry delivers to Dorothy about his brother and father is cut. Instead Jerry tells Dorothy's son Ray (Jonathan Lipnicki) a very short story about his father, to which Ray responds by telling Jerry that his father is dead. In the film, the simpler lines contrasted with Ray's provide insight into Jerry's character and make for a more poignant scene. We never find out (in the screenplay or film) how Ray's father died, and it really isn't important. The effect is felt.

The "Show me the money" and "Quon" scenes are in the screenplay but they are not presented quite in the same way as in the film. Each scene is far more developed in the film, taking them to extremes that the script only suggests.

13

THE MIDDLE—THE RISING ACTION

Study Film: *North by Northwest*

In the best films, tension escalates as the plot builds. The bulk of this increase in tension should occur in the second act as the author balances the important plot elements—action, character and theme—to keep the story moving and to develop its meaning. Strong conflict opposes the protagonist which he faces in obstacles, complications, reversals and crises. Relationships develop, upping the stakes for the characters and increasing the audience's emotional involvement. The new developments of the plot, introduced at the start of Act Two, lead to startling revelations which either deepen the bonds between the characters or tear them apart.

The middle, the rising action, is generally the longest section of a film and the hardest to keep focused. The action in Act Two rises, falls, and rises again to a climax which focuses the development for Act Three. The action should orchestrate a believable character arc while maintaining tension and plot momentum as the protagonist pursues his goal; it should build a plot which is logical but unpredictable. In the best films, the orchestration of the second act should generate suspense and surprise, two qualities a great film cannot do without.

SUSPENSE

Suspense is a mental state of excited uncertainty, generated by an impending decision or outcome. Suspense is created as the audience becomes increasingly concerned about the welfare of the characters, worried that they won't achieve their goals.

Alfred Hitchcock, whose sobriquet was "master of suspense," brings in the audience on issues or incidents the characters know nothing about; then, he exploits that knowledge by sending the characters into situations fraught with danger from the undiscovered circumstances. Viewers fret as they anticipate what terrible things might entrap the characters.

This type of suspense builds perfectly in *Diner*. Recall the sequence in which Boogie schemes to have Beth impersonate the sick Carol Heathrow. Tension mounts because we know what Boogie intends and we anticipate Beth finding out. But when Beth's husband Shrevie tags along with Fenwick to verify the bet, the stakes are raised. Now we squirm in our seats waiting for the inevitable—for the characters to be caught in the act. The characters escape and we breathe a collective sigh of relief, having been glued to our seats in anticipation of the outcome. Suspense is that glue.

Suspense can be created in a variety of ways.

The Antagonist

The best representation of the protagonist's problem and obstacles is the antagonist. A strong antagonist greatly contributes to a film's overall tension and suspense. The stronger he is, the more we wonder about the protagonist's ability to succeed in his ultimate mission. In *Witness*, Schaeffer and McFee present strong forces against Book; in *Casablanca*, the Nazis have the power; in *Chinatown*, Noah Cross holds all the cards and seems to have the whole city in his back pocket; in *Jerry Maguire*, Bob Sugar is omnipotent in his ability to anticipate Jerry's moves and steal his clients.

Jeopardy

To compound suspense, great films put their protagonists and/or other main characters in jeopardy—and keep them there. Jeopardy can be personal, as in the character's risk of losing love or respect. In *Quiz Show* and *Tootsie*, both protagonists (Charlie and Michael, respectively) are in danger of losing respect and love if they're discovered; in *Witness*, Rachel puts her reputation in personal jeopardy with her community by caring for Book; in *Jerry Maguire*, Jerry is in danger of losing everything if he can't sell his only client and rediscover his self-respect.

Jeopardy can be physical, as in a bodily attack or the threat of an attack. In *Witness*, Book, Samuel, Rachel and Eli are in physical peril due to Book's presence (if Schaeffer and McFee find him on the farm, several lives could be lost); in *Chinatown*, *Diner* and *Reservoir Dogs*, characters face physical dangers at one point or another; in *Casablanca*, the characters are in personal and physical jeopardy at different points in the film; in *The Piano*, Ada puts herself in personal and physical jeopardy (who knows what Stewart might do if he discovers her with Baines). Audiences anticipate reactions to dramatic situations, which contributes to the plot suspense. (So, when Ada accepts Baines' arrangement, the audience naturally begins worrying, "What will happen if they are discovered by her husband?")

A negative consequence awaiting the protagonist if he fails to solve the plot's problem adds to the suspense. *Witness, Diner, Annie Hall* and *Parenthood* set up negative alternatives for the characters. For Book, it's his life and the lives of others; for Boogie, it could be his life or at least his limbs; for Alvy and Annie, it's their relationship; for Gil, it's his job. The price of failure in each case is high enough to generate genuine suspense. These consequences are generally set up early enough in the plot to create mounting concern. But if they are established too early, before the main conflict has engaged, or if they fail to increase as the plot progresses, they will not effectively increase apprehension in the audience.

Unexpected Complications
Chapter Two defined a complication as any factor entering the world of the film that makes matters more difficult for a major character and causes a change in the course of the action. Complications do not pose an apparent threat, but they generally arise when an unexpected problem confronts the character which then causes repercussions.

The unexpected complication adds suspense to any story because the sudden surprise produces a new and additional obstacle for the protagonist. *Risky Business, Tootsie* and *Jerry Maguire* are films in which the protagonists are confronted with unexpected complications. In each one, the complications produce more obstacles to be overcome which, in turn, keeps the suspense building. From Lana stealing the Steuben egg to the Porsche rolling into the lake to Guido stealing Joel's furniture, the complications in *Risky Business* constantly present Joel with new obstacles to conquer before his parents get home. In *Tootsie*, complications include Dorothy's persona, Michael's feelings for

Julie, Michael bedding Sandy, Van Horn's and Les's feelings for Dorothy, to name a few. *Jerry Maguire* also jumps from one complication to another, beginning with Jerry's Mission Statement, to the client who sells him out, to Marcie trying to convince Rod to become a free agent; these complications add tension and make us wonder how in the world our hero will prevail.

Complications can be specific incidents. In *Casablanca*, Ilsa walks into Rick's saloon and complicates his life; in *The Piano*, Stewart leaves the piano on the beach, creating Ada's major complication; in *Chinatown*, Escobar continually dogs Gittes, complicating the private detective's job; in *Quiz Show*, Enright tricks Charlie into winning, complicating Charlie's life; in *Diner*, Carol Heathrow comes down with the flu, putting a kink in Boogie's plan. *Reservoir Dogs* bases its plot on a complication—Mr. Orange getting shot—and continues from there.

Complications can come in the form of new attitudes and character feelings. In *Chinatown*, Evelyn's desire to take care of her child is a complication, as are Gittes' feelings for her; Goodwin's growing affection for Charlie in *Quiz Show* complicates his job; in *The Best Years of Our Lives*, the feelings Fred and Peggy develop for each other complicate their lives while Al's new attitude complicates his job at the bank; in *Grand Hotel*, the Baron falls in love with Grusinskaya, thus complicating his problem of stealing her pearls to pay off his debt.

Great films lace their plots with more than one type of complication for many characters, not just the protagonist. Besides contributing conflict and suspense, complications often lead to deeper characterizations and more involving plots. By devoting attention to how a particular character deals with complications, that character's arc comes into focus and better defines him. This leads the audience to a deeper involvement in the plot, especially if we come to care more strongly for the characters. Complications also break up the linear plot by forcing it to take unexpected turns. A good complication twists the plot in a new way and, in the process, tightens the knot around the protagonist by placing more obstacles in his path and raising additional problems.

Predictability—The Suspense Killer

The enemy of suspense is predictability. If viewers easily foresee what is going to happen and their expectations are met without surprise, they become bored. While the possibility of impending crises needs to be foreshadowed, it is the possibility—not the certainty—of these crises that generates suspense and anticipation. We know conflict is going to take place, but if we can predict how and when it will happen and to whom, the story loses interest, momentum and value.

A protagonist who is so strong and smart that he can solve any problem through physical might or intellect will not engender much suspense. A protagonist needs to be challenged to be great. Think of Superman without kryptonite: how interesting would the Man of Steel be if he could never be defeated? The greater the odds against the protagonist, the more the audience will root for him to succeed.

Losing the antagonist too early in a film can seriously undermine the uncertainty and excitement which should surround the main climax. For suspense to keep building, the antagonist needs to be viable until the final climax. In *The Fifth Element*, the antagonist Zorg (Gary Oldman) dies halfway through the third act; audience involvement significantly decreases in the film. If the antagonist is removed from contention before the final crisis and climax, momentum will be slowed and suspense will be lost.

SURPRISE

A key element in any great film is surprise—to take unawares, or to affect with unexpected wonder. When we discover something unknown or if a plot takes a sudden turn, when a character behaves in a startling way or does something inexplicable, our attention is caught. Audiences anticipate the action to go one way or a character to behave in a certain manner; when suddenly something different happens, expectations are dashed.

Surprise can startle or shock. It can make the audience laugh or scare the pants off them. When we first see Homer's hooks in *The Best Years of Our Lives,* we are shocked; his initial attitude toward them surprises us even more because he makes a joke out of them. In *The Piano,* Ada surprises us when she agrees to Baines' deal; the plot then turns in a new direction. Most often, surprise finds shape in complications, discoveries, reversals, revelations.

Discoveries

A discovery is when a character or the audience learns something unknown, such as a clue or evidence, that advances the plot. The information contained in the discovery is unforeseeable by the characters and the audience, which is why its discovery comes as a surprise.

In *Chinatown*, discoveries play an important role in figuring out the mystery. Gittes discovers Mulholland's "affair;" then, he discovers that he was used and set up; he discovers the meaning of the obituaries and the word "apple core;" he discovers the glasses in the pond; he learns it is saltwater that the pond holds, not freshwater; later, when he forces Evelyn to tell the truth, he discovers the revelation of the girl's true identity. All of these discoveries surprise and shock us and hold our attention as we try to determine their ultimate meaning.

Mysteries are not the only genre to use a discovery. In *Witness*, Samuel discovers McFee's photograph on the police precinct bulletin board and it surprises us to learn that the killer is an honored policeman. When McFee attacks Book in the garage, surprise turns to shock because we realize that Schaeffer, Book's mentor, is in on the crime. This surprise reverses the plot, sending it in a new direction, as Book goes from hunter to hunted. In *Casablanca*, Rick discovers that Ilsa was married to Laszlo when he knew her in Paris. In *Quiz Show*, Goodwin finds Snodgrass who reveals that he also got the answers, thus setting the plot on a new course. In *Diner*, Boogie learns he lost the bet and Billy learns that Barbara is pregnant—both are important discoveries. In *Parenthood*, when Gil discovers that Karen is pregnant, we groan along with him, knowing that he has only just quit his job.

Reversals

One of the strongest surprises occurring in film takes place when things seem to be headed in one direction, then something happens and the film suddenly veers off in the opposite direction. This is called a reversal. More often than not, the situation created by the reversal is not only unanticipated but unwanted; and as a result tension is added by leading the protagonist to other obstacles. A reversal can also turn a bad situation into a good one (although this does not produce as much drama and tension as when a good situation turns bad; it can provide needed comic relief). Often, a bad situation that turns good comes near the close of the film, or just before a major reversal sends the action back into more conflict.

Reversals can be major or minor. A major reversal can force the protagonist into an entirely new and unforeseen direction, while a minor reversal might cause him to reconsider his plan of action and discard it in favor of something else. Most films have at least one major reversal, sometimes more. Reversals are strongest when placed near any of the five key focal points in a film's structure because they maximize momentum and help focus the plot. (See the example from *Witness* above; note how the reversal comes at the end of the first act.)

Risky Business has several important reversals. The first comes at the midpoint, when Joel kicks Lana and Vicki out of his house only to let them back in when he rescues them from Guido. Another reversal comes at the Act Two climax, when Joel agrees to go along with Lana's plan after first refusing; a third comes at the main climax when he thinks he has solved his problem but walks into his house to find it empty of all furniture.

At the end of the second act in *Casablanca*, Ilsa enters, gun in hand, to get the Letters of Transit from Rick; instead, she winds up in his arms. In the main climax, Rick sends Ilsa off with Laszlo at the last minute, which is a complete reversal because it goes against his plans and everything he said during the course of the film. In *Tootsie*, the first reversal is seen when Michael puts on a dress; another is when the show picks up Dorothy's option; a third occurs when Michael wants off the show. In *Diner*, a reversal occurs when Boogie decides he can't go through with his plan to use Beth to impersonate Carol Heathrow.

A reversal works best when emotion connects it with an action and/or the consequence of an action. Emotion can fuel and cause a reversal; emotion can also result from a change in a situation. Emotion adds depth to the reversal and therefore enhances the drama. For example, at the midpoint of *The Piano*, Baines returns the instrument to Ada; this functions as a reversal in the plot action. Suddenly, Baines no longer wants to go on with the agreement; it is too painful because of his feelings for Ada. This causes another reversal, this one for Ada: she realizes what Baines means to her, which sets the film on a new course. At the end of *The Piano*, the reversals mount: Stewart sets Ada free, reversing his course with her; Ada goes but jumps off the boat to kill herself; sinking, she suddenly realizes she wants to live and fights her way to the surface.

Revelations

In drama, revelation means to reveal or expose something startling or shocking that is not previously known or realized by the characters or the audience. It is a discovery, but of greater importance; a moment in the film when information, crucial to understanding the story, can no longer be hidden or withheld from the characters and audience. This information may come as a shock but it always makes sense as it sheds light on the main characters and the plot by illuminating their motivations and back story. A major revelation causes the action to be dramatically different than if it had never surfaced. A minor revelation tells the audience about motivations that are not necessarily dramatic but which contribute to the audience's understanding of the story.

One great example of revelation in film is in *Chinatown*, when Evelyn reveals that her sister is also her daughter. This dramatic piece of information changes everything for the protagonist. It also changes how the viewers see the story, for now they understand why actions were taken (despite the risks) and they realize what the plot was truly about.

Revelation takes place generally in the film's second half, although it can come as early as in the main exposition. In *Jerry Maguire*, six minutes into the film, the protagonist has a revelation about his life in his breakthrough/breakdown. Revelation is more powerful when linked with another element, such as a reversal, crisis, climax, resolution or any of the key focal points in the structure. At the midpoint in *Casablanca*, Rick learns a startling piece of information—that Ilsa was already married to Victor Laszlo during the time he knew her in Paris; in the second act climax of *Chinatown*, Evelyn reveals the girl's identity; in the main climax of *Parenthood*, Gil has his epiphany that life *is* a roller coaster and there's nothing he can do but enjoy the ride; in the resolution of *Risky Business*, Joel realizes that Lana used him from the very start even though she denies it; and, at the very end of *Citizen Kane*, the audience is allowed the revelation of the sled—"Rosebud."

The best revelations work emotionally on the characters and the audience. Ada's response when Baines returns the piano to her at the midpoint is the revelation of her true feelings for him. Gittes responds to Evelyn's startling revelation with the emotions of sympathy and understanding. Often there are consequences to the revelations which motivate the characters to react. Book's reaction to his betrayal by his mentor is shock and anger and he vows he will get him. In *Casablanca*, Rick softens once Ilsa makes her revelation about Laszlo; now he knows there was a good reason why she had to leave him in Paris.

A revelation which has a direct relationship to the main exposition is truly dynamic because it strengthens cause-and-effect relationships as well as the overall sense of dramatic unity. The revelation, while hidden, contributes to the reasons why the protagonist encounters difficulties when trying to achieve his goal. Once the revelation occurs, it can free him to attain his goal—or, at least allow him to meet his fate more consciously. Again, *Chinatown* offers a great illustration of this point. Once the revelation of Evelyn's relationship with her father is exposed, everything in the movie makes sense; we know who the real antagonist is.

Revelation of character can proceed in a variety of ways. If information is first hidden from the audience, then exposed, the character is illuminated—for better or worse—as in *Chinatown*. In film, behavior is the most effective way to illustrate character essence. In *The Piano*, Ada's revelation of her feelings for Baines is illustrated in her behavior toward him and her changed feelings for her piano.

In a sense, exposition continues until the end of the film because, in each new scene, the writer gives the audience new information, revealing and exposing certain facets of the characters and the story. But the main revelation is held back until the time is ripe with dramatic possibilities. From the beginning, the writer has the details needed by the protagonist and audience but withholds them, revealing them only when the impact will be greatest or when the audience truly needs them in order to follow the story. Withholding the revelation, helps to maintain tension by keeping the audience guessing about what is really going on.

North by Northwest

Written by Ernest Lehman, produced and directed by Alfred Hitchcock, *North by Northwest* tells the story of a self-assured Madison Avenue executive mistaken for a nonexistent spy and who is then chased across the country. It is a fairly straightforward yarn, spun with plenty of plot twists and suspense. The structure breaks down like this:

The first minutes of Act One introduce Roger Thornhill (Cary Grant), a confident, successful advertising executive who is a bit of a womanizer and Mama's boy. Four minutes into film, Thornhill is at the Plaza having lunch with business associates when he is mistaken for a "George Kaplan" and kidnapped (the inciting incident). He's taken to meet a "Mr. Townsend" (James Mason) and accused of being a spy. Thornhill's denials mean nothing. When "Townsend" cannot get the information he wants, he sends his men to kill Thornhill, who manages to escape, but cannot convince the police or even his mother (Jessie Royce Landis) of the truth behind his crazy story, especially when they learn that "Townsend" works at the U.N. Thornhill returns to the Plaza with his mother to find "Kaplan" and clear up the misunderstanding, but the same men try to capture him and he escapes. Angry, Thornhill goes to confront "Townsend" at the U.N., and learns that the diplomat is not the same man who orchestrated his kidnapping. The real Lester Townsend (Phillip Ober) is mistakenly killed (Thornhill is the real target) and Thornhill is photographed holding the knife, making him the prime suspect. Act One ends 35 minutes into the film, with Thornhill running for his life.

Act Two opens at a U.S. intelligence agency, with agents offering story exposition in a meeting with the Professor (Leo G. Carroll), during which they reveal there is no "George Kaplan;" he was created to divert suspicion from their own agent. But there is nothing they can do for Roger Thornhill.

Thornhill decides he is not going to take this lying down. He heads for Chicago by train with hopes of finding the elusive "Kaplan" and clearing up the whole mess. The police are after him, making his travels difficult until he is rescued by the beautiful Eve Kendall (Eva Marie Saint), who hides him in her drawing room compartment and covers for him. During the night, feelings seem to develop between Thornhill and Eve, but in the morning she sends a note to Vandamm (James Mason)—the man who masqueraded as Townsend at the beginning. Eve works for Vandamm. Thornhill arrives safely in Chicago and Eve calls "Kaplan" for him, arranging a meeting place. Thornhill follows her elaborate directions, out to the middle of nowhere. He waits until a cropduster attempts to mow him down with a machine gun. Thornhill dodges the plane in a terrific action sequence, finally flagging down a tanker truck which causes the cropduster to crash.

Back in Chicago, Thornhill discovers that "Kaplan" left his hotel before Eve placed her call to him. Thornhill now realizes that Eve must be working with the men who are after him—she set him up (the film's midpoint, at 75 minutes). He finds Eve, following her to an auction where Vandamm waits. Thornhill confronts Vandamm over Eve while Vandamm and his associate Leonard (Martin Landau) track the bidding on a primitive statue (their bid wins). Vandamm's other men again try to apprehend Thornhill, but Thornhill creates a scene and gets himself arrested. When the police learn Thornhill's identity, they do not take him to the police station, but to the airport where he meets the Professor, who reveals what's going on, including the fact that Eve is his agent. Eve is in danger of Vandamm discovering her identity because she has fallen in love with Thornhill. The Professor now needs Thornhill to play Kaplan, to save Eve from Vandamm's suspicions. Thornhill agrees. Below Mount Rushmore, he shows up, as "Kaplan," forcing a confrontation with Vandamm over Eve. But Eve suddenly shoots Thornhill and runs away before the authorities reach her. This is the end of Act Two—97 minutes into the film.

Act Three begins in a forest, with a meeting between Eve and Thornhill (she used blanks when firing the gun at him earlier). Both declare their love, but Thornhill is surprised to learn that Eve is going back to Vandamm now that her cover is safe. He argues with the Professor, but Eve drives off before he can stop her. The Professor confines Thornhill at a hospital, but he manages to escape and he makes his way to Vandamm's estate where he overhears that Leonard has discovered Eve's ruse with the blanks. Vandamm decides he will get rid of Eve while flying out of the country. Thornhill manages to warn Eve but can't get to her before Vandamm and Leonard take her away to meet the plane. Thornhill now is captured by the maid, but he breaks away once he realizes that she is holding Eve's gun on him. He and Eve flee with the primitive statue while Vandamm and his men chase them down the face of Mount Rushmore (the main climax). The statue breaks, revealing its contents—microfilm. Two of Vandamm's men die trying to reach Thornhill and Eve; but the two manage to elude them until Eve slips down the cliff and dangles over the edge, Thornhill trying to pull her up. Leonard tries to kill them both, but the Professor shows up with enforcements; a sharpshooter gets Leonard while Thornhill pulls Eve with all his might. The film ends as he pulls her up, not to safety on Mount Rushmore, but onto the upper berth of a train drawing room, with the two already wed (127 minutes).

Suspense in *North by Northwest* doesn't wait for the second act. It begins four minutes into the film and doesn't let up until the very last moment of the film. And it uses all of the elements discussed above. Let's see how.

The mistaken identity which starts the film (the inciting incident) is an unexpected complication in Roger Thornhill's day. Suddenly, he's caught up in a cat-and-mouse game he neither cares about nor understands. Jeopardy increases when Vandamm's men threaten him with a gun. Right away, viewers want to know what's going on. They know a mistake has been made, but they see that Thornhill can't get out of it. When Thornhill seems to have murdered the real Mr. Townsend (another unexpected complication), the stakes increase immeasurably. Now Thornhill must run from the police as well as Vandamm.

The suave and sinister Vandamm is a potent antagonist—he is in control, with several men working under him. Even though, in the first act, his men lose Thornhill before they can kill him, Vandamm seems in control of the situation, especially when we discover him on the same train as Thornhill and allied with Eve (a revelation).

Several sequences milk the suspense for all it's worth. The first time Vandamm's men want to kill Thornhill, they poor a fifth of bourbon down his throat, then set up a car crash (jeopardy). Thornhill is intoxicated, but able to kick one of the men out of the car before being sent over a cliff. But now he's driving drunk on a dangerous road. Miraculously, Thornhill steers the car through a string of hazards before crashing into a police car which forces his adversaries to back off.

In the second act, suspense mounts in small and large doses. For example, there is a scene in which Thornhill tries to buy a train ticket: the ticket agent clearly knows who he is because the "wanted" picture is revealed to the audience but kept from the fugitive—this creates more jeopardy. When Thornhill dodges the police and the conductor on the train and then jumps off, the uncertainty continues to mount. Each of these events are obstacles that create jeopardy and stand in the way of Thornhill finding "Kaplan" in Chicago.

Thornhill's feelings for Eve create complications for him. He tries to set up a time to see her again, until the risk of getting caught sends him off. Later, he discovers that Eve set him up with Vandamm (a reversal) and he wants to confront her, which leads to further complications at the auction. The audience's earlier knowledge of Eve's connection to Vandamm increases suspense, causing us to wonder what Thornhill will do when he discovers who she is. When Eve gives Thornhill elaborate directions to meet "Kaplan" on a deserted road, we know something is up. Apprehension builds while Thornhill waits in the middle of nowhere. Because of Eve's ties to Vandamm, we expect that something bad is about to happen. But Hitchcock takes his time, making us squirm before he introduces the cropduster far in the distance. (The farmer further foreshadows trouble ahead by saying, "That plane's dustin' crops where there ain't no crops.")

The sequence at the auction also builds suspense. Thornhill's confusion over his feelings for Eve causes him to put himself in danger. As Vandamm's men close in, we wonder how he will get away. Thornhill does it by causing a disturbance and getting arrested. This leads to a surprise because the police don't arrest him; instead, they bring him to the Professor. Thornhill learns that Eve is really a government agent (another reversal and revelation). Now Thornhill understands how his own actions have put her in jeopardy and he risks his life to go back and save her. Instead, at the end of Act Two, she shoots him (a surprise *and* a reversal).

Tension keeps building when Thornhill's expectation that Eve will be free of Vandamm proves to be wrong. Again, Thornhill is put in a situation where suspense builds: he's locked in the hospital room. How will he get out and away from the Professor? Thornhill escapes through a window (with a nice piece of comic relief—he meets a woman who would like Cary Grant in her bed).

The last act, leading up to the chase down Mount Rushmore, is filled with suspense. The most important event involves Leonard's discovery that Eve used blanks on Thornhill. Now *her* life is in danger and Thornhill must find a way to keep her off the plane. This is orchestrated to great effect, with a series of near-misses, until finally Thornhill gets a message to her on the back of his matches. But Eve is forced to leave, and Thornhill is discovered by the maid who holds him hostage until he realizes she is holding Eve's gun. The shooting distracts Vandamm and

Leonard, allowing Eve to make a break for it with the statue. A chase ensues, leading down the top of the monument. The danger of the situation creates suspense, for there is no way to go but down and it is a treacherous cliff, a fact emphasized by several people who fall off it. At the end, Eve slips and dangles over the cliff as Thornhill struggles to hold her. When Leonard arrives, Thornhill asks for help. Instead, the gunman steps on Thornhill's hands. Surely, it looks bleak, but then a shot rings out and Leonard topples. Still, can Thornhill save Eve? The question is left in doubt until the last seconds of the film when suddenly, through a match cut, we find ourselves on a train: Thornhill pulls Eve up onto the upper berth to join him there.

SPECIAL NOTES

A case might be made that *North by Northwest* is the prototype for contemporary action pictures. Certainly, action films were made before 1959, but mostly in the western and war genres. Detective and film noir stories had chases and shoot-outs, but nothing of the nonstop caliber seen in this film. In fact, most of Hitchcock's earlier films emphasized suspense over action (*Saboteur* and *The 39 Steps* utilized action and had a protagonist falsely accused, but the energy and activity were of a different quality). Some scenes might seem slightly dated today, and a good 10 minutes could easily be trimmed from its 136-minute length (the total length, with credits: the actual story is 127 minutes). However, the film still stands as a masterpiece of suspense, with a terrific beginning that gets us off and running, and doesn't stop until the last frame.

On the screenplay used for comparison, the title page is not dated, but inside, the earliest date is 7-13-58, with revisions dated through 10-27-58. It is 179 pages long, with a few "A" and "B" pages throughout. It is clearly a shooting script: establishing shots, close-ups and angles are noted and numbered. The scene descriptions and action are dense, telling us exactly what we're going to see as well as showing the director's input. The structure of the film and the screenplay are the same and, in fact, very little has been changed. A few short scenes with minor characters have been trimmed or cut. The length of the screenplay is caused by the description of almost every shooting angle and by the ample stage directions. The auction scene, for instance, includes everything the auctioneer says on one-half of the page while the dialogue between Thornhill and Vandamm occupies the other half. This lengthens the script considerably.

The screenplay begins with an opening narration, asking us if it would not be strange if one man was never mistaken for another. This was cut from the film. The last shot of the film, the obvious sexual metaphor where the train disappears into the tunnel, is not in the screenplay. In the script, the train simply disappears into the night. Another shot not indicated in the screenplay but which exists in the film is the ultra high-angle shot of Thornhill leaving the U.N. after Townsend's murder. (Hitchcock could not obtain permission from the United Nations to shoot on location, though he sneaked a few camera shots from the street.) These constitute the only "major" changes from this script to film. The story and screenplay of *North by Northwest* was nominated for an Academy Award in 1959.

14

THE MAIN CLIMAX AND RESOLUTION

Study Film: *One Flew Over the Cuckoo's Nest*

Great films know how to end: they build until the audience can't take it anymore. Then, at just the right moment and in a surprising way, they bring together the conflicting elements of the main crisis and climax by arriving at a solution, thus resolving the film. A great ending is the sum total of everything that has gone before. Every scene, every decision (or lack of one) creates and shapes the climax and resolution. It's the moment toward which the audience has been traveling since the beginning. It's the moment they have been waiting for since introduction of the main conflict—how will it end?

Why are some climaxes and resolutions profoundly more satisfying than others? Why do some move us, make us hold our breath in expectation and doubt? Even after the film is over, why do some make us reflect upon our experience, whether we want to or not? It's not just the action, though great action and spectacle can certainly take one's breath away. What really sustains a film story and keeps it timeless are the people involved in the action. We've been with them. Because of their commitments and values demonstrated through the plot, our empathy was engaged. Good traits and bad, they have won us over through the relationships they have formed with other characters. A great film ending is satisfying because we care about the people involved in it.

There are no set formulas for writing the main climax, no paradigm that can create the scenes. The main climax of a great film is created by a writer who has realized characters on the page whom the audience can care about and who has invented action for them in order to resolve the plot. Chapter Two defines both the main climax and the resolution; Chapters Eleven and Sixteen cover sequence and scene construction. Here, then, let us examine the elements needed to make a great ending.

THE MAIN CLIMAX

The main climax is found at the moment the final crisis reaches its greatest intensity and the main conflict resolves. In it, one character wins and one character loses (*Witness, Casablanca, Chinatown, North by Northwest*); or, a character succeeds despite the odds (*Risky Business, Tootsie, Diner, The Best Years of Our Lives, Jerry Maguire*); or, the characters lose to the system or life (*Quiz Show, Citizen Kane, Chinatown, Reservoir Dogs*); or the characters resolve the problems within themselves or each other (*The Piano, Parenthood, Annie Hall*).

The main climax is the culminating point for both the conflict and the theme. In telling us who succeeds and why, the main climax determines the simple meaning of the film. The climax of *Witness* shows that adherence to a nonviolent code can defeat violent men; for *Casablanca*, it's that love defeats cynicism; for *Chinatown*, it's that absolute power corrupts absolutely. (See Chapter Five for a more extensive discussion of the theme's relationship to the climax.)

The origin of a powerful main climax starts considerably before the beginning of the final crisis: the groundwork is laid with the characters as they evolve through the plot. In order for the main climax to be riveting, the audience must care what happens to the characters and this must happen on the page, before an inch of film is shot. Unless compelling characters inhabit the plot, it doesn't matter what kind of pyrotechnics the special-effects wizards will concoct or what else the director tries to do—the climax will not be satisfying.

Audience Identification and the Main Climax

In great films, climaxes are emotional and cathartic because the audience has found a character to identify with and cares what happens to him. Identification causes viewers to become so wrapped up in the characters that they experience the characters' emotions as their own. That's what audience identification really means: during the course of a great film, the audience feels the emotions of the characters and therefore experiences the film more intensely. (Usually the audience identifies with the protagonist, but not always. In *Hud*, the protagonist is compelling but thoroughly unsympathetic; the audience instead identifies with his innocent nephew.)

Through identification, the audience not only cares about the characters and their problems, but also strongly hopes the characters will resolve their problems favorably while fearing, in light of the obstacles, they will not. The interplay of hope and fear causes the viewers to anticipate the plot's direction as they process the story's information. (See Chapter Four for more on the importance of emotion in fostering audience identification.)

In *Casablanca*, we want Rick and Ilsa to get together, but fear it will happen at Laszlo's expense. In *The Piano*, we want Ada to accept Baines' love, but fear she will be unable to. The same is true in *Jerry Maguire*—we hope he'll be able to open his heart to Dorothy, all the while dreading that he's incapable of it. The doubt about the outcome for the characters keeps viewers engaged in the film and sustains the tension until the climax actually satisfies the plot.

The Relationship Between the Protagonist's Inner Conflict and the Main Climax

In many great films, we see a powerful relationship in the structure between the development and solution of the protagonist's personal problem and the resolution of the main conflict. For Rick to save Ilsa and Laszlo from the Nazis in *Casablanca*, he must overcome his personal problems (his anger and bitterness); in *The Piano*, for Ada to say no to the abyss, she must open her feelings to another person; in *Jerry Maguire*, Jerry can accept all Dorothy has to offer only after he learns to relate honestly to himself and to others; In *Parenthood*, Gil straightens out his life and gets his job back by letting go of his need for perfection; in *The Best Years of Our Lives*, Homer and Fred must overcome their respective fears before they can start their lives (Homer fears no one can love him because he's crippled; Fred fears that he'll never find a good job and live up to the potential he saw in himself during the war).

In all these films, plots establish characters with internal conflicts. Each character must deal with his inner conflict before he can resolve the main conflict in the climax. (Rick must know why Ilsa left him in Paris before can he save her and Laszlo;

Ada must reconnect with her own feelings and discover love from another being before she can find a reason to live; Jerry must do what his heart tells him—care about his one client—before he can understand and accept Dorothy; Gil must accept the fact that parents aren't perfect; Homer must expose his fears to Wilma before he can accept her love while Fred must get a real job and recapture his self-respect before he can go to Peggy. As the protagonist struggles with his personal problem, he will become more interesting, unpredictable and, ultimately, more sympathetic.

As characters try and fail and keep on trying to solve their outer problems, they earn our respect. When the characters are forced to deal with their inner conflicts in order to solve their outer problems, our relationship with them grows and strengthens. Audiences understand that change is an heroic undertaking. Therefore a character who confronts his own psychic problems which results in change, pulls the audience deeper into the film.

However, not all great films have characters who are transformed by the end of the story. In *Citizen Kane*, Charles Foster Kane is unable to change. Though he meets with great success in the outer world, his inner life is a shambles. This is the point of the film—Kane wants most of all is to be loved, but he has no idea how to achieve this. The characters in *Reservoir Dogs* are unable to change and this could be considered the reason they meet with disaster at the end.

The struggle to change and the resistance to it are at the heart of many great films. It is precisely because viewers intuitively understand how difficult it is to change—and they fear that a character will not be able to do it—that their bond with the character and film is strengthened. (For a complete review of character transformation and how the character arc relates to structure, see Chapter Four.)

What's at Stake?

Great films have clearly defined stakes for the characters. As the climax approaches, the audience understands what the protagonist risks if he does not successfully deal with the main conflict. Clear, identifiable stakes increase the tension and suspense over how the plot will end. In some films, the stakes are obvious. *Witness, Casablanca, The Piano, Chinatown, Reservoir Dogs* and *North by Northwest* all have plots in which the characters' lives are at stake. In other films, the risk is more subtle. In *Quiz Show*, Charlie's and Stempel's respect and love are in jeopardy; in *Tootsie*, Michael's career and love life are at risk; in *Diner*, *Parenthood*, *The Best Years of Our Lives* and *Grand Hotel*, it is the characters' happiness and sense of self worth which is at stake.

The specific situation at the main climax is usually a result of action set in motion as early as in Act One, but most commonly in Act Two. Often, the stakes at the final climax have a direct relationship to the jeopardy the protagonist experiences during Act Two. (As the protagonist's jeopardy increases during Act Two, the stakes rise.) Boogie, in *Diner*, is not threatened with bodily harm until after he has missed a payment in the second half of the plot; Gil's job in *Parenthood* is not in jeopardy at the first act climax, but the situation which will later threaten it is created there. Increasing the stakes makes the conflict escalate with clear cause-and-effect relationships between the major developments.

Stakes are highest when lives and relationships are involved. At this level, the film turns into a test of commitment—what price will the protagonist pay for maintaining it? The climax is the point at which the protagonist demonstrates he will pay the price—or is unable to. Many great films involve another character's fate in the climax, either directly or indirectly. In *Witness*, *Casablanca*, *Chinatown*, *Reservoir Dogs*, *North by Northwest*, the lives of the protagonist and other characters are directly at stake. In *The Piano*, *Quiz Show*, *Tootsie*, *Diner*, *Parenthood*, *The Best Years of Our Lives*, *Grand Hotel*, *Citizen Kane*, *Annie Hall* and *Jerry Maguire*, the psychological lives of the protagonists and other characters are in emotional jeopardy.

Action and the Main Climax
Chapters Eleven and Sixteen discuss at length the mechanics of sequence and scene structure. But here let us emphasize a few points about the main climax.

Action usually comprises a portion of the final crisis and main climax and should keep the ending in doubt while also bringing together the opposing elements of the film. Here, in their final clash, the outcome of the plot will determine the film's true meaning. In films where the antagonist clearly opposes the protagonist, the climax is more obligatory. (In *Witness*, *Casablanca*, *Chinatown*, *Reservoir Dogs*, *North by Northwest*, each has a climax that must involve the protagonist and the antagonist or the audience would feel cheated.) The main source of the protagonist's conflict also must be the conflict of the main climax. The only real issues in doubt are where the climax will play out and what kind of action it will need. Once a location is determined, action must be conceived to excite and rivet the audience, keeping viewers uncertain about the ultimate ending until the last possible moment. Can Book save Samuel and Rachel from Schaeffer and McFee? Will Rick get Ilsa and Laszlo on the plane and away from the Nazis? Can Gittes save Evelyn and her daughter from her father? Will Mr. Orange and Mr. White outlive Joe and Eddie? Can Thornhill save Eve? These questions focus the action on a specific course and keep the audience guessing to the end, when the characters either achieve their aims or not.

But, in other great films, the antagonist is not the true source of the main conflict for the protagonist, only part of it, so his presence at the final crisis and main climax is less mandatory. In this case, what is most important is the understanding of the forces working against the protagonist and how these forces relate to the theme. In *The Piano*, Ada's principal conflict is within herself; the problems with Stewart and Baines are outer manifestations of her inner struggle. The film surprises us by having an incredibly dramatic second act climax—Stewart chopping off Ada's finger—and leaves us wondering where the plot will go from there. In the last act, Stewart's guilt overcomes him and, wanting to repress the memory, he sends Ada off with Baines. However, Ada still hasn't faced her ultimate adversary—her despair. That comes in her suicide attempt. But, when she faces death and chooses life, we are then able to understand the true meaning of the film.

The main conflict in *Quiz Show* is within Charlie himself. Although *Quiz Show* has a strong antagonist (Enright) who leads Charlie astray, the main climax does not involve a showdown per se between these two characters. The main conflict peaks at the end, when Charlie is forced to testify and tells the truth; he doesn't do this to destroy Enright but to clear his conscience. This is his defining moment—when integrity wins out over fame and fortune.

Tootsie, too, does not have a central antagonist working against Michael. His primary conflict is whether or not he can maintain his deception. In the second half of Act Two, more and more obstacles and complications are thrown at him (Les's and Van Horn's feelings for Dorothy, Dorothy's feelings for Julie: Sandy's conflict with Michael) and threaten to undo his charade. The main conflict is over once Michael "unmasks" and reveals his true identity, even if Julie rejects him at the end of the scene.

Jerry Maguire is yet another film with a terrific climax that does not rely on an antagonist as the source of its main conflict. Jerry's conflict is over how to integrate outer success with inner fulfillment. At the end of Act Two, he loses Dorothy because he can't open up to her. In the third act, it looks as if he might lose Rod, too, not because he hasn't succeeded in relating, but because Rod is injured in a football game. Real worry sets in for Rod's welfare—and not because Rod is Jerry's meal ticket. When Rod recovers, relief purges Jerry of his inner fears and he realizes what Dorothy means to him. He is able to go back and fight for her, asking her to stick it out with him.

One of the most moving main climaxes in film literature is in *The Best Years of Our Lives*. There is no antagonist involved—there is only Fred's problem of finding a good job. Everything he tries has failed and his wife is leaving him. This would normally free him to go to Peggy, but he is so dejected about his unemployment that all he wants to do is leave town. What he needs is a measure of self-respect. He packs up and goes, giving his father his medals and citations. At this point, he is asking himself why he fought in the war.

Fred goes to the Air Transport Command and decides to take the first flight out of town. The film cuts back to Fred's father reading his son's citations of wartime heroism. Then, the film goes back to Fred on the airfield and Fred's emotional pain sets the tone for what we are about to see. Waiting for his flight, Fred walks through rows and rows of disassembled planes, engines lined up, giant propellers—all ready to be junked. As the music rises, we sense that Fred feels like the old planes—used up and good for nothing. He stops at a bomber, like the one he flew, and climbs inside. In one of the most stunning and memorable sequences committed to film, Fred's emotional turmoil is revealed without him uttering a word (everything is communicated through acting, camera movement and music): we sense his pain and see his panic as he relives his ordeal in the bomber's seat. Fred's experiences were horrible and he just can't shake them.

These memories might be holding him back. Fred is interrupted by a contractor he mistakes for the junkman. Then, he learns that the planes are not being junked: they will be used to make prefabricated homes. Fred seizes this opportunity, fighting his way to a job, the one thing he wants and needs in order to hang onto his self-respect. This moment (Fred getting a job) is the climax of the film. Now the three men—Fred, Homer and Al—each have dealt with the problems or worries introduced in the first act. All that's left is the resolution.

THE RESOLUTION

The resolution ties up the loose ends of the story, and fixes the fates of the main characters involved in the struggle, especially those the audience is most interested in. All the other characters are affected by what happens to the hero. The job of the resolution is to demonstrate how they are affected. The resolution can appear in a scroll at the end, as in *Quiz Show*, or it can include one last insight or action that develops the theme's final and ultimate meaning, as in *Tootsie*. (In *Tootsie*, the resolution completes the theme. With his line, "I was a better man with you as a woman than I ever was with a woman as a man," Michael finally gets Julie to understand what he learned as "a woman." This underscores the theme, hitting it one last time to illuminate the full meaning of the film.)

The best resolutions work in two distinct ways. When there are few questions regarding the main characters which need clearing up at the end, the resolution should be quick and to the point. The characters will face a specific set of circumstances which establishes how they have fared because of the climax. Look at how quickly the resolutions of *Casablanca*, *The Piano*, *Chinatown*, *North by Northwest* play out. These resolutions might take a page or two at most to wrap up their films. Sometimes they take as little as a line of dialogue.

When the fates of important characters have yet to be shown, or if several lines of action are left dangling (as in subplots or mini-plots), or if there are other questions which need to be answered, the action of the resolution should still make the audience wonder what is going to happen next. *Tootsie*, which is 113 minutes long, climaxes at 106 minutes into the film; it then spends seven minutes in its resolution. What holds the audience's interest? First, we care about the characters involved in the subplots so we want to know what happens to them. Second, we don't know how these minor conflicts will be resolved. In the individual scenes of subplot resolutions with characters like Julie's father, Michael still has obstacles to overcome; he must be absolved. The film's most important subplot conflict (Julie) is held until the very end. All this keeps the audience wondering—what's going to happen with Julie? Will Michael get the girl after all?

The resolution in *Parenthood* is particularly noteworthy since it keeps us guessing while visually establishing what has happened to the characters. The climax of *Parenthood* really only deals with Gil and his inner struggle but the rest of the characters need resolutions. Previously each one has had his or her own climax: Nathan serenades Susan, proving he can change and winning her back; Helen helps Julie accept Tod and so in doing wins her son's respect and love; Larry escapes to South America. But what happens next to them? The final resolution ends in the hospital with a gurney being wheeled down a corridor. We realize a baby has been born, but we don't know who had it. Then we see Susan standing by, pregnant; Karen is holding an infant; and finally Julie and Tod cuddle their baby. The new mom turns out to be Helen, who has had a baby with Garry's biology teacher (a character we've met only once in the film). The structure of the resolution makes the audience wonder about the identity of the new mother and therefore keeps them engaged for the final moments of the film. *Parenthood* closes with all the families gathered for the birth, having weathered their crises and reaffirming the notion of family by extending it.

One Flew Over the Cuckoo's Nest

Adapted from Ken Kesey's novel, *One Flew Over the Cuckoo's Nest* was written for the screen by Lawrence Hauben and Bo Goldman; it was directed by Milos Foreman and produced by Saul Zaentz and Michael Douglas. The 1975 film tells the story of Randle Patrick McMurphy (Jack Nicholson), a spirited misfit who feigns insanity to escape a jail sentence only to collide with the strong-willed head nurse of his psychiatric ward. McMurphy's inherent humanity conflicts with the cold tyranny of Nurse Ratched (Louise Fletcher) in a battle over nothing less than the freedom of the human spirit.

The basic structure holding the scenes together sets up simply. Act One begins with McMurphy entering the mental hospital for evaluation (the new "force" entering the hospital universe). The main exposition comes eight minutes in and establishes a problem: Is McMurphy faking insanity to get out of his work detail or is he really mentally ill? Dr. Spivey (Dean R. Brooks) suspects that he is pretending (as does the audience), but McMurphy will remain in the ward until the evaluation is complete. The main exposition establishes that McMurphy wants to ride out his jail time in the asylum with ease but his manic temperament raises a question: Can he do this without getting into more trouble and making things worse for himself?

As McMurphy gets acquainted with the ward, so does the audience. He meets the cast of characters and sees that Nurse Ratched controls the ward with surface concern but with cruel indifference underneath. By the end of McMurphy's first group therapy session (20 minutes into the film), he sees Nurse Ratched as the ball-buster she is; and, she is clearly anticipating trouble from him. McMurphy has his first real run-in with her when he attempts to turn down the pervasive ward music so he can hear himself think and she prevents him. Then he finds himself in conflict with her over taking his medication. She gives him a choice—he can take it himself or it will be given to him forcibly. He defers but secretly doesn't swallow his pill. Harding (William Redfield) chides McMurphy about backing down; McMurphy responds by betting he can get her goat by the end of the week. Now the sides of the main conflict are drawn and a time frame is delineated.

The heart of Act Two takes up this conflict while showing how McMurphy handles the patients—warming to them and winning them over with his unlimited enthusiasm even in the face of defeat. This creates more conflict with Nurse Ratched who sees McMurphy as a threat to her authority. After McMurphy absconds with several patients on a fishing trip, the medical evaluation team sees him as dangerous but still not crazy. They want to send him back to the work farm but Nurse Ratched persuades the doctors to let her keep him. This is the midpoint: Nurse Ratched has McMurphy securely in her clutches—the antagonist will not let go.

McMurphy then learns the reality of his prison sentence: he's not serving time while at the hospital—the authorities can keep him there indefinitely. Suddenly, the reality of his actions hits him. At group therapy, McMurphy lets the others know how upset he is with them, figuring they must have known what was at stake for him. Only now does he find out that almost all the patients have voluntarily committed themselves. Incredulous, he tries to convince them that they are no crazier than the average Joe on the street. As tempers flare and patients openly defy Nurse Ratched, the session disintegrates into chaos and ends with McMurphy defending Cheswick (Sydney Lassick) and brawling with the aides. The Chief (Will Sampson) comes to McMurphy's rescue and all three patients—Cheswick, McMurphy and the Chief—end up cuffed and taken for special treatment. While awaiting their fate, McMurphy discovers that the Chief has been faking his deaf-mute routine. The two plan to escape to Canada and then are taken in for electroshock therapy. Act Two ends.

Act Three begins when McMurphy returns to the ward as his old self, but promising Nurse Ratched that he is gentle as a puppy. That night, however, he puts his escape plan into action, bribing the night attendant with booze, cash and a woman, only pausing to show his buddies a good time (and to wreak a little havoc in the ward) before he goes. With the night attendant's keys, McMurphy unlocks a window and says his good-byes. But Billy (Brad Dourif) steps forward, clearly smitten with McMurphy's girlfriend Candy (Marya Small). Amused yet concerned about Billy, McMurphy arranges for the kid to sleep with her before he goes. Billy needs a little coaxing, but soon disappears with Candy while the others continue partying.

In the morning, when the staff arrives, McMurphy and the others are asleep. The window is relocked and the aides round up all the patients except Billy, who is soon discovered in bed with Candy. Billy's evident pride over his sexual initiation is stripped away by Nurse Ratched with the mention of his mother. Hysterical, Billy is locked in an office with an aide. Now McMurphy, still holding the night attendant's keys, tries to break out. The aide goes to prevent him, but they are both stopped by a scream: Billy has killed himself. McMurphy jumps Nurse Ratched, trying to kill her. He is knocked out just in time.

Life goes back to normal on the ward—music plays, card games continue—even though Nurse Ratched now wears an orthopedic collar. Rumors abound that McMurphy killed two guards and escaped. But, this is not the case. When McMurphy is brought into the ward late one night, the Chief realizes his friend has had a lobotomy. Distraught, the Chief smothers McMurphy with a pillow, then escapes.

The main climax of *One Flew Over the Cuckoo's Nest* is clearly the most dramatic and defining moment in the film. In the climax, McMurphy attacks but cannot kill Nurse Ratched. When he is dragged off, we do not know what will happen to him—that will take the resolution to explain. But since he has attempted to murder her, we know this action will weigh heavily on his fate.

In McMurphy, and in all of the characters in the ward, the audience finds someone to care about. McMurphy, despite his past, deals with the other patients compassionately; he tries to help them in his own way. Even at the beginning, when he attempts to take advantage of them (through the card games and bets), he still sees them as human beings and is able to form bonds with them. The audience sees this behavior as a demonstration of McMurphy's true character. It makes him sympathetic; he is a good person, even if he does "fight and fuck too much" on the outside. Here, on the inside, he stands up for the little guy against the insurmountable odds and un-wavering authority.

We also care about the other characters. Their vulnerability and illness make us feel sorry for them and their childishness makes them endearing. Most of them are good-humored and the ones that are not are often comical. Many times throughout the film, we are struck by the poignancy of their situation.

McMurphy's inner conflict comes in the form of his person-ality: He is rash and excitable; incapable of passivity or follow-ing orders. He thinks he is smarter than he is and he has to do things his way. He is his own worst enemy. He never resolves this inner conflict and so never changes. He confronts an ob-stacle stronger than he—the institution personified in Nurse Ratched—and cannot change to get around or through it. Instead, he battles, as usual, with the same results: defeat. When the cli-max comes, McMurphy has a choice. He has the window open, but the death knell sounded by the nurse's scream tells him what has happened. Why doesn't he escape in the chaos? Because he is enraged by what happened and must fight back. The anger and hate he feels for Nurse Ratched is so strong that he wants to kill her. He has not learned to control his raging emotions and this leads to his ultimate downfall—the lobotomy. The reason he has to die in the end is because he cannot change. This is often the fate of the antihero—death rather than change—because change means capitualation.

The stakes in the main climax are clearly drawn—freedom or perpetual imprisonment—and action leading to the confrontation between the protagonist and antagonist makes it all the more compelling. The action starts when the hospital staff arrives in the morning. Tension escalates when Billy is discovered with Candy, then when Nurse Ratched berates him and threatens to tell his mother. In the hysteria, McMurphy decides this is a good time to leave. He looks for the key to unlock the window but one of the aides tries to stop him. McMurphy punches him, alerting Nurse Ratched who calls the other aide for help. This action leaves Billy unattended. Moments later, his body is discovered and McMurphy, blaming Nurse Ratched (his antagonist), attacks and tries to kill her. The action keeps the ending in doubt until the final moments of the sequence but it ends before we know what will finally happen to McMurphy.

The resolution sets the ultimate meaning of *One Flew Over the Cuckoo's Nest*. As life returns to normal in the ward, nothing appears to have changed. Rumors of McMurphy's escape are spread by the inmates but only Harding seems to know what has happened to him. Late at night, McMurphy is brought in; he is in a vegetative state and only the Chief is awake to see him. McMurphy has lost his battle with the institution and its demand that all patients conform to a standard of "normalcy" to exist. The Chief physically kills McMurphy, but it is the institution that truly murders him. (The Chief's action is merely an act of mercy.) Yet McMurphy's struggle has not been in vain: he is both protagonist and agent for change. McMurphy's soul, confidence and life spirit have liberated the Chief from his own self-doubt, enabling him to break through both the physical and emotional prisons holding him. McMurphy ultimately triumphs because he enables the Chief to assert himself and his right for freedom.

SPECIAL NOTES

One Flew Over the Cuckoo's Nest was nominated for ten Academy Awards in 1975 and took home the top five: Best Picture, Best Director, Best Adapted Screenplay, Best Actor and Best Actress. (Only two other films have accomplished such a feat: *It Happened One Night* was the first to capture all five top honors and *Silence of the Lambs* was the third.) *One Flew Over the Cuckoo's Nest* won British Academy Awards for Best Picture, Best Director, Best Actor, Best Actress and Best Supporting Actor (Brad Dourif). It swept the top five awards at the Golden Globes besides winning many more awards from critics societies, etc.

The film was difficult to launch, understandably so in light of the depressing backdrop and downbeat ending. Saul Zaentz and Michael Douglas mounted the film independently and United Artists came in to distribute. Despite all this, it was not only a critical success but a box-office success as well.

The screenplay used for comparison is dated July 26, 1974 and labeled "Revised." It is 127 pages long. There are numerous changes throughout, but the basic structure seen in the film is laid out in this draft. Most of the changes involve shadings. In the screenplay, for instance, the aides are presented in a much more menacing light. The first time we meet them, on pages 1 and 2, they are brutally hassling the Chief (called Bromden in the script). In the film, this brutality is cut, relying instead on the situation itself to convey the gross inhumanity of the patients' circumstances.

The film, through casting, more clearly differentiates the patients. In the screenplay, it's hard to distinguish between them; only Harding stands out with his own voice.

The most drastic changes are quite small ones and involve streamlining McMurphy's introduction and making the subtext less obvious. In the screenplay, McMurphy has almost two pages of dialogue with Harding about who is the top dog in the ward. This is cut from the film. Instead, McMurphy is more circumspect during his first time on the floor—watching and trying to figure out the lay of the land on his own. In the screenplay, McMurphy's first interview with Dr. Spivey, laying out the main exposition, is changed. In the script, McMurphy is more obviously trying to convince the doctor that he is crazy. In the film, McMurphy is more clever: he does not say anything about being crazy until the end of the scene when he compares his behavior to what is expected of him at prison.

Most of the group therapy scenes allowed the actors to ad-lib lines to create a more natural feel but the basic thrust in all of these scenes is found in the screenplay. The basketball scenes are slightly altered in the film from the screenplay, but are basically the same, as is the fishing sequence.

There are a number of cuts in the screenplay, especially in the first 40 pages of its translation to film. The end of Act One comes on page 40, corresponding to 30 minutes in the film; roughly, 10 pages have been cut. These are the scenes mentioned above, as well as some dialogue and transitions which are obvious or unnecessary. In fact, the film runs about 10 minutes faster than the screenplay—until the last act. By the time the night supervisor arrives on the ward (page 104), the film has reached the 98-minute mark. In the resolution, the scene in which the Chief decides what to do about McMurphy takes a page and a half; it takes another page to reach the end. In the film, the director affords the scenes the time needed to deepen their emotional impact, taking up six minutes.

15

THE STRUCTURE OF PLANTING AND PAYOFF
Study film: *Groundhog Day*

In great films, all elements feel connected: every aspect, character, incident, thematic concern—from the main exposition to the final resolution—relates to each other and to the whole. This connection is created in the way plot information is managed and in the construction of strong cause-and-effect relationships between the scenes: every scene, every action, every line of dialogue advances the plot to the point where everything will ultimately make sense.

Chapter Six discusses the principles of action in terms of cause-and-effect scene relationships, rising conflict and the use of foreshadowing, the principles which form the basic strategy behind building an effective plot. This strategy can be refined by thinking in terms of planting information within the plot structure that will be used later for specific purposes. This is referred to as planting and payoff.

Planting and payoff are based in causality, as are the other three principles of action, and are most closely associated with foreshadowing because time elapses before the consequences of the set-up are felt (in the payoff). Planting and payoff weave connections through a film, but their real contribution to effective plot construction is in the strengthening of overall dramatic unity by creating specific connections between disparate sections of the plot.

THE PLANT AND THE PAYOFF
The idea of planting and payoff has to do with the details of a story, which can be visually or verbally related to the audience.

A "plant" can be an object, action, place, line of dialogue—anything to set up information which will have a later effect in the plot. Sometimes, the consequence of the plant will lead to a greater understanding of the story or to a credible plot action; other times, it will pay off with a laugh. It depends upon the type of plot being constructed. However, when it occurs, planting and payoff make a plot feel tight.

Informative Planting

The informative plant and payoff, which is the most straightforward type, sets up what is going to happen and what should be expected. For example, in *Diner*, the guys meet Billy at the train station and tell him about the football quiz Eddie plans to give Elyse before they get married; if she doesn't pass, the wedding is off. Sure enough, this is exactly what happens in the second half of Act Two: Elyse flunks the test and Eddie calls off the wedding.

At the beginning of the second act of *North by Northwest*, Thornhill calls his mother and tells her he plans to go to Chicago and find Kaplan. The audience already knows that Kaplan does not exist and so tension rises as we wonder what will happen. Can he make it to Chicago? He does, to find out Eve is working with Vandamm—a payoff. In *The Best Years of Our Lives*, Fred outlines what he wants and what he expects upon returning from the war; one by one, these wants and expectations are dashed.

Planting a Place or Prop

By establishing early in the script a location or object which later plays an important role in the plot, the film's plausibility will be increased. The important location or prop does not simply materialize when needed; its significance must be introduced earlier so when its importance is identified it feels like a natural part of the setting.

In *Witness*, the silo is established in Act Two, when Samuel shows Book around the farm; then, in Act Three, when McFee and Fergie chase Book through the barn, Book uses the silo to entrap Fergie and get him out of the way. *North by Northwest* sets up both Chicago and Grand Rapids when Thornhill meets Vandamm for the first time at the Townsend estate; later, Thornhill goes to both places, the first on his own, the second at the behest of the Professor. In *Diner*, Fenwick's preoccupation with the nativity scene at the church pays off when he discovers the baby Jesus figure is stolen; he strips, then gets into the manger himself. Each of these locations was incorporated into its plot well before it was used.

Objects are planted as props to advance the plot and paid off in almost every film. In the first act in *Chinatown*, the photographs taken by Gittes and his associates appear in the newspaper; then, late in Act Two, they turn up again at the home of Ida Sessions, implicating Gittes in her murder. Gittes also takes a few business cards of Deputy Chief Yelburton (John Hillerman), using one to get past the policeman at the Oak Pass Reservoir and arriving in time to see Mulray's body dragged out of the water.

In the First Act of *One Flew Over the Cuckoo's Nest*, McMurphy notices a group of patients going on a bus trip; in the second act, he sneaks onto the bus and escapes with his fellow patients to go deep sea fishing. In *North by Northwest*, we see that Thornhill's matchbooks have his initials on them (when he meets Eve in the train dining car). They are used as a cute device illuminate a trace of the self-loathing Thornhill seems to feel. However, the matches are used again during the final crisis—this time with a message warning Eve of danger.

In *The Piano*, an attack with an ax is foreshadowed in the Blackbeard play. At the end of Act Two, when Stewart strides down the hill carrying the ax to confront Ada, we know what could happen. In *Rashomon*, the rope, dagger and woman's hat are planted in the woodcutter's account of finding the body; these articles, particularly the dagger, pay off later in the others' versions. (The dagger is the most critical because it plays a role in every version. Even the framing story—the three men at the gate—uses the dagger when the commoner accuses the woodcutter of stealing it.)

In *Citizen Kane*, Jed keeps Kane's handwritten declaration of principles. Jed sends the paper back after Kane has fired him as a reminder of all he (Kane) once stood for. In *Witness*, when Book gives Rachel his gun, he sets up a payoff which comes when he wants to go to town and needs his gun (and she must dig the bullets out of the flour bin).

Characterization and Planting
Planting a character trait early in a film and then developing it through expansion or contrast strengthens the characterization.

This type of character development enhances the plot or can be used for comic effect, paying off substantially either way. In *Diner*, Bagel's respect for Boogie's father is set up early in the film; at the end of Act Two, when Bagel rescues Boogie by paying his gambling debt, the plot development is entirely credible. Also from *Diner*, Eddie's mother, Mrs. Simmons (Jessica James), wants her son out of her house, the focus of a very funny scene in the first act; at the end of the film, this set-up pays off comically when she asks Eddie when he's coming home again.

In *One Flew Over the Cuckoo's Nest*, the Chief plays a deaf mute through two-thirds of the film; the payoff comes when he speaks to McMurphy, showing he's not crazy. Billy's suicide attempts are established in the first half of the film and so his suicide is a dramatic payoff.

Using Character Actions in Planting and Payoff

In great films, dramatic action pays off to enhance the plot and to emphasize character growth. In some films, one character may perform a task, or try to; later, a different character may do the same thing (or similar), emphasizing the second character's growth. In *One Flew Over the Cuckoo's Nest*, early in the second act, McMurphy bets the other patients that he can pick up the sink apparatus in the tub room and throw it through a window to escape. The sink is impossibly big and heavy, and try as he may, he cannot budge it. He walks away defeated but the other characters clearly admire his courage. At the end, after the Chief has smothered McMurphy, he heads for the tub room and picks up the sink, throws it out the window and escapes. This action demonstrates that the Chief carries McMurphy's torch, thus affirming McMurphy's life.

As an example of action used to show character growth, at the beginning of *Witness*, Eli says to Rachel as she leaves for her trip, "You be careful out among them English." At the end, Eli repeats the line to Book when he leaves the farm, showing the change in his attitude toward the policeman.

A simpler, but no less effective, version of planting and paying off is used in *The Best Years of Our Lives*. In the second half of the film, Homer runs into Al at the bank and says he's taking piano lessons from Butch. The payoff comes when Homer demonstrates "Chopsticks" for Al while Fred places his telephone call to Peggy in the background. As Homer plays, the audience watches Fred make the difficult call and feels his pain without hearing him utter a word. The music provides an ironic counterpoint to the actions of the other two men and makes the scene more powerful.

Planting in Dialogue

Of course, the easiest way to plant information is through dialogue. In *North by Northwest*, the scene between Thornhill and his secretary sets up his mother's attitude toward his drinking. The set-up is paid off after he has been arrested for drunk driving and stands before the judge. Even his mother disbelieves his preposterous story.

In *Tootsie*, Julie sets up her attitude about men and her wish that men and women could just be honest with each other during a conversation she has with Dorothy. She offers a specific line as an example, "I could lay a big line on you, but the simple truth is, I find you very attractive and I'd really like to go to bed with you." Later, when Michael meets her at a party, he uses this line on her, hoping for a positive response. But she doesn't respond as predicted and the payoff doesn't come via dialogue; instead she hurls her drink in his face.

In *Citizen Kane*, "Rosebud" is the first word uttered in the film. The audience is reminded of it throughout the film, as the reporter searches for its meaning. The payoff comes in the last scene when the sled with the brand name "Rosebud" is tossed into the furnace.

In *One Flew Over the Cuckoo's Nest*, McMurphy uses dialogue to plant the idea of escaping to Canada with the Chief before their electroshock treatments. When McMurphy returns to the ward after his lobotomy, the chief realizes there is no way he will ever be able to leave the country. The payoff comes when the Chief breaks out and runs away.

In *Chinatown*, the title itself and then a scene between Gittes and Evelyn plant his troubled past in Chinatown. In dialogue, Gittes tells Evelyn that the reason he does not like the place is because once he tried to keep a woman there from getting hurt but he "ended up by making sure she was hurt." To Gittes, the place represents a feeling of doom, of not knowing what's going on even "if you think you do." The ending plays out tragically—in Chinatown—and the last line from one of Gittes' associates is: "Forget it, Jake. It's Chinatown." This final line completes the metaphor begun with the title and developed in the scene with Evelyn that one cannot possibly rectify all that is evil.

The Best Years of Our Lives also pays off its title in a line of dialogue. Toward the end of the third act, when Fred's wife Marie decides she is leaving him, she says, "I gave up my job when you asked me. I gave up the best years of my life. And what have you done? You've flopped!" The title's ironic use in dialogue makes it all the more memorable.

Combining Different Types of Plants
Planting information in different ways—through dialogue, objects, place—and paying off each in a different context makes the information more interesting and surprising.

In *Tootsie*, Van Horn is set up as a lecherous old man through dialogue. But then, Dorothy realizes that she has to kiss him in a scene and is told by April (Geena Davis) that he kisses all the women on the show. A panicky Dorothy tries to address it with Ron, but he puts her off so, during the scene, she slaps Van Horn instead of letting him kiss her on TV, shocking everyone. She takes flak from Ron, but it seems that Dorothy has escaped Van Horn's lips until Van Horn, out of character, welcomes her to the show with a full-lip kiss.

The scene in which Dorothy slaps Van Horn also serves to set up her spontaneity during filming; i.e. she changes lines when she feels she has to be true to her character. (On several occasions, Dorothy changes her lines, developing this action throughout Act Two.) Later, in dialogue, the audience learns that the soap opera must sometimes be broadcast live. At the climax, both these plants come together and are paid off when the party scene on the show must be done live, allowing Dorothy to take advantage of the live-feed and spontaneously "re-write" her dialogue to reveal she is a he.

In *Chinatown*, before the close of Act One, Gittes sees something in the pond at Mulray's house (an action) and hears the gardener say, "Bad for glass," when referring to the water (dialogue). Toward the end of Act Two, Gittes finds the glasses in the pond (a prop) and discovers that the pond is filled with salt-water (information: saltwater is bad for the grass and it also connects to the fact that Mulray was drowned in saltwater). Gittes takes the glasses to Evelyn and accuses her of killing her husband (the glasses are proof). This leads to the sister/daughter scene. When the truth is revealed, Evelyn tells Gittes that the glasses didn't belong to her husband—he didn't wear bifocals (new information). Gittes then meets with Evelyn's father, discovering that Cross wears bifocals.

These incidents are separated by sequences that allow other aspects of the story to develop (characterization, theme). When isolated, they form a chain of causality leading Gittes and the audience to the conclusion that Noah Cross is not only responsible for Gittes' initial set-up with the phony Mrs. Mulray, but for Mulray's death, as well.

Variety in planting information makes the plot less predictable and generates more audience participation by enticing the audience to keep the information in mind and processing it as new developments occur. Viewers will instinctively try to put it all together and determine where the plot is leading. But a great plot continually surprises viewers with new revelations and discoveries which cannot be predicted.

An Irrelevant Plant Becoming an Important Payoff

Another way to disguise a plant and surprise the audience is setting up information which seems irrelevant when it first occurs in a scene, like a throwaway line or an incidental prop. However, in a different context, the plant pays off when it is more fully understood. Again, from *Chinatown*, the "Bad for glass" line used in Act One seems innocuous at first, a throwaway bit of business to make the scene funny (as we laugh at the Japanese gardener's English). Only later, when Gittes finds the glasses and the gardener explains the line does its significance emerge. In another instance, "apple core" means nothing to Gittes in Act One when Walsh tells him of the argument between Mulray and Cross. But in Act Two, when Gittes and Evelyn arrive at the Mar Vista Inn and Rest Home, he understands that the reference must have been to the "Albacore Club," the club Noah Cross owns on Catalina Island.

Mysteries thrive on set-ups and payoffs. The clues have to be factored into the plot throughout its construction and should be paid off at different points to keep the audience engaged in the mystery, even if particular clues seem insignificant or misleading when they first arise. The detective needs to continue finding pieces of the puzzle, even if they lead him to erroneous conclusions before the truth comes out. As the detective tries to figure out the mystery, so does the audience.

Groundhog Day

Directed by Harold Ramis, who co-wrote the screenplay with Danny Rubin (story credited to Rubin), and co-produced with Trevor Albert, *Groundhog Day* tells the tale of a smug TV weatherman caught in a personal time warp on the worst day of his life. The whole film relies on set-ups and payoffs to develop its comedy and meaning. Its structure is fairly simple but the execution is pure genius.

Smug, superficial TV weatherman Phil Connors (Bill Murray) is sent to Punxsutawney, Pennsylvania, to cover the annual Groundhog Day festivities. With him is cheery producer Rita (Andie MacDowell) and smart-aleck cameraman Larry (Chris Elliot). Phil detests the small-town schmaltz and announces this will be his last Groundhog Day. The next day, they cover the festivities and the groundhog predicts six more weeks of winter. At Phil's urging and despite blizzard warnings, the group heads home. (Phil predicts the blizzard will miss them; "I make the weather," he omnipotently proclaims.) All Phil wants to do is get out of town. But on their way out, the blizzard hits and forces them back to Punxsutawney (the inciting incident—16 minutes into the film). Rankled, Phil ditches his two cohorts; he wakes up the next morning to find that it's Groundhog Day all over again.

Incredulous, Phil hurries to Gobblers Knob and tries to convince Rita that something is wrong. He again performs his Groundhog Day routine and makes it through the day hoping it is all a dream—only to wake up once more to that same Sonny and Cher song on the radio. He refuses to do his job; he later tells Rita what is happening to him and asks for help. She doesn't buy his lame excuse for not doing his job. Phil sees a neurologist (Harold Ramis) who sends him to a psychologist (David Pasquesi)—but no one believes him or can help him (Act One climax, 34 minutes into the film).

Act Two begins with Phil at Punxsutawney's bowling alley, where he meets two young drunks, Gus (Rick Ducommun) and Ralph (Rick Overton). With them, he wonders, "What if there were no tomorrow?" He realizes that if there is no tomorrow, there are no consequences. So, the first half of Act Two is comprised of episodes showing Phil going wild: driving a car down the railroad tracks with the police giving chase; putting the moves on a girl; stealing money; and living his Clint Eastwood fantasy.

Finally, he turns his scheming toward Rita. This leads him to a perfect day with her, but he ruins it by pressing too hard to get her in bed. "I could never love someone like you," Rita says, "because you could never love anyone but yourself!" And, she slaps him (the midpoint, 53 minutes into the film).

Now Phil tries harder than ever to duplicate that day, but he fails miserably each time. He grows embittered, kidnaps the groundhog and tries to kill himself, the first of many attempts. But, each day he awakes again, leading him to believe that he must be a god. Phil talks to Rita, predicting what is about to happen and telling her about all the people in the diner; he tells her about herself and convinces her to stay with him for the rest of the day; he amuses her with card tricks and anecdotes. By the end of the night, Phil admits he has been a jerk and that Rita has influenced him with her optimism. She falls asleep with Phil telling her that he loves her. The morning comes, Rita is gone and it is still Groundhog Day! End of Act Two (75 minutes into the film).

Act Three begins with Phil honestly trying to make a difference in the world and improve himself. He brings coffee to Rita and Larry, he reads, takes piano lessons, learns to ice sculpt; he tries to save an old homeless man (Les Podewell); he deepens his TV commentaries with references to Chekhov; rescues a falling child; changes a tire; saves a man from choking. Finally, at the Groundhog Day dinner, Phil is auctioned off and Rita "buys" him. On their date, Phil makes a beautiful snow sculpture of Rita's face and he tells her, "No matter what happens tomorrow or for the rest of my life, I'm happy now because I love you." They kiss. The next morning Sonny and Cher's "I Got You, Babe" fills the room once again, but the deejays' banter is different. Phil wakes up and finds Rita beside him (95 minutes into the film). The film ends with Phil and Rita leaving the inn together, Phil saying, "Let's live here" (at 97 minutes).

Broad movements really define the structure of *Groundhog Day*. The first act sets up Phil as impossibly egotistical then sticks him in the time warp. The first part of the act also establishes Phil's dislike for Punxsutawney and how he wants to get out of town. Phil, in fact, equates himself to God, saying, "I create the weather" (and one might argue that this is the inciting incident because it may be what brings on the Phil's warp) The snowstorm forces them back to town where he continues to behave badly with Rita and Larry. The next section of the film moves the story into Phil's initial responses to the time warp. He's incredulous, but it could be a dream. By the third time around, Phil falls apart and tries to get help from Rita. She tells him to get his head examined. So Phil does just that, but no one believes him. Phil is stuck and Act One ends.

Act Two has three broad movements to its construction. The first deals with the idea that if there is no tomorrow, there are no consequences. Phil breaks the rules and tries to get whatever he wants, including Rita. The second segment shows his depression turning suicidal when he can't win Rita's love. But, he cannot kill himself. He is doomed to relive this day for eternity. This leads to him the thinking that he is a god and his day with Rita. Phil tells Rita he loves her, but only when she is asleep. When he wakes up the next morning, it is still Groundhog Day.

Act Three has two broad movements. Through Rita (at the end of Act Two), Phil is directed to find the best in himself. He reads, takes piano lessons, tries to save a life, tries to make a difference in people's lives. He changes. The second Act Three movement shows Rita's new appreciation of Phil which leads to their union and breaking the time warp.

Groundhog Day would not work as well without the inventive and expert use of planting and payoff. The entire first day sets up the basis for much of the humor which pays off in the plot execution time and again: meeting the large man (Ken Hudson Campbell) in the hallway, finding Mrs. Lancaster (Angela Paton) in the dining room and Ned Ryerson (Stephen Tobolowski) on the street; stepping in the puddle, taking the cold shower, and, of course, the clock playing "I Got You, Babe" every morning—these incidents all pay off in spades throughout the film. The payoffs differ, depending upon Phil's emotional state and where they come in the film. But all of the encounters evolve to varying degrees throughout the plot, increasing their humor and depth. When Phil steps in the puddle three days in a row, it gets a laugh because we remember it so well from the first day and understand how, in the state he is in, he would forget. By the fourth time, Phil dodges the puddle and someone else steps in it, showing us he has remembered and we laugh at the change. Ned Ryerson's final payoff—telling Rita that Phil has bought a lot of insurance from him—is not only funny but it meshes with Phil's transformation.

Humor isn't the only aspect of *Groundhog Day* that relies on set-ups and payoffs. Real pathos comes when Phil tries to save the homeless man. At first it seems like an irrelevant set-up; only later do we realize how important the man truly is. We have seen him throughout the film, so when Phil finally gives him money (in Act Three), we feel this is the payoff—there to mark Phil's transformation and we do not expect anything more. But, late that night, Phil discovers the old man in the alley and helps him, creating very dramatic circumstances. The old man's death surprises and subdues us, for it is the last thing we expect. But it develops even further and, because this is a comedy, we expect a happy outcome. But this is not the case: try as Phil may, he cannot save the old man. "Sometimes people die," the nurse says, and we realize that this film has a lot more to say to us about life than we expected.

Planting in the film is done in various ways: with people (Ned Ryerson, Mrs. Lancaster, the homeless man), information (the storm), dialogue (insurance, the sweet vermouth with a twist, people's backgrounds, Rita's ideas about what to do with one's life), actions (stepping in the puddle, the dishes crashing, Rita's slaps), props (the fudge, the clock/radio). All are used several times over, with different effects.

For instance, Phil sees Nancy (Marita Geraghty) in the diner and asks about her background and the pay off would appear to be their date. But later Nancy has another pay off when Phil, dressed as Clint Eastwood and with another woman, says hello to her outside the theater and she doesn't know who he is. She is used yet again at the end, with Larry and Phil.

Sonny and Cher's "I Got You, Babe" wakes Phil up on every Groundhog Day. But the song really pays off when it plays again at 6 AM, February 3rd, followed by new banal banter from the deejays and Phil's reaction.

SPECIAL NOTES

Groundhog Day provided Bill Murray with the perfect role: a haughty TV weatherman who is brought to an awareness of his own humanity in his own personal "Twilight Zone." *Groundhog Day* was released in 1993 and became an immediate hit, grossing over $70 million domestically.

The screenplay used for comparison is dated April 27, 1992, and contains revisions from March 5 through April 24, 1992; it is 128 pages, with only 2 or 3 "A" pages (the film is only 101 minutes long). The title page reflects the following credits: screenplay by Danny Rubin, final revisions by Harold Ramis. As noted above, the screenplay is credited to Danny Rubin and Harold Ramis, from a story by Danny Rubin (who wrote the original screenplay).

There are many changes in this screenplay from the finished film, too numerous to name individually, though much of the screenplay is intact on the screen, if reordered; however, many scenes have been cut. The major structural changes occur in the opening and first half of the script. The screenplay begins with Phil, Rita and Larry already on the road; the film begins with Phil's weathercast and introduces him to Rita, his new producer. The action in the film proceeds as in the screenplay, but is more streamlined (dialogue with a bartender, business in the diner all cut or trimmed in the film). In the script, the groundhog actually gets loose and runs around on the first day. (This is cut; there are so many minor cuts that page 22 corresponds to 16 minutes of film.) The first act break in the screenplay occurs on page 41; in the film, Act One ends at minute 28 (thirteen pages have been cut). In the screenplay, Phil's encounter with the therapist is followed by a trip to a science teacher and watching a group of school children perform in a play, thus lengthening the section; these are cut entirely from the film.

In the "I live by my own rules" section of the screenplay, there are a few additional episodes, one showing Phil partying all night and another buying a Mercedes with cash. The midpoint in the script comes at page 67; in the film, it comes at about 53 minutes (cutting approximately 14 pages). In the first half of Act Two, the screenplay has Phil breaking the clock on three separate days; in the film, it comes in the second half as he begins to feel more and more lost after Rita's rejections. In the script, scenes showing Phil playing pool, bowling a perfect game and counting the cracks in the sidewalks are cut; instead, the film relies on Phil acing "Jeopardy!" to convey the idea that he has been watching the show over and over. A scene in the script of Phil praying in church is cut from the film. These cuts leave the most essential parts of the story intact, creating a stronger unity in the film. The plot is simplified by focusing on the cause-and-effect relationships between set-ups and payoffs.

16

THE STRUCTURE OF SCENES

Study Film: *Se7en*

Scenes—the basic, individual parts of a story in which a single main point is made or one principal effect is obtained—are the building blocks of drama. A great scene introduces an idea and builds upon it, creating tension and uncertainty over how the idea will evolve or resolve, and leads the audience toward the next scene. During the action, we sit in rapt attention, wondering where the scene is going and what we are going to learn from it. The most unforgettable scenes not only give us interesting character action but reveal to us who the characters really are through the difficult choices they must make. Great scenes contain emotion, which stems not so much from the "activity" of the scene, but from how the activity reveals the characters.

Viewers define favorite scenes as those in which something noteworthy "happens." Screenwriters and filmmakers know that memorable scenes are those in which characters—despite or contrary to what they have said or done so far in the plot—are ineluctably drawn to perform heroically by the force of their personalities. Great scenes are defined not so much by what happens but by what unforgettable characters face in them and how these characters respond.

UNITS OF ACTION

Screenplays are constructed from scenes, building to and falling from a main climax. A scene is a unit of action, a single event or exchange between characters, with unity of time and place, which propels the plot forward toward the final climax and resolution. The organization of scenes comprises the plot which, in turn, moves the story. Whereas the plot is the blueprint from which a film is designed, the scenes are the specific building blocks for that blueprint while the theme is the mortar which holds everything together.

Chapter Six tells us that plot is structured—not random—action. Individual scenes are structured action, too. Action has been used in several capacities throughout this book e.g., the rising action of the middle, the driving action of the full screenplay. The action of a scene shares many of the same ideas with these other uses of the term. Obviously, action is movement, but here we mean it as progression: whatever is happening in a scene is moving the whole story forward.

The action of a scene accomplishes at least one of three goals:
1) It advances the plot toward the climax;
2) It advances the audience's understanding of the main characters by illuminating them through behavior;
3) It advances the audience's understanding of the overall story by providing expository information.
When a scene is properly conceived, all three scene goals relate directly or indirectly to the plot.

Stories are dramatized by showing characters probing, investigating and interacting with other forces in the film. This relates directly to the plot, which should grow out of these actions. Showing something that is important to understanding a character and his motivation relates indirectly to the plot: the audience needs to understand or intuit motivations in order to make sense of the overall story. Finally, another possible scene ingredient is exposition, which is crucial to the plot because it represents information vital to the audience's understanding of the conflict or characters. If too many scenes fail to achieve one or more of these objectives, the plot structure crumbles.

The best scenes utilize some combination of these goals by revealing character while advancing the plot and contributing to the audience's understanding of the story. Good scenes are always true to the characters, even if their main goal is to communicate plot information. In Act One of *Chinatown*, Gittes spots the glasses in the pond, though he doesn't yet know what they are, and exchanges lines with the gardener ("Bad for glass"). This plant of the glasses is inserted clearly for plot reasons but Gittes' actions are true to his character—his response to the gardener, "Yeah, sure. Bad for glass," confirms for the audience his cynical nature. (And the notion of a Japanese gardener helps root us thematically in an historical Los Angeles.)

Film Scenes vs. Theater Scenes

Films, unlike plays and situation comedies, are not made up of fully developed scenes. Films have both more freedom and more limitation.

In theater, the proscenium separates the audience from the play. The audience will accept many theatrical conventions and contrivances, but a play succeeds primarily for two reasons. First and foremost, it succeeds to the extent that the spoken word moves the audience. And second, depending upon the relationship established between the actors and the audience, success comes if the experience is immediate and powerful.

In a movie, the camera sits in place of the audience. Anywhere the camera can fit offers the audience a view of action it otherwise does not have from a theater seat. The camera places the viewer inside a malfunctioning space capsule thousands of miles from earth (*Apollo 13*), in the eye of a tornado (*Twister*) or in the face of raw emotion (*Old Yeller*); it can create a sense of freedom with wide open spaces (*Dances with Wolves*) or a feeling of claustrophobia (*Titanic*); the camera records several different characters' reactions to a brutal incident by the use of the close-up (*Rashomon*); it transcends geography by cutting from continent to continent in seconds (any of the James Bond films). Because most films strive for realism, the close proximity the camera provides on the drama increases the viewer's involvement in the film. The successful film experience then, can be infinitely more intense and visceral than the theater experience because it can take you right into the heart of the drama.

But conversely, this freedom to move anywhere the production budget permits can create certain limitations. No matter how interesting a scene is, it should not play on and on if it does not perform any of the functions described above or it does not conform to the theme. (The average length of a scene in a film is one to four pages). What is important is that the scene fit the rhythm of the whole film.

We expect films to rely more heavily on visuals while plays and sitcoms are allowed wide latitude with dialogue. A filmmaker is not limited only to the visual, however; what characters say and how they say it are also important. But the filmmaker's use of all materials—space, time, color, light and sound—creates and defines the film's world. The visual and aural quality of the medium (space, color, light and sound) and its plasticity (time) can create the appearance of reality or even hyper-reality. While theater scenery and props only suggest reality. As characters in film move through space and time, illuminated to appear saintly or satanic, they conjure specific visual images to create the audience's experience. The more powerful these images, the greater the impact on the viewer because they appear so real and so close. Although a screenplay is more a blueprint than a completed structure, it should provide the inspiration for powerful imagery in order to successfully move the composition from the storyboard to screen.

THE PRINCIPLES OF SCENE CONSTRUCTION

A scene is constructed with a number of different considerations, each contributing to its overall effectiveness. A writer must understand the point of the scene, where the tension comes from, how each scene should progress and how the scene visually looks. In a scene, something should happen which furthers the action of the plot; and at least of one of the three scene goals should be accomplished. Whatever happens should change the previous circumstances in some way, by adding or subtracting something from the situation at the start of the scene. At the scene's end, characters are either closer to their story goals or further away from them. If nothing changes by adding new information to the story or developing existing information, the plot becomes static and the audience gets bored.

One Main Point Per Scene

Every good scene has a purpose. It exists to advance the plot by revealing information or by emotionally impacting the audience. It should have one main point the writer wishes to communicate to the audience. This can be an incident or event in the development of the plot—as when Gittes and his associates discover Mulray and the girl (*Chinatown*) or when Phil, Rita and Larry get forced back to town because of the blizzard (*Groundhog Day*). The point of a scene can be an aspect of character necessary for the audience to understand him, such as Homer confiding to Butch how difficult life is at home (*The Best Years of Our Lives*).

Sometimes, the main point of a scene is to make the audience feel something—to empathize with or be repulsed by a character. Homer jokes with other servicemen about his prosthetic hooks when he signs his name; his self-effacing courage makes us admire him. How he acts with his family and Wilma makes us feel his pain. In *Jerry Maguire*, Bob Sugar lies to Jerry's clients to keep them in his agency, thus making us detest him. The actions in a scene can dramatize the emotional impact on a character. In *Jerry Maguire*, when Jerry says good-bye to Dorothy's son Ray after Dorothy has told him their relationship is over, we see how deeply hurt Jerry is. A scene can show the results of a character's earlier effort to achieve a goal, as when Phil cannot save the old man in *Groundhog Day*. Other times, the point is to move characters closer to each other, as when Jerry and Dorothy go out on their first date.

Other information can be factored into the scene, but not so much that it detracts from the scene's main purpose. Too many important ideas in a scene can compete for audience attention and cause viewers to lose focus on what is truly important. Other noncentral ideas can be addressed in a scene—and should be—but they must complement and not obscure the main issue.

If too many scenes combine ideas of equal importance, the film will seem fuzzy. Great films solve this problem by creating separate scenes for each important point. Even if a character walks from the outside to the inside of a house (in what would seem to be a continuous movement), the different locations can represent a division of the important ideas, thus focusing the points. In *Chinatown*, recall when Gittes arrives for the first time at the Mulray estate, looking for Mulray. The butler leads him to the garden where he waits and spots something in the pond. In the distance, Evelyn approaches on horseback preventing him from digging the object out of the water. When she arrives, he asks to see her husband. They move, to a patio table where the reason for Gittes' visit is made clear—he thinks someone is after her husband and wants to find out who.

Scene Goals

In every film, the protagonist wants something; he has a goal. Will Book save Samuel? Will Joel get the egg back before his parents come home? Will Gittes figure out the mystery? The goal directs the main action of the film.

In every scene, the characters also have goals which direct the action of that scene. (The goal is what the characters want, consciously or unconsciously, within the parameters of a specific scene.) These objectives do not have to be the same as the overall story goal. The character may want information, as in *North by Northwest*, when Thornhill questions the real Townsend at the U.N.; the hero may want to prove something, as in *Groundhog Day*, when Phil demonstrates to Rita why he thinks he is a god.

Sometimes a character's need directs the scene's flow of action. The protagonist may need comfort or prodding, as in *Jerry Maguire* when Jerry wonders why Rod stays with him when all his other clients defected. In *Quiz Show*, Charlie's unconscious need for his own unreflected glory allows Enright to achieve his own conscious objective.

Sometimes a character's goal can be defeated by his own inner problems. In *Casablanca*, Rick's anger conflicts with his need to understand what happened in Paris in more than one scene. Scene subtext deals with these underlying needs. (Chapter Eighteen deals exclusively with subtext.)

In many great scenes, the characters have conflicting wants and needs. The conflict in these scenes is not limited to the protagonist and antagonist; the protagonist often clashes with other characters (who form obstacles and complications to be overcome). Conflict is what makes the scene interesting. In *Chinatown*, Gittes tries to get some information from a snotty county clerk. The clerk is an obstacle that Gittes finally overcomes—by borrowing the clerk's own ruler and ripping out a page from a record book. The conflict and what Gittes does to overcome it make the scene more memorable than if the clerk had been as docile as a lamb.

Some scenes do not rely on conflict between the characters to create tension. Instead, the external conflict established in the prior scenes or the threat of what will happen next can create tension for a scene that might otherwise only reveal character information or give straight exposition. At the beginning of Act Two in *North by Northwest*, there is a scene of a group of people sitting around a table, giving us naked exposition about Thornhill's predicament. Because of the tension and curiosity created in the first 35 minutes, we sit and listen—still to get straight information to understand what's going on. In *Tootsie*, six minutes into the film, as Michael and Jeff walk home from the restaurant, they discuss Jeff's play. Before this, we had seen Michael being rejected for every part he was up for. It makes us wonder—how will he ever be able to put on this play?

Every scene has its own protagonist who directs the action through his specific wants and needs; the scene protagonist is not necessarily the protagonist of the entire film. In *Chinatown*, the first time Evelyn turns up at Gittes' office with her lawyer, she directs the action of the scene; her objective is to sue Gittes for making the photographs public. In *The Piano*, when Baines returns the piano to Ada and sends her away, this is the action that dominates the scene (forcing her to react). In *Quiz Show*, the scene in which Enright tries to convince Charlie to challenge Stemple on *21* belongs to Enright. In *Casablanca*, Ilsa shows up with a gun to get the Letters of Transit from Rick—she commands the action of the scene. In the next scene, which takes place in the same location but a short time later, Rick directs the action when he finally learns why Ilsa left him.

Scene Progression

Just as action in a screenplay builds to the most dramatic point in the climax, the movement within a scene must build from the least important ideas to the most. If the significant point is given at the beginning of the scene, all that follows will be anticlimactic: instead of growth, amplification or development in the drama, there will be a letdown for the audience. Once the main point is made, the scene is effectively over.

Every good scene has a point when the substance or action of the scene begins. It is like the inciting incident of the plot. A few lines of dialogue or a few seconds of visuals may set the scene, but once the catalyst engages, the action of the scene starts; this can be overt conflict, as in a crisis or, more covert, as in a seduction. Within a few seconds of the scene's opening, the action should engage and send the scene toward its the main point: a plot development, character revelation or sometimes just a funny line.

In *Witness*, Book tries to get his car working one night, Rachel beside him, holding a lantern. Finally, he gets the battery to connect and music fills the barn; he has succeeded in his initial goal. But that is not the point of the scene. A golden oldie, Sam Cooke's "What a Wonderful World," plays and he gets caught up in it, whirling Rachel around. Sexual attraction and tension build until finally Eli enters and interrupts them. He scolds Rachel and she leaves. As Eli follows her outside, we learn that she is in danger of being shunned by her community because of her relationship with Book.

This scene progresses by using several levels of conflict. The first is estabished right away, with Book trying to fix the car without the benefit of modern technology. The second is the clash of cultures—Book's world of modern music vs. Rachel's world which forbids it. He beguiles her into dancing, increasing the sexual tension that was present in the beginning of the scene. Both Book and Rachel are acutely aware of the attraction. Then suddenly, Eli enters, reminding Rachel of who she is and driving her from Book. The scene ends with Book and Rachel fully aware of their feelings for one another and also of the obstacles that separate them.

If a scene deals with a character's emotional life, or if it is a love scene, it can take longer to set up and get to its main point; these scenes are often used to provide some breathing room after a scene of action. Generally, they follow very dramatic ones. (Think of the love scenes in *Chinatown*, *Jerry Maguire* or *North by Northwest*.)

Tension in a scene can come from what has just happened or what we anticipate will happen. In *One Flew Over the Cuckoo's Nest*, McMurphy, the Chief and Cheswick sit in a hall outside the electroshock therapy room. McMurphy does not really know what is in store for him but Cheswick does. He moans and struggles as he is led away. McMurphy and the Chief are left alone in the hallway—now comes the revelation that the Chief can really speak. Before the orderlies come for McMurphy, the two talk about escaping to Canada. The tension comes from us as we anticipate what is about to happen to these men. The next scene shows the electroshock therapy and what it does to McMurphy.

The middle section of a scene usually shows the struggle or conflict involved as the scene protagonist attempts to achieve his goal. The flow of the scene may appear to head in one direction but then, as a result of new information or a surprise, it may suddenly veer off on a new course (similar to the plot line of a film). The dancing scene from *Witness* illustrates this.

The most problematic areas of scene construction can be the beginning and ending. Very few great scenes begin with introductions, entrances or exits, instead, they'll cut right to the action. The main questions of each scene—which have to be answered are, where will the tension come from and is it overt conflict or is it subtle? Wherever the tension originates, the scene must develop dramatically (or comedically) to its point.

Visual Actions

Scenes are strongest when they do not depend upon dialogue to communicate their entire meaning. It is the action that creates interest, drama and meaning. Look at how many different layers of conflict are used in the dancing scene from *Witness*: the contrast of the cultures, the sexual tension between Book and Rachel, Eli's sudden arrival. In the scene between McMurphy and the Chief (after Cheswick is led away), the Chief does not suddenly begin talking to McMurphy; it's a simple action—McMurphy offering a piece of chewing gum to the Chief—that leads to the revelation that the Chief has been pretending to be both deaf and dumb. Actions make scenes more interesting and realistic. In *Citizen Kane*, Kane does not tell Susan that Jed has refused the $25,000; instead, he shows the audience when he dumps the torn pieces of paper out of Jed's letter.

Characters involved in physical movement are more dynamic than people just sitting and talking. When Charlie, in *Quiz Show*, comes to his parents' home late at night to find refuge in a piece of cake, he is doing something that emphasizes the emotional state he is in. His father discovers him and the two share a piece of cake as they talk. We wonder if Charlie is going to confide in his father. Will he ask the older man what he should do? The scene ends with nothing truly resolved for Charlie but, for the audience, the bond is deepened between father and son, making the later scene between the two men even more compelling.

The scenes of a plot need to be conceptualized as units of action rather than as windows of dialogue. Each scene should show what the character is trying to accomplish in relation to the main conflict—whether it is developing the actual events of the plot or developing characterizations through the relationships.

Dramatizing a story through actions instead of through dialogue deepens audience involvement. When we watch characters struggle to achieve what they want, we are immediately involved in this active process. We wonder if they will succeed which is a more emotional response than simply wondering about the importance of the information dispensed in the dialogue. When characters do more and talk less in a scene, the audience must interpret what those actions mean, which actively includes the audience in the story. But for viewers to understand fully, the film must provide hints to the actual motivations. It is this active participation in the story that makes a viewer deeply feel for and identify with the characters. When characters tell too much about themselves or the story, audiences tend to tune them out or disbelieve them.

CONSTRUCTION TECHNIQUES

Writing a great scene is a special talent, like having an ear for funny dialogue or innovative action. Some screenwriters are just more naturally inventive and skillful than others. Still, few scenes start out fully formed. Good scenes are the product of careful planning, hard work and reworking. Successful screenwriters tend to utilize particular techniques when composing their scenes. Discovering these techniques can save the novice screenwriter time and anguish.

Starting Off

Before writing a scene, spend a little time thinking about it. Clarify the topic and main point. You need to know:

1) What is the scene's purpose?
2) Who is in the scene?
3) Where will it play?
4) What do the characters want in the scene?
5) What do they need (the subtext) in the scene?
6) What are their attitudes?
7) Where is the conflict or tension coming from?

Clearly, who is in a scene and where it plays seem self-evident. But the screenwriter must go beyond the obvious. Often first thoughts and choices about a scene are familiar or clichéd. So it's important to take time to examine a number of other questions at the onset. Not only must you know which characters are in the scene, but you also must know what their relationships are. Husbands and wives, siblings, employer and employee—all of these groupings may have varying relationships, depending on their back stories or previous scenes in the film. (Not all husbands and wives are loving and not all employers are bossy to their employees. If they are, the characters are generally stereotypes and boring.) Additional characters in a scene, other than the primary participants, can lend values not readily apparent; the main characters can play off minor characters for either comedic or dramatic purposes. Minor characters also can provide a counterpoint to the main characters or can reinforce them. Think about Van Horn and April in *Tootsie* or Martini (Danny DeVito), Taber (Christopher Lloyd) and Fredrickson (Vincent Schiavelli) in *One Flew Over the Cuckoo's Nest*.

A character's initial attitude as he enters a scene can create tension or humor. Is he happy or sad? Has he just had a minor fender-bender or suffered a major bankruptcy? Should our next meeting with the character be influenced by what just happened to him? These are good questions you should ask yourself to see if tension or humor might play well in the scene.

Think Visually

As you approach a scene, always keep in mind how it is going to look on screen. As it plays, try to see it in your mind's eye. What does the setting look like? What is on hand for the characters to use that will make it more interesting and more real? Mentally picture the action as fully as possible. Then think about how you would communicate the scene's important ideas if you didn't use dialogue. Try to find meaningful actions for the characters and audience.

The skilled screenwriter often takes advantage of what is available in the setting for the characters to relate to and use. Giving the characters scenery to connect with or physical props to hold enlivens the scene and increases its level of reality. The gum McMurphy offers the Chief (*One Flew Over the Cuckoo's Nest*), the fish Jerry takes from the sports agency (*Jerry Maguire*), the knife Eddie's mom picks up and threatens him with (*Diner*), all make the scenes feel more real, spontaneous and interesting.

Where a scene plays greatly affects its mood. An open field at dawn, midday or sunset, during summer, winter, spring or fall, yields different interpretations to a picture. (Claude Monet's paintings of grainstacks at different times and seasons demonstrate the effect of light on mood.) In *Citizen Kane*, the journalist Thompson goes to meet Susan Alexander for the first time at night, in the pouring rain; this helps create an oppressive mood.

Writers often don't give enough thought to the setting for a scene; they sometimes use the first locale that occurs to them.

Setting adds color and depth to screenplays. It enhances dramatic value by offering opportunities for the characters to engage in revealing activities. It reflects their emotions. Always consider exactly where a scene should play to maximize the location's contribution to the screenplay.

You should also ask yourself if you have seen this type of scene done before. Determining this before writing can save time and aggravation by eliminating clichés and unconscious imitations. (How many ways can a love scene play under a harvest moon?) Ask yourself if you can do it differently. Try to be as original as possible. Originality and inventiveness surprise the audience and make for a better film.

Of course, before visuals come the words to describe them. Words are the screenwriter's first and only tools. Unlike all other steps in the production of a film, writing is what conveys the imagination in words. The closer words describe the images and characters actions, the stronger the power, excitement and passion a viewer will feel when watching the completed film.

Business

In a scene, the personal actions of a character are referred to as "business." These specific actions might be pouring a drink, eating an apple, fixing a meal—anything people occupy themselves with. Business contributes a number of valuable functions to the overall effectiveness of a film. Day-to-day activities help create a sense of reality on the screen because people seldom engage in head-to-head discussions except in very specific situations. In *One Flew Over the Cuckoo's Nest,* the patients play cards or Monopoly while they interact; that is their business. In *Parenthood,* Karen, Helen and Susan are in the kitchen preparing food for the birthday party; this business contributes to the sense of reality and makes the exposition more interesting to hear. In *Rashomon,* a bit of business is the tramp making a fire to keep warm while listening to the various stories. Actions also lend physical movement to the scene and keep it from becoming static. Since you should think in visual terms, it will help if you keep the characters' business in mind.

A scene which includes business that specifically suits the character helps define that character and gives us clues to his personality. We all know that actions speak louder than words; audiences tend to give greater credence to what they *see* as opposed to what they *hear*. In *Diner*, the way Eddie gets dressed while talking to Billy reveals much about his character besides making the scene more interesting. Homer, in *The Best Years of Our Lives*, is seen shooting a rifle in the garage which shows us that he is trying to reclaim aspects of his life experienced before the loss of his hands. (Cleaning his rifle occupies him so he can avoid dealing with Wilma, thus dramatizing his inner conflict.)

Because of the strong influence actions make on assessing the characters, business should not be considered incidental, nor should it be viewed as just movement. Business should reinforce the characterizations. If a character's business contradicts his dialogue, the scene will make a stronger impression than having him deliver a speech that tells us exactly what he is thinking. If a character wants to hide his emotions but the writer wants us to understand and empathize with him, his business can provide the telling actions. Although dialogue is extremely convenient for expressing inner thoughts and feelings, it often undermines the power of the character and the scene when it tells us too much.

Humor

A writer should consider using humor anywhere it fits naturally into a scene, regardless of genre. However, the humor should be organic to the situation and not merely an excuse to be funny. Jokes which turn the protagonist into a stand-up comedian tend not to advance the action, but rather slow down the story. Effective comedy is not based on quips or mechanical gimmicks—the banana peel is not funny, but the character who slips on it is.

Even the darkest tragedies benefit from a little comic relief. In a serious or tragic work, the writer often purposely uses a humorous scene, incident or remark to relieve the emotional intensity while simultaneously heightening the seriousness or tragic implications of the action. In *Chinatown*, Gittes is told a funny joke by the barber which he uses in the next scene and embarrasses himself; the natives in *The Piano* are used for comic relief when they mock Stewart; *The Best Years of Our Lives*, *Reservoir Dogs* and *Grand Hotel* all have scenes which make us laugh or chuckle.

Humor, of course, can be broad or realistic, light or heavy-handed—it all depends upon your story. Filmmakers David Lean and Ronald Neame worked together on several films early in their careers (*Great Expectations, Oliver Twist, Brief Encounter*). Mr.

Neame is fond of saying that after they identified the point and conflict of a scene, the last thing they would do is determine if humor would fit organically into it. After all, films are entertainment.

Economy

It is an unwritten law that films must move forward: every scene must advance the action, every line must keep sight of the climax. One of the best tools a screenwriter can utilize to help him achieve this momentum is to use an economy of words. Words, descriptions and dialogue must be as focused as everything else in the screenplay. Random descriptions of every detail will only derail the scene. Usually, when setting a scene, the heading provides much implied detail.

```
INT. ARTIST'S STUDIO - DAY
```

This heading gives the reader important details. A line or two of description (i.e., noting blank canvases scattered around the large room or an expensive bottle of cognac lying amidst paint brushes), will give the reader more necessary information. Descriptions should always be kept to a minimum.

Another way to keep screenplays lean is to enter the scene at the latest possible moment. A scene that starts close to the most relevant plot topic dispenses with boring or superfluous material. As soon as its goal is accomplished, the scene should end. Stay away from entrances, exits and introductions. These take up time and contribute little to most scenes.

Se7en

Written by Andrew Kevin Walker, directed by David Fincher and produced by Arnold Kopelson and Phyllis Carlyle, *Se7en* tells the disturbing story of a serial killer pursued by two detectives. It is as suspenseful as it is unsettling and offers a terrific structure holding together action and theme. The individual scenes are masterfully constructed, delivering important exposition while deepening the characterizations and maintaining tension every step of the way. As gruesome and unsettling as the film is, the violence in *Se7en* is not gratuitously shown. The acts of violence are often only suggested; it is the aftermath—when the detectives are picking up the pieces, following the leads and trying to make sense of the violence—that the filmmakers are concerned with.

Se7en's basic structure sets up like this:

Act One introduces Somerset (Morgan Freeman), a meticulous detective with seven days to go before he retires. On a Monday, charged with breaking in Mills (Brad Pitt), an ambitious young detective who just transfered to the big city, Somerset begins an investigation which should be his last. An obese man has been murdered in a ghastly way—made to eat until his insides burst (inciting incident, nine minutes into the film). Somerset immediately suspects a serial killer and wants off the case and he does not think Mills should take it either. The Captain (R. Lee Ermey) does not buy Somerset's scenario but notices the conflict between the two men. He reassigns Mills but leaves Somerset on the case to wrap it up.

On Tuesday, Mills gets his first case: The murder of the city's most prominent criminal defense attorney. Written in blood near the victim is the word "Greed." The Captain tries to talk with Somerset about this crime, but Somerset resists—it's none of his business anymore—so the Captain hands over a new piece of evidence from the first murder. Somerset returns to the obese man's house and discovers behind the refrigerator the word "Gluttony" written in grease with a note that says: "Long is the way, and hard, that out of hell leads up to light." Now Somerset knows the two crimes are connected. He explains to the Captain and Mills his theory about the Seven Deadly Sins; then, he refuses the case. Mills forcefully asks for it and the Captain gives it to him (Act One climax, 24 minutes in). Somerset, though, is unable to sit at home. He goes to the library and methodically researches the Seven Deadly Sins while Mills, in his home, sorts through his crime scene evidence, disorganized and frustrated. Somerset finishes putting together some notes for Mills; he leaves them on Mills' desk. End of Act One, 30 minutes into the film.

Act Two begins on Wednesday. Mills' wife Tracy (Gwyneth Paltrow) invites Somerset to dinner, hoping for a truce between the two men. She succeeds and the two detectives again work on the puzzle (although Somerset assures Mills that he's still leaving at the end of the week). The detectives go to the defense attorney's widow and discover a painting hanging upside down. When they check out the painting, they find it has handprints behind it asking, "Help me." The fingerprints lead them to a suspect (Victor) but the suspect turns out to be another victim,

"Sloth," who was tortured and starved. Angered, Mills feels the killer is playing with them . Somerset tries to calm Mills, telling him that he must divorce his emotions from his work—something that Somerset is expert at doing, but which Mills is not. Then, a reporter snaps a photo of Mills who explodes and curses the man. Somerset walks away from Mills, disgusted.

Tracy calls Somerset, asking if she can talk to him the next morning, Friday. She confides in Somerset her hatred for the city—which are the same reasons he hates it—but she is boxed in because of her husband's work. Also, she is pregnant. Somerset reveals a little about himself. Then he advises Tracy to never tell Mills if she chooses not to keep the baby; but, if she decides to have the child, she should spoil it every chance she gets.

Waiting for the killer to strike drives Mills crazy and again, Somerset tries to calm him. In Mills' furor, Somerset finds a lead. They make a reading list at the library, then take the list to a contact of Somerset's. This leads to the revelation that the FBI monitors the public's reading habits. In an hour, they have a name: Jonathan Doe (midpoint, 68 minutes).

They find the apartment, but argue over barging in. John Doe (Kevin Spacey) turns up and fires at them. The two cops give chase. The killer gets the upper hand with Mills, attacking him but sparing his life. Feeding on his emotions, Mills breaks down the door to Doe's apartment, only afterward thinking of probable cause and paying a drug addict to lie. The search of John Doe's apartment turns up photographs of all the victims, other evidence, but no fingerprints.

Saturday finds Somerset and Mills following up on a receipt from "Wild Bill's Leather Shop" found in Doe's apartment. The proprietor (Martin Serene) identifies Doe as the man who picked up a package the night before and shows them a polaroid of the apparatus. The detectives are called away to the latest victim at a sex parlour, "Lust." Interviews of the surviving victim (Leland Orser) and the sex parlour proprietor (Michael Massee) lead nowhere, and that night Somerset and Mills have a drink. Mills will not buy into Somerset's defeatest world view. The young cop's belief that he can make a difference creates a crisis for Somerset. At home he is unable to sleep. He breaks the metronome he has used to numb himself to sleep with and starts throwing a knife. End of Act Two, 93 minutes.

Act Three starts on Sunday which brings the discovery of "Pride's" crime scene. Somerset decides to stay on the case till it is over. Right on their heels, John Doe enters the precinct and turns himself in. The police have no way to trace who he really is since he has ritually sliced off his fingerprints. He has no history, no idenity beyond John Doe. John offers to reveal the last two bodies only if Somerset and Mills will accompany him. The detectives agree and this leads into the final crisis. They follow John's directions out of the city. During the drive Mills tries to belittle John, but the prisoner gets the better of him as he explains his ideas. They arrive at their destination and wait. A van arrives and drops off a package which Somerset takes and opens, gasping in horror. He runs back to Mills and John, trying to convince Mills to put his gun down. Through dialogue it is revealed that John killed Tracy and her unborn child, and now wants Mills to kill him out of wrath (sin #6) because he (John) is guilty of envy (sin #7). Somerset is unable to stop Mills who shoots and kills John (Act Three climax, 2:02). In the end, Somerset decides to remain a police detective (resolution, 2:04).

Se7en is made up of scenes from beginning to end that create tension and produce suspense. Filmic atmosphere contributes to the sense of foreboding, but individual actions in the scenes and how they fit together as a whole carries the tension. Let's look at four scenes and examine how each contributes to the advancement of the plot and reveals characterizations and exposition to the audience.

Se7en begins by introducing Somerset. It is his story. He wants to quit. Let's look at the first crime scene which shows him in action and introduces him to Mills. This scene starts about a minute into the film, on a man's dead body at a tenement apartment. Somerset listens to a detective give him the details of the murder: a couple was arguing for two hours, nothing new to the neighbors until the shotgun went off. A crime of passion. Somerset responds ironically: "Yes. Look at all the passion splattered up on the wall here." The line establishes his skepticism. Somerset asks if the kid saw it and this causes another detective to reveal how happy the other precinct workers are that Somerset is quitting. Clearly, he irritates them with the questions he asks. They do not know want to consider the human side of the equation. We have seen in the previous scene Somerset is meticulous, now we see in this scene he is thoughtful. At the end of the scene, Mills enters and asks for Somerset.

The main point of this scene is to communicate that Somerset is retiring at the end of the week. In the process, Somerset's way of working, his unusual questioning, is established. The one policeman's point of view toward Somerset establishes ongoing conflict, causing the audience to wonder more about Somerset's character—why has he pissed these people off so much? It also helps us to empathize with him because we, too, might wonder the same thing about the child. Somerset's scene goal is to understand why. He does not understand the violence and apathy. The other detective's goal is to wrap up the case without upsetting himself. Somerset's business in the scene is his looking around for clues to understand what went wrong.

In the screenplay, this scene runs a total of 12 exchanges before Mills enters. In the film, these exchanges have been cut down to five. The following scene outside in the rain begins the story of Somerset and Mills. It establishes the initial conflict between the two men. Somerset wants to take a moment and talk, Mills wants to go right to the precinct and get the feel of things. Through dialogue we learn Mills fought to get himself transfered down state. Somerset cannot understand why and wants to find out (his scene goal). Mills, on the other hand, does not want to consider reasons, he wants to get to work (his scene goal), to the action—to be the hero as Somerset says later in the film.

At the end of a very strong scene sequence leading to the discovery of Victor, Somerset tries to calm Mills down in the slum stairwell. He tries to make Mills understand they have to divorce themselves from their emotions, but Mills states: "I feed on my emotions..." They are interrupted by a photographer who snaps a picture of Mills, causing the young cop to explode and curse the photographer. Somerset watches, appalled. The scene clearly contrasts the two men. Somerset's scene goal is to make Mills focus on the facts of the case and not let his emotions lead them astray. Mills' goal is to vent, to release his emotions. But the real point of the scene is to create a visual and personal connection between killer and cops. First, the audience anticipates the photos landing in the newspaper and making Mills a target for the killer. Later, when the detectives discover John Doe's apartment, Mills finds photos of himself and realizes they let the killer slip away. This personal connection causes the tension to increase even more. We fear and anticipate the very real possibility of the killer targeting Mills in some way.

The last scene we'll consider comes in the third act. John Doe has turned himself in and the detectives have agreed to his terms to find the last two bodies. The two men are getting ready in the precinct house bathroom, shaving their chests for the wires they will wear. The tension of the situation is very high and Somerset is still schooling Mills. He says, "If John Doe's head splits open and a U.F.O. flies out, I want you to have expected it." Mills says he will and they continue shaving. Then Mills wonders, "Hey, man, if I were to accidentally cut off one of my nipples, would that be covered by workman's comp?" The two men break out laughing and it eases some of the tension. The scene ends with Mills trying to tell Somerset something, but unable to.

This scene is a good example of using humor to ease the unrelenting tension established by the rising conflict in the plot. The audience wants not only an ending for the story but to understand why it happened. The intensity of the plot has increased radically, making it difficult to wait to the end. It will take another 20 minutes to reach the final climax. Humor gives the audience a breather, it relaxes the tension now so it can build up again to the climax. Once this scene ends, and the protracted scene sequence begins, tension starts mounting. Due to the grisley nature of the murders and the intelligence and insanity of the killer, the audience knows anything could happen and they expect a trap—just as Somerset and Mills do. This creates the tension for the nine minute car scene when John Doe explains the little he can about his crimes without giving himself away.

SPECIAL NOTES
Se7en met with a mixed critical response when it opened in 1995, but the public could not be put off from seeing it, despite its unsettling nature. It grossed over $100 million domestically and more than $200 million abroad. It was the film that truly established Brad Pitt as a star.

The screenplay used for comparison is dated August 8, 1994, 122 pages with no revised pages indicated. The basic structure is laid out in the screenplay; most of the changes are seen in the opening, the structure of the first act and the resolution.

The opening of the screenplay takes place at a country house Somerset is buying, then shows him returning to the city and the urban decay. The next scene shows him getting ready to go out and this is where the film starts. The first half of Act One builds the same in film and script. But in the screenplay, the coroner gives Somerset and Mills the plastic pieces which sends them back to the crime scene where together they discover the note behind the refrigerator. Somerset tells the Captain they have a serial killer and he wants off the case. The Captain gives in to Somerset and hands the case over to Mills. The film changes this. The two detectives do not get the plastic pieces at the end of the autopsy scene. Somerset still thinks that this is the first in a series of killings just starting, but he has no proof. He wants off the case, but his Captain will not let him off. Instead he reassigns Mills. On Tuesday, Mills begins his murder investigation of the defense attorney without Somerset (in the screenplay, the discovery of the second murder does not come until the start of the second act). The Captain fills Somerset in on the new killing and ends by giving him the plastic pieces. This sends Somerset back to the first house alone where he discovers the note and the word "Gluttony." Now Somerset goes back to the Captain and shows him the connection between Mills' new case and his. Clearly this is the work of a serial killer. He again refuses the case (the climax of the first act). But Somerset cannot just leave it, and so goes to the library to research the Seven Deadly Sins.

After this, the screenplay and film run pretty much the same. A few scenes are changed, either in dialogue or backdrop. But the substance of the scenes and screenplay are the film. The midpoint in the screenplay, when they get Victor's name, comes on page 65 of the script and happens about 68 minutes into the film. The bar scene at the end of Act Two in the film cuts out background Somerset gives about himself and his father, starting the scene with Somerset's line, "You know, this isn't going to have a happy ending." The film also adds important lines by Mills to Somerset in this scene. Mills tells Somerset: "I don't think you're quitting because you believe these things you say. I don't. I think you want to believe them, because you're quitting. And you want me to agree with you, and you want me to say, 'Yeah, yeah, yeah. You're right. It's all fucked up. It's a fucking mess. We should all go live in a fucking log cabin.' But I won't. I don't agree with you. I do not. I can't."

The climax of the screenplay and film play out pretty much the same except for two important details. In the screenplay, Somerset does not put his gun down voluntarily, but threatens to shoot Mills if he does not put his weapon down. It is Mills who returns the threat and makes Somerset throw his gun down.

When Doe reveals to Mills about the unborn baby, Somerset gets ready to throw his switchblade, but Mills shoots him in the shoulder first, then kills John Doe. The actions are changed in the film, but most of the dialogue from the screenplay remains. The resolution in the screenplay takes place in the hospital, then finally showing Somerset come back to work at the precinct. In the film, the resolution plays out at the final crime scene with Mills, in shock, being taken away.

17

DIALOGUE

Study Film: *It Happened One Night*

The previous chapter discussed the various aspects of scene construction except for the most obvious one: dialogue. Dialogue is probably the most prominent part of any screenplay. It must convey important elements of the plot but still work as conversation. Great dialogue gives each character his own individual voice. It should be clear and understandable the first time you hear it, yet also create the illusion of real conversation. In actuality, real conversation, is random, repetitive and often pointless whereas, dramatic dialogue is ordered and purposeful. Often, great dialogue is funny or witty. When we hear a great line, we often wish we were clever enough to have said it.

Some screenwriters have a natural gift for writing great dialogue, for turning a phrase, for using humor or innuendo to deepen the meaning of a film conversation. However, with hard work, a dedicated student can go a long way toward developing good dialogue. He can learn to actively listen to different speech patterns and develop an ear for words. This chapter defines the main function of dialogue in a visual medium, examines what makes it good and presents certain techniques to aid a screenwriter in his pursuit of the perfect line.

THE FUNCTION OF DIALOGUE
The role of dialogue in a screenplay is to:
1) Advance the plot and conflict leading toward the climax;
2) Reveal the characters;
3) Advance the audience's understanding of the story by providing information which can't be shown;
4) Set the tone for the film (especially in comedy).

Film dialogue is crafted within the context of character and conflict. It gives the appearance that this is what a specific character would say in a specific situation, while staying close to the main topic of the film.

Advancing the Plot and Conflict

Film plots grow out of the interaction between conflicting characters; these exchanges involve dialogue. Dialogue makes up the largest portion of a screenplay and of most scenes. When dialogue advances the plot, it relates directly to the conflict, which doesn't mean that dialogue only describes specific plot-oriented details, but that it helps illustrate the progress of the conflict by showing how the conflict affects the characters and what they do as a result.

It's easy to see how dialogue advances the plot in films like *Chinatown* and *Se7en*: clues are found and explained in dialogue and the characters are able to move ahead in their investigations. More specifically, in *Seven*, Mills sees the photograph of the defense attorney's wife (Julie Araskog) with her eyes circled. He shows it to Somerset who thinks the killer might be telling them she is supposed to look at her husband's office, an example where dialogue moves the plot. In *Tootsie*, dialogue is used to fill in character background. Michael is told that someone else on the soap got the part in the O'Neill play that Michael had coveted. Michael sees his agent who tells him no one will hire him because he is too difficult to work with.

> Michael: "Are you saying no one in New York will work with me?"
> George: "No, no, that's too limited...no one in Hollywood wants to work with you either."

This exchange motivates Michael to put on a dress and become Dorothy. From that moment on, almost every scene advances the plot and conflict and dialogue plays a big part in the overall advancement. Michael has problems with Jeff at home, with Ron at work; he must dodge the lecherous advances of Van Horn and stay in character; he must resist his own impulses with Julie while wearing a dress. Dialogue plays a large role in defining Michael's problems as he continues his masquerade.

In *One Flew Over the Cuckoo's Nest*, the therapy session (in which McMurphy learns that the other patients are free to leave

SECRETS OF SCREENPLAY STRUCTURE

the hospital) uses dialogue to advance the conflict and the plot. The scene first shows McMurphy telling the patients they are not crazy. As a result, the other patients openly challenge Nurse Ratched instead of each other. Scanlon (Delos V. Smith, Jr.) asks, "I wanna know why the dorm has to bc lockcd in the daytime and on weekends." Cheswick wants to know why she has taken his cigarettes. The scene builds until it finally explodes, leading to McMurphy, the Chief and Cheswick being taken away for therapeutic punishment.

Revealing Character

What people say—and what they don't—is a primary way the writer defines them. How a person speaks can be very telling about where he comes from, his level of education, and so on. His diction or choice of words provides hints into his deeper nature. In *Se7en*, Somerset chooses his words precisely while Mills does not seem to think at all before he speaks (showing that one man is in complete control of his emotions while the other is at the mercy of them). Their respective dialogue reflects their differences.

Dialogue should be thought of as a function of character. Within the context of film unity, dialogue is action; it should not be looked at as merely a device to tell the story. Dialogue allows the audience to more specifically comprehend the character and distinguish him from others.

Of course, not all characters have deep natures. Consider Avery Bishop's admission in *Jerry Maguire*: "There is a sensitivity thing that some people have. I don't have it. I don't cry at movies, I don't gush over babies, I don't buy Christmas presents five months early, and I DON'T tell the guy who just ruined both our lives, 'Oh, poor baby.' But I do love you." Motivated by Jerry's loss of the number one NFL draft pick, Avery exposes her true soul.

Though physical action is considered the best revelation of character in a film, sometimes only dialogue can expose real character motivations. In *Chinatown*, the only way we can comprehend what the title means is by Gittes telling us. In *Se7en*, John Doe's motivations can only be understood through dialogue, almost 20 minutes of it in Act Three, and we still don't know all we want to know.

When dialogue is the only way to understand motivations, it must be crafted carefully. A speech too precise in its description

264

of past events rings false and loses impact because, in real life, these disclosures are rarely made. The right circumstances must be created for a character to reveal himself. In *Chinatown*, when criticized by the mortgage banker, Gittes says he makes an honest living trying to help people. Evelyn reveals that she was raped by her father only after Gittes has forced it out of her with threats and a beating. When character revelation is properly motivated, it provides a powerful comment on the character—all the more so when it portrays the character in a radically different light from what the audience expects. The Chief finally drops his guard in *One Flew Over the Cuckoo's Nest* and reveals he can talk only after he and McMurphy have been through an ordeal on the ward and face the electroshock therapy. Later, when McMurphy is ready to leave, he wakes the Chief and asks him to join him in an escape. The Chief declines and tells McMurphy why.

> Chief: "My poppa was real big. He did as he pleased. That's why they worked on him. The last time I saw my pa, he was blind and diseased from drinking. And when he held the bottle to his mouth, he don't suck out of it, it sucked out of him till he shriveled up so small that the dogs don't even know him."
> McMurphy: "They killed him?"
> Chief: "I'm not saying they killed him. They just worked on him. The way they're working on you."

Providing Information

Dialogue plays some part in conveying the main exposition (Chapters Two and Twelve describe the nature and importance of expository information), but as a film progresses, additional information is needed. Characters make discoveries about each other and the dramatic situation. Many of these discoveries are visual but they often need confirmation and elucidation through dialogue. Gittes finds the glasses in the pond and draws the conclusion they must have been Mulray's; in dialogue, Evelyn reveals that her husband didn't wear bifocals.

Information can also have to do with a place or a situation. In *Parenthood*, Helen discovers that Julie has married Tod only because her daughter tells her, which is the same way she learns about Julie's pregnancy. In *Witness*, Rachel explains to Book about the Amish:

Rachel: "I should tell you this kind of coat doesn't have buttons. See? Hooks and eyes."
Book: "Something wrong with buttons?"
Rachel: "Buttons are proud and vain, not plain."
Book: "Got anything against zippers?"
Rachel: "Are you making fun of me?"
Book: "No."

Setting the Tone

In film, a sense of foreboding or catastrophe is best achieved through visuals and the drama, not through poetic or overly dramatic dialogue. Comedy, however, relies on humor, funny lines, jokes and gags (visual and verbal). When dialogue crackles with quips and jokes, audiences respond with laughter. It can, in seconds, effectively establish a film's tone. Look at the openings of *Tootsie*, *Parenthood* and *Groundhog Day*. Each one starts with funny or amusing characters or situations illustrated with dialogue. Both Gil and Phil in *Parenthood* and *Groundhog Day* are funny men; *Tootsie*'s Michael is serious, but the situations he finds himself in and his reactions create the humor.

THE CHARACTERISTICS OF GOOD DIALOGUE

Dialogue is not real conversation but rather the illusion of it. As anyone knows who has read a court transcript or taped a college class, the best dialogue is not an edited version of real speech; it is invention, contrived conversation that satisfies the demands of its scene. But it must sound real if it is to work. If dialogue sounds stilted, false, corny, or clichéd, it can destroy a worthy story. Dialogue is at its best when it differentiates characters, when it is clear, when it advances the tension in a scene, when it is to the point but not "on the nose."

Voice

A character's individual voice is one of the most important ways he reveals himself. Voice is more than just how he talks. It reflects where he has come from and where he has gone. It gives an indication of how he thinks, what's important to him and what's not; it gives, to some degree, an insight into of his psychology.

A character's behavior will differ if he is born in Scarsdale or the South Bronx and so will his dialogue. Patterns of speech show where a person comes from, as do accents and dialects. Certain phrases and expressions are particular to specific ethnic backgrounds and classes. Look at the differences between Charlie, Goodwin and Stemple in *Quiz Show*. Or, in *Witness*, the differences between Book's speech and the Amish distinguish their backgrounds and worlds.

Grammar—good or bad—usually clues us in to someone's education; the use of special jargon characterizes occupations; slang often identifies time and place. Understanding and using the special way people talk brings dialogue to life and makes it colorful and real.

Through dialogue, a writer illustrates differences between people. One can be philosophical or literal, make allusions or be direct. Listen to how Somerset and Mills differ in *Se7en*. Jerry Maguire, who went to law school, sounds different from his client Rod, a black football player. Even characters of similar backgrounds often have different speech patterns, depending on their interests and the way they think. Look at the differences between Al and Millie in *The Best Years of Our Lives*. A sense of humor can define one character while the lack of one defines another.

To understand how different people speak, a writer needs to develop an ear for words. As long as a writer works within his own scope, dialogue should not be a problem. But when characters are introduced with backgrounds divergent from his, research becomes a true ally. Research lends authenticity to a plot and milieu, but it also often produces colorful and esoteric language which gives any screenplay authority and brings it to life. Again, look at *Witness* and how language helps define the Amish world.

Simplicity

In a film, dialogue needs to be understood the first time it is heard. You can't rerun a scene in a movie theater and take time to think about it the way you can reread a passage in a book. The audience is listening to the dialogue and must grasp its meaning before the film moves ahead. The best dialogue is usually simple, coming in short, ordered sentences that give the illusion of real speech.

In real life, people tend to talk in short sentences or in sentence fragments, with simple, direct words. They interrupt each other, repeat and overlap. Effective dialogue, however, cannot literally follow these patterns or it will lose momentum and power.

SECRETS OF SCREENPLAY STRUCTURE

Realistic dialogue uses interruptions and repetitions sparingly to emphasize what a character is saying and to show another's reaction, thus adding to the appearance of reality. In *One Flew Over the Cuckoo's Nest*, Martini interrupts and distracts McMurphy and the poker game when he tries to place a bet with a broken cigarette. The interruptions serve to establish that McMurphy is dealing with people who are not right in the head.

Poetic, flashy and complex words and sentences generally confuse the dialogue's meaning and make it hard to follow—whether listening or reading. This doesn't mean that a character should never use poetry or flashy phrases, express complex thoughts or use esoteric language; a character distinguished by verbal cunning or abstract logic would use this type of language. Think of Somerset and John Doe in *Se7en*.

Progression

Just as a scene progresses to its most dramatic point, so should dialogue. Lines must build from least significant to most, exploiting the innate tension such a progression contains. Whether the speech is dramatic or comedic, the principle is the same. The most dramatic or important point should come at the end. ("Jimmy fell and hit his head. He's at the hospital—In a coma.")

In comedy, dialogue develops to a punch line, the funny twist that makes you laugh. A perfect example is found in *Tootsie*, when Jeff (Bill Murray) responds to Michael who refuses to let him answer the telephone for fear whoever is calling might get the wrong impression of idea about Dorothy: "Look, I didn't complain when you kept threatening my life as 'Duke Mantee.' I didn't complain when you hopped around ranting about your hump and pretending this was a bell tower! But I'll be goddamned if I sit here pretending I'm not home because you're not 'that kind of girl!'"

Good writers save the joke until the end of a speech. If it comes at the beginning and the audience laughs, it can get in the way of or conceal important material that follows. Also, in comedy, jokes tend to need a line or two to set up. "It's not like I'm picky," the lady lawyer says. "All I want is a guy who's tall, dark—and has no prior felonies."

Whether it's comedy or drama, the strongest lines often come at the end of a scene to maximize their impact. When McMurphy learns from Nurse Ratched's aid Washington (Nathan George) that he is committed and what it means, it is spelled out in the last exchanges of the scene. In *Parenthood*, Nathan learns that Susan is leaving him when she uses flash cards to get his attention. She holds up a number of cards and he reads: "...this is...(new card) the only way...(new card) I can get your attention..." He stops reading: "Isn't this a little too basic. She's way beyond this." Susan just keeps turning over new flash cards. Nathan continues reading: "I'm leaving you..." He stops reading. "What? You're leaving me?" She holds up another card and Nathan reads: "Yes." The scene ends.

Economy

Many screenplays depend too heavily upon dialogue to communicate every aspect of their story. Film is a visual medium and dialogue does not need to tell the viewer (reader) what he will learn by watching the screen. Therefore, the best dialogue is lean. Brevity is more valuable than amplification, especially in dialogue. The best films rely more on action and the visual aspects of a story than on dialogue to move the plot. Remember, a person's behavior and deeds are stronger indicators of his character than his words. Extraneous words, lines and even whole speeches should be cut whenever possible. As long as clarity is not an issue, these cuts will strengthen the runaway dialogue, not weaken it.

Long speeches work better in novels and plays than in films. Monologues are a theatrical device, not a filmic one. But whenever a lengthy speech is used in a film, there should always be a good reason: it should be used to emphasize character revelation or important exposition, whether dramatic or comedic. In fact, the circumstances surrounding a long speech are often very dramatic. For example, the characters in *Reservoir Dogs* all have long speeches throughout the film, but they occur in tense situations. (Someone has set them up but they don't know who; Mr. Orange is bleeding to death and they don't know if they will get away.) Long speeches generally are not used in everyday circumstances.

A good rule is to examine carefully any passage that runs more than three or four lines—to see if anything can be cut. If a character uses a long speech to explain how something works, it can slow the action. If there is a simpler and more visual way to get the information across, you need to consider it.

"On the Nose" Dialogue

When dialogue is too direct or too clear, it often rings false, especially when it involves an emotional issue. In real life, most people have difficulty expressing emotion; they tend to conceal or deny it. Because film strives to capture the appearance of reality, real-life verbal responses are most crucial when they involve issues which the audience can identify with.

The heart of a great film is its emotional wallop. So emotion must be forced into the open where the audience can identify with the characters who are feeling it. Many unsuccessful films either avoid emotion and conflict in their scenes or are too obvious in their use. Either extreme can jeopardize whatever goodwill the audience may feel on behalf of the film.

The art of scene construction and dialogue involves capturing characters' natural indirection so the audience intuits a deeper explanation for what they see. Audience intuition will be confirmed or proved wrong when the characters force each other to reveal their real motivations. When viewers make the associations for themselves from their own lives and backgrounds, the characters' experiences take on greater significance and so does the film. When characters imply rather than state "on the nose" what they are feeling, it allows the audience to make these associations and connect more deeply with the characters. We know that Fenwick in *Diner* has some real problems because we saw him break windows and stage a car crash to get attention. In *The Best Years of Our Lives*, Homer does not walk into his home and tell his parents how bad he feels—but he acts it; Al is happy to be home, but restless and ill at ease with his wife Millie. In *Chinatown*, Evelyn does not reveal to Gittes that she was raped by her father: she hides it until Gittes forces it out of her. Ada's behavior in *The Piano* tells us that she has some deep emotional troubles but we never find out why she has stopped speaking. All of these characters have issues which are best revealed in action; their dialogue provides a final nuance.

Clichés find their way into almost everyone's speech now and then, and into almost every writer's first draft. The trouble with hackneyed phrases in written form is that they stand out, however common they are in daily speech. The best films turn a cliché on its head. A man might talk about being "strong-armed" by a thug while another might describe the thug's methods as "a little strong in the arm." Instead of using, "Dead as a doornail" try instead, "Dead as a thumbtack." Or consider Daffy Duck's: "Just shows to go you!"

Nonverbal Language
Not all communication is verbal. In a scene, much can be said by the way a character looks at another and through other non-verbal actions or reactions. Remember, in film, the camera sits in place of the audience. By taking us into the face of a character, we can read a reaction as easily as we can understand words. Through the use of action, mood, music, editing, film can amplify small gestures which would otherwise be missed on stage. Nine times out of ten, the action will be stronger than dialogue. However, in the screenplay, the description of the reaction and quality of the action should be succinct. It is better to suggest and imply, rather than be absolute because this gives the reader an opportunity to use his own imagination and allows the actor room for personal interpretation.

TECHNIQUES AND TIPS
To create dialogue that sounds natural and rolls effortlessly off the actor's tongue, there are a few techniques and tips that will assist the beginning writer.

Rough It Out
Once the formal idea for a scene is in mind (and you have answered many of the last chapter's questions), you are ready to begin writing. A good idea is to rough out the scene without censoring any thoughts. It does not matter if the speeches are long and full, if they are too flowery, too direct or too pedantic; it is not yet important whether ideas are repeated and clichés abound. Sometimes the characters just have to speak in order for you to discover the heart of a scene.

Out of these flabby speeches one or two lines will surface and say everything necessary. Save these lines for the most significant places within the scene and cut the others.

Next, look at the dialogue and the scene, word by word. Most of the speeches should be no longer than one or two lines. (At this point, formatting is very important to determine the proper line length. For a complete manual on screenplay format, see *Elements of Style for Screenwriters* by Paul Argentini, Lone Eagle Publishing.) Take out anything that sounds clichéd and look for better ways to express your ideas. Then rewrite. Don't be afraid to juggle the beats of the scene around; use a piece of dialogue at the beginning that was initially written for the end. This may show you that the whole first half of the scene is extraneous and can be dropped.

Read It Out Loud

Always read your dialogue out loud. The best indication of how it will sound is by how it rolls off your own tongue. Dialogue is written to be spoken; it must sound natural. It is totally different than dialogue in a book which is written to be read. (Book dialogue often sounds stilted and unreal when it is read aloud.)

Reading the dialogue out loud will also help you determine if all the characters sound alike. Depending upon how good an actor you are, saying the dialogue aloud can also indicate whether or not the emotion builds through the scene. Acting out the lines will illustrate the emotional points. Listening tells you if your dialogue moves to the most dramatic point or jumps from one emotion to another.

Miscellaneous Tips

Wherever possible, find the specific emotions behind not only the scene but each speech. Actors will do it, so you should, too. The emotion in a scene usually grows or diminishes according to what is happening. If Character A tries to mollify an upset Character B, Character A's actions could instead actually annoy Character B. If the point of the scene is an angry explosion, the speeches should join the actions to show its progression. Grounding each speech on its suitable emotional moorings will strengthen the progression of the dialogue within the scene.

Dialogue is best in face-to-face confrontation. Confrontation is conflict. Whenever characters are in conflict, emotion enters the picture. Emotion makes characters say and do things that calmer heads would not. Emotion always makes things more interesting because characters act (and say things) more unpredictably.

If you listen to the dialogue of people who know each other well, you learn several things about dialogue and interrelationships. First, when addressing each other, they rarely use their names. They already know who they are talking to, so what's the point of calling more attention to it? Who would they be signaling except the audience? If one person wants to emphasize an issue, he might use the other's name, but this would be an exception. When names are used in every other line of dialogue, it sounds clumsy and unnatural. (Listen carefully to the dialogue in the film *Bringing Up Baby* and you hear the two characters use each other's name in almost every other line. Ask yourself if it sounds real.)

In a formal situation, people tend to use names more frequently, and this can be accommodated in the dialogue—to some extent. When a writer overuses character names in dialogue, it is usually an indication that he does not know his creations as well as he should.

When characters are introduced for the first time in a screenplay and film, their names do not have to be used right away in dialogue to make sure the viewer gets them. Names can be held until an appropriate moment—when it comes up naturally in the dialogue. Within the story, there will be a moment when the important characters meet; names can be exchanged at this time. You do not have to be in a rush to label all the characters. In fact, if a few lesser characters are never named in dialogue, the economy of the film benefits. Think of how many people you interact with each day whose names are unknown to you.

However, when several people are talking in a scene, it can be confusing if you don't use names, especially when one character is speaking directly to another. Still, using a name each time a character talks to someone else sounds false. To simplify this situation, use dialogue cues to indicate who the character is talking to:

>   PHIL
>   (to Ed)
>   Hey, let's go!

Or:

>   PHIL
>   (faces Sally)
>   Please, let me go.

These cues show the reader and actor what to do. On film, the viewer sees the speaker physically turn to Ed or face Sally and thereby understands who is talking to whom. However, do not to overuse these cues. If a scene and its dialogue are well-written, the emotion will flow. A good rule of thumb is to keep dialogue directions short and use them only if they add something to the speech that is not obvious.

The words "yes" and "no" are used less than one expects in real conversation. People nod or shake their heads to answer yes or no questions. Therefore, whenever a visual reaction is possible, use it.

This is true for expressing anger as well. Too often writers allow their characters to curse indiscriminately. When these words are used too frequently in dialogue, the dramatic value is lessened. It is better to find actions which express a character's anger than to have a character call someone names. Then, when a character really wants to swear a blue streak, his words will have power.

Soliloquy and asides do not work well in films and they are very hard to pull off authentically. In film, people don't talk to themselves; most times, a soliloquy will seems forced, unnatural. It's better if the screenwriter finds another way to get the information across to the audience. The same is true for the non-sequitur. These are hard to follow (when reading or hearing) so their relevance is often lost.

Another good rule is to always take time to make the film's last line of dialogue count. If the final moment is strong, viewers will leave the theater with something they take with them.

It Happened One Night

Based on the story, "Night Bus" by Samuel Hopkins Adams, *It Happened One Night* was written by Robert Riskin and produced and directed by Frank Capra in 1934. A classic comedy, the first of the '30s screwballs, *It Happened One Night* has spawned many imitations and is one of the best boy-meets-girl, boy-loses-girl, boy-gets-girl films of all time. It tells the story of a spoiled heiress whose desperate bus flight away from her father's clutches to reach her newly wedded husband is derailed by a newshound desperate for a scoop. The dialogue crackles with wit, insults and warmth. Characters from all levels of society are represented. The comedy begins with conflict and does not let up until the climax.

Act One opens with Ellie Andrews (Claudette Colbert), a "prisoner" of her wealthy Wall Street father (Walter Connolly) on his ship in Florida. Andrews wants his daughter's marriage to society aviator King Westley (Jameson Thomas) annulled. But ever-rebellious Ellie jumps ship and swims for shore. She eludes the detectives that her father sends after her and boards a night bus headed for New York and King Westley. Ellie steals the bus seat belonging to a slightly intoxicated Peter Warne (Clark Gable), a reporter from a New York tabloid who has just lost his job, while he argues with the bus driver (Ward Bond). When Peter discovers her, he forces her to share it. At the rest stop, Peter tries to catch a thief making off with Ellie's valise but fails. When he approaches her, she rudely dismisses him until she realizes her valise is gone. Then, when he wants to help her report it to the bus line, she adamantly tells him no, coming off like an ungrateful, spoiled brat. They get back on the bus and Ellie finds another seat but is forced to return to the one next to Peter and awakes the next morning cuddled up beside him.

The bus stops in Jacksonville and Ellie takes off, telling the bus driver to wait for her. Peter overhears. When she returns, the bus is gone but Peter is not. He has found her ticket on the seat and gives it to her, revealing that he knows who she is. She offers to pay him to keep quiet, but Peter pretends to be indignant. He stalks off, then sends a telegram to his ex-editor Joe Gordon (Charles C. Wilson), saying he knows Ellie Andrews's whereabouts but will not give Joe the story (inciting incident, 17 minutes into the film).

That night, Ellie boards the next bus and sits beside a lecherous and annoying Mr. Shapeley (Roscoe Karns). Peter rescues her by pretending to be her husband. A washed-out bridge stops the bus and Peter gets them a room at an auto court for the night. Ellie becomes suspicious of his motives, which creates a crisis for her—until he tells her what he really wants is her story (Act One climax). He strings a line for a blanket that will divide the room—the "Walls of Jericho." Act One ends, 31 minutes into the film.

In the first half of the second act, Ellie grows comfortable with Peter. She roughs it on the road, taking outdoor showers and learning the fine art of donut dunking. Together they pretend to be married and get rid of a couple of detectives looking for her. But when Shapeley figures out who she is, their plans are upset. Peter puts a scare into Shapeley and then ditches the bus with Ellie, knowing that Shapeley will wise up soon enough.

Ellie and Peter spend the night in a haystack where they both become aware of feelings for each other (the midpoint, about 56 minutes into the film).

The conflict between them now takes on a different cast: Peter criticizes her as if he is trying to convince himself of her worthlessness, while Ellie finds herself drawn more intensely to him and what he represents—freedom. In the classic hitchhiking scene, Peter fails to stop a single car, but Ellie flags down a Ford and gets them a ride with Danker (Alan Hale, Sr.), a singing highwayman. Danker stops at a diner, and Peter and Ellie only stretch their legs. Peter finally apologizes to her, just as Danker comes out and drives off with Peter's bag. Peter chases him and runs out of sight, returning triumphantly with his suitcase and the car. Now the two of them head off to New York.

After three days, Ellie's father is worried sick. He withdraws his objection to her marriage to King Westley, which the newspapers then announce. Ellie sees the headlines as Peter gets them a room for the night. As he puts up the "Walls of Jericho" again, it is clear that he is just as upset about returning her to King Westley as she is to be going back, but the blanket dividing them hides their feelings from each other. Ellie, however, finally breaks down and says she loves him. Peter does not know how to respond—he sends her back to her own bed. After awhile, he comes to her to see if she means it but Ellie is asleep. He drives to New York, writes his story and convinces Joe that he's got a scoop. Joe pays him a $1,000, because "a guy can't propose to a girl without a cent in the world, can he?" But back at the auto court, the proprietors have discovered that Peter is gone and they turn Ellie out. She now calls her father. Peter, driving as fast as the Ford will carry him, is overtaken by the motorcade of Andrews and Westley. They pick up Ellie and are already on their return trip to New York before Peter reaches the auto court. He pursues them but they leave him in the dust (Act Two climax, 85 minutes into the film).

Act Three begins with headlines announcing Ellie's return and her upcoming wedding to Westley. Once home, Ellie's father sees that she is different and he tries to find out what's wrong; he even tells her that she does not have to go through with the wedding. Finally, she reveals she is in love with Peter but that he despises her; there is no use in doing anything but marrying Westley. Meanwhile, Peter has contacted Andrews about a financial matter. Ellie tells her father to reward him well, for he took good care of her. Andrews sees Peter before the wedding and learns that he wants only to be compensated for losses amounting to $39.60. Surprised, Andrews asks if Peter is in love with Ellie and finds out that he is. Andrews tries to stop Ellie from marrying Westley, but she does not go for it. The Minister (Neal Dodd) then asks, will she take Westley as her wedded husband? She pauses, then takes off running to the car outside the front gate (Act Three climax, 101 minutes into the film). The film ends with Andrews sending a telegram to Ellie and Peter announcing the annulment and saying the "'Walls of Jericho,' let them topple." The last scene shows the proprietors of another auto camp talking about bringing a couple a blanket and a trumpet. A trumpet blasts and the cabin lights go off as a blanket drops to the floor (103 minutes).

It Happened One Night's structure is as simple as it is timeless and archetypal, providing us with an amusing look at the battle between the sexes. The first exchange of dialogue, between Ellie's father and his ship's captain, immediately sets the tone of the film.

Andrews: "Hunger strike, eh? How long has this been going on?"
Captain: "She hasn't had anything yesterday or today."
Andrews: "Send her meals up regularly?"
Captain: "Yes, sir."
Andrews: "Well, why don't you jam it down her throat?"

In the exchange above, conflict between Ellie and her father is immediately established, though we do not yet know what the conflict is about. Throughout the film, conflict livens up the dialogue between all the characters and it helps advance the plot. For example, once she hits the road, Ellie steals Peter's seat and insults him, creating an initial dislike.

The characters reveal themselves through their dialogue. Peter tells Ellie of his hopes and dreams; Ellie admits that she has never been free to do what she wants. We learn that Peter has hopes of writing a novel; that Ellie's father thinks she is too clever for the detectives.

The film's cast includes characters from the highest to the lowest social classes and the dialogue reflects this. Each scene, each speech is crafted for the character speaking the lines. Ellie's voice is different from Peter's which is different form Shapeley's; the bus driver's speech defines his attitude and is differentiated from Peter's, as noted in the following exchange on the bus:

> Peter: "Look here, partner. You may not like my nose. But I do. I always keep it out in the open where anybody can take a sock at it, if they can do it."
> Driver: "Oh, yeah?"
> Peter: "Now, that's a brilliant answer. Why didn't I think of it? Our conversation could have been over long ago."
> Driver: "Oh, yeah?"
> Peter: "If you keep that up, we're not going to get anywhere."
> Driver: "Oh, yeah?"
> Peter (exhausted): "You got me. Yeah!"

Peter is a bit grandiloquent, reveling in words; the bus driver is a monosyllabic ape.

Or, consider Shapeley's speech when he puts the moves on Ellie:

> Shapeley: "You know, there's nothing I like better than to meet a high-class mama that can snap back at you, 'cause the colder they are, the hotter they get! That's what I always say, yes sir! When a cold mama gets hot, boy, how she sizzles!"

We can see that each of these exchanges or speeches builds to its payoff. They are sharp, to the point, clear, yet hardly on the nose or clichéd. There are moments in the film when words fail our two heroes. For example, the end of the haystack scene relies upon the characters' attitudes to communicate nonverbally what they feel.

SPECIAL NOTES

It Happened One Night took home the top five Academy Awards in 1934, Best Picture, Best Director, Best Screenplay, Best Actor and Best Actress. Oddly enough, it was a picture that had trouble getting actors. Capra wanted Robert Montgomery to star, but he turned the role down. Louis B. Mayer, upset with Clark Gable (an MGM contract player) for wanting more money, agreed to lend the young star to Columbia Studios to punish him. Claudette Colbert originally turned down the role of Ellie until they offered her $50,000 to do it. The comedy did not make enough money in its opening wcck at Radio City Music Hall, New York, to be held over for a second, but word of mouth spread. Critics praised the fast-paced farce while undergarment manufacturers complained that sales plummeted when Gable took his shirt off and was seen wearing nothing underneath! The demand for the film was so great that Radio City Music Hall brought it back for a return engagement where it then played to packed houses.

The screenplay is published in "Great Film Plays," Volume 1, edited by John Gassner and Dudley Nichols. It is not presented in true screenplay format but rather in play format (stage), and divided into nine parts. Essentially, everything in this version of the screenplay is in the film. Lines have been changed here and there, a few were edited out. The beginning has been changed, but the film version is included at the end of the screenplay. A section of the script which is not in the film is noted by brackets, indicating the cut.

The dialogue crackles on the page, with all the characters given their own voice, from the colloquialisms of the boy on the bus to King Westley's formal English. Most of the characters are funny and their dialogue reflects their humor—in the insults they throw and the jokes they tell. King Westley is the only character who does not have a sense of humor, allowing him to play Andrew's straight man in a number of scenes.

18

THE SUBTEXT OF MEANING

Study Film: *Thelma and Louise*

In great films, a subcurrent runs just beneath the action of the plot. This subcurrent helps maintain tension when crises, climaxes, and plot action slows. Its presence, just below the surface of a scene, keeps the action unpredictable and the audience wondering where it will all lead. In *Witness*, when Book and Rachel dance in the barn, a subcurrent of sexuality charges the scene and we anticipate them getting together. Eli arrives and dashes our expectations, but the subtext of the scene has kept us riveted.

Scene subtext is what is going on below the surface, the undercurrent of emotions and thoughts that truly motivates characters to behave as they do. Most of the time, scene subtext connects to characters' needs, just as the theme does. Scene subtext sometimes relates to what characters consciously know and want, yet cannot reveal. Subtext answers the question why characters act the way they do and say what they do, before and after plot requirements are considered. For the plot to work, certain actions and dialogue must unfold. But it the layer of meaning beneath plot mechanics that goes to the heart of who our characters really are and why they find themselves in a particular story.

Directors and actors bring a scene to life by determining the feelings, thoughts and motives which lie behind the actual words and actions of the characters. If the screenwriter lacks sufficient understanding of the subtext, his scenes will lack purpose and power. Action that's all on the surface frustrates the director's and actors' task of "realizing" the scenes—making them life-like. A screenwriter who understands subtext provides clues in the script for the director and actors on how to dramatize for the audience this deeper level of the story.

Subtext is not what you write, it's what you write around. It is the deeper level of the story which cannot be told so much in words but must be shown in actions, often the slightest reaction in an actor's face.

THE ROLE OF SUBTEXT

In real life, people rarely say what they feel. More often, they try to hide what bothers them, their personal weaknesses, minor transgressions. They lie about small troubles and big problems. They may be motivated to protect the ones they love or themselves, to gain power or prestige. Because motives are hidden, they often are misperceived. When this happens to us and problems arise, many of us find ourselves playing the episode over in our minds, trying to figure out what exactly happened and why. The reason? We are astounded, and usually upset, that our real desires remain so obscure; that we have been so misunderstood. What has happened is our words and deeds have miscommunicated our true intentions. The real meaning of our actions, the subtext, has been muddled by a pattern of behavior designed to show what we want. But what we are really after is to get people to give us what we need, even if we are not conscious of what that is.

In drama, where art imitates life, our aim is to illustrate a version of reality. The ultimate goal, however, is not to be obscure, but to be understood, to avoid the confusion between needs and wants in everyday life. Filmmakers must know their characters better than they know themselves, and then demonstrate this knowledge through subtext by letting the audience see what the characters really need beyond what they say they want.

One way to understand this elusive concept of subtext is to see it as the connection between how the characters, moving according to their desires in a story, end up with what they have needed all along. Cinderella doesn't need a day off work, new slippers or to take revenge on her family. She needs recognition that comes through love. Somerset, in *Se7en*, does not need to give up and retire, though he says so throughout the film. What he really needs is to overcome his own apathy, to feel and care what happens to others. We see this as *Se7en* progresses: Somerset becomes more emotionally involved with Mills. As a result, he keeps changing his retirement date until at the end, he decides to stay on. Phil in *Groundhog Day* does not just need to get out of the time warp; he must discover his own humanity to find love and give to meaning his life. Jerry in *Jerry Maguire* does not need to get back on top in the sports agency world. He needs to learn how to truly connect with people to make his life more fulfilling.

Subtext is used to reveal needs which cannot easily or honestly be told in words. These needs surface in the character in the form of feelings and thoughts which generate motives for his actions. In Chapter Four we defined need as the unconscious motivation of a character. The protagonist has a conscious goal and an unconscious need. If a character's unconscious need contradicts his stated goal, the scene will play differently than if conscious and unconscious minds are in total accord. Need comes from a deep part of a character's psyche and he may not be conscious of it. But it is this need that drives the subtext, reinforces the theme and tells us if the plot resolves happily or tragically. Why does Charlie allow himself to be used by Enright in *Quiz Show* when it causes him to abandon the very ideas his family stands for? Because he needs his own renown and not the reflected glory of his famous father.

Of course, a character's need is not always unconscious. Gittes tells Evelyn in *Chinatown* that when he worked for the DA's office, he tried to help a woman in Chinatown and failed. Gittes is conscious of this fact, but his need to help is what propels him in helping Evelyn in her own mystery.

The character's need may be the real motivation behind everything he does in a film. But for the audience to grasp this fact, the need must be shown in a credible fashion.

Feelings, Thoughts and Motives

To understand a story, certain exposition must be overtly presented to the audience, while other pieces can be implied. Subtext compliments exposition, conveying feelings, thoughts and motivations which are too complex to tell in words, but are crucial to understanding the plot. If this information is clumsily handled or just dumped in the audience's lap, viewers doubt its veracity the same way you might be skeptical of a person who tells you his life story at the drop of a hat. A character's motivation carries more weight if it is closely guarded—the way true motivations in life are. When viewers have to figure out for themselves why characters do something, they become active participants in the dramatic process. When they identify with characters and feel what they are feeling, they are in an active relationship with the material, and this participation leads to a deeper involvement in the film.

Filmmakers allow the audience glimpses or hints through subtext of the protagonist's and other characters' true feelings and motivations. In *One Flew Over the Cuckoo's Nest*, Nurse Ratched never says that she will stand for nothing short of complete control over her ward. But the way she deals with the patients, especially in their therapy sessions, shows how she divides them from each other to maintain her authority. Her power over the group is threatened when McMurphy enters the ward and, through his leadership, starts to bring the men together. After the first therapy session disintegrates into screaming and name calling, the subtext of a searing look between McMurphy and Nurse Ratched (which the director focuses on) illustrates the undercurrent of tension beginning.

Subtext and Theme

The overall subtext of a great film often carries a direct relationship to its theme. It is an important means for getting the main ideas across when it is unrealistic to do so in dialogue. In *Witness*, subtext defines the theme about how violence in our society affects us. We see it most specifically when Book cannot control his emotions and hits the local punk, contrasting with how the Amish handle the problem. In *Citizen Kane*, subtext defines the theme: the search for love and the impossibility of finding it if one is not loved and taught to love early in life. We see it in the subtext of every scene where Kane essentially is trying to get people to love him, most of the time by using his money. Leland talks about Kane's need for love, but never gets to the reason why his friend is incapable of giving it. It takes the audience's discovery of the meaning of "Rosebud" to understand.

When a story is successful, audiences feel satisfied. When we feel satisfied, usually something is working on a deeper level. Even if we can't completely articulate what the story is about, it has touched us in some unaccountable way and feels true. When we take the time to analyze it, to think about the characters, their feelings and motives, we are able to make associations that allow the deeper meaning of the film to emerge.

THE EMOTION BENEATH THE LINES

Dialogue is the most obvious way to reveal emotion. "I'm really mad," one character says. "I feel sick at heart," says another. Yet dialogue is rarely the best way to express emotion unless it is forced out into open conversation.

As already noted, when characters tell too much, especially regarding difficult issues, audiences often do not assign the matter the proper emotional weight. Seeing a character avoid a troubling issue or unable to find words to express his feelings engages our interest more deeply, because we do the same. When our curiosity is whetted, we watch more carefully to see what the character will do.

In a scene, the emotion carrying the lines may:
1) Support the dialogue;
2) Contradict the dialogue;
3) Have little relationship to the dialogue.

Emotion Supporting Dialogue

When emotion supports the dialogue, the lines reflect what the characters feel. It's hard for characters to suppress happiness. Their feelings will effect attitude, actions and easily filter into the conversation. When McMurphy arrives at the hospital and the corrections officer unshackles him, he jumps with joy and kisses the officer. He does not need to say "I am happy" for his actions tell us. When Grusinskaya in *Grand Hotel* returns from her triumphant stage performance with an armload of flowers, her whole attitude is transformed to one of sheer happiness and her dialogue reflects this.

Anger also is hard to control and it ultimately infiltrates what is said. In *Parenthood*, when Gil arrives home after quitting his job, he is in a fit. He barks at the children and then at his wife, upsetting her and making her angry as well.

Depression is hard to hide, too. In *Jerry Maguire*, Jerry does not tell Rod in the airport lounge, "Gee, I'm depressed." Instead he drinks and whines, asking, "What are you doing with me, Rod?" His dialogue and actions convey what he is feeling.

Emotional states find expression in the dialogue, but in elliptical ways. Characters talk around the cause of their emotional condition. Even though the dialogue in these scenes is an indirect indication of mood, it must still be properly motivated, usually in a progression of emotions within the scene or in the progression of scenes that builds emotion.

Emotion Contradicting Dialogue

When emotion contradicts the dialogue, it forces a character to take action contrary to what he says. He might feel fear and want to hide it; he might be angry, yet unable to show it. In *North by Northwest*, Thornhill is very upset with Eve when he finds her after the crop-duster scene, knowing she set him up. Yet he cannot reveal his anger. His dialogue contradicts how he really feels and increases the tension in the scene.

In *The Best Years of Our Lives*, Al's dialogue on his first day home with Millie disputes the clear uneasiness demonstrated in his actions, the same way Homer's words at home with his family and girlfriend deny his true feelings.

Emotion With Little Relationship to Dialogue

Sometimes the whole point of a scene is the emotion it contains. The scene is needed to move the audience one way or another, to get them to better identify with or oppose a character as he approaches a problem. In *Tootsie*, Dorothy accompanies Julie to her father Les's farm for the Easter holiday. The three of them chat and sing into the evening. What's being said really isn't important, but the warm feeling created between the characters is.

In *The Best Years of Our Lives*, Al convinces Fred to break off his relationship with his daughter Peggy. As Fred makes the telephone call, Homer arrives and drags Al over to hear the results of his piano lessons with Butch. Al's conversation with Homer and the music that follows are really incidental. What is important is that the audience witness Fred's call, which they do not hear, and experience the emotion and pain behind it.

Jerry Maguire is packed with moments designed to make the audience feel for the characters. Jerry driving in his car trying to find a song to sing along with after signing Cush helps us feel his pleasure. The dialogue when Jerry brings presents to Ray isn't important, but Ray kissing Jerry before he leaves on his date with Dorothy is and moves us.

Remember, to the audience, your characters are initially strangers. Do not expect viewers to believe everything they say. The audience needs to see your characters in action and under pressure to discover who they really are. Only in conflict is one's true self revealed. Viewers evaluate a character from what he does and what he says. The audience measures the truthfulness of the dialogue and weighs it against the actions performed to discover who each character really is.

REVEALING THE SUBTEXT

In scenes, emotions motivate characters to act the way they do. The protagonist may be cool and calm, but if all the characters reflect this same indifference, the scenes will not be very interesting. In most scenes, someone is in the grip of an emotion, positive or negative, and this emotion influences the scene, how he behaves and how others interact with him. It also creates interest. It appeals to the voyeur in us as we witness a person feeling joy and making a fool of himself or feeling anger and saying things he will regret. Because the audience needs to become aware of the emotions and thoughts affecting the story, filmmakers externalize them.

Dialogue

The characteristics of good dialogue have already been discussed in Chapter Sixteen. Asking a few questions about the characters and the emotion can help insure the dialogue strengthens the subtext of a scene. First determine:

1) What must be said in the scene?
2) What can be implied?
3) What doesn't need to be said at all?

Then ask:
4) What is the key emotion motivating the characters in this scene?
5) How will their respective emotions specifically affect the characters? What would each do? For example, would one suppress or vent his anger?
6) Would the character have a conscious or unconscious strategy for dealing with this emotion? Would he use understatement or directly contradict his feelings in words?
7) Is there a progression or a shift in the emotion experienced by a character?
8) Where is the conflict or tension coming from?

Any or all of these questions help clarify what is going on beneath the surface of the characters present. Once these questions have been answered, you should have a better idea of the subtext and how a character might react to it. Dialogue may be the perfect way to bring the subtext out into the open. But if it's not, consider the following:

Physical Attitude

Physical attitude refers to a character's outward disposition or mood representing his inner emotional state. Body language, facial expressions, gestures fall under this heading. All provide hints to a character's state of mind. Film is interested in showing what a character is like as opposed to telling us what he feels as novels or short stories do. Screenwriters cannot rely on the narrative to explain complex personalities, emotions and attitudes. They must figure out ways to show the audience what is really going on through the external action which can be seen and heard.

When McMurphy is introduced at the beginning of *One Flew Over the Cuckoo's Nest*, everything about him—from the clothes he wears to his physical attitude—suggests he is cocky and self-assured. In *North by Northwest*, Thornhill's smug confidence and unflappable demeanor are established not only in his dialogue but in the physical pace he sets for himself and his secretary. In *The Best Years of Our Lives*, Homer cannot look his parents in the eye when he comes home and later it is hard for him to maintain eye contact with Wilma.

Screenwriters describe the characteristics of what the audience sees and hears in the action and parenthetical directions. Most of the description is of an external state. In the following portion of a scene, note the words used to describe the characters' attitudes in the action and parenthetical directions.

```
EXT. TURNER HOUSE - DAY

Indignant eight year-old ALEC TURNER, dark
eyes flaring, grips the collar of his old
black dog, KING. Across the grass, towers
forty-five year-old nerd, TED McCLURE. He
stands over a recent brown spot on his
immaculate lawn.
```

```
                    McCLURE
                  (red-faced)
        I am sick and tired of
        finding a new pile of crap
        on my way to work every
        morning!


                    ALEC
        King didn't do it!


                    McCLURE
        Look at this!


   He points with real emotion at the small
   circles of dead grass.
```

"Indignant" and "dark eyes flaring," describe the eight year-old boy Alec. He "grips" his dog by the collar as he defies his neighbor. Does he grip the dog to hold him back or for protection? The "nerd" McClure "towers" over brown spots on his lawn. The parenthetical cue clues in the reader to McClure's attitude: He is "red-faced" with anger.

This short introductory description sets the tone for the rest of the scene. As long as the lines maintain or build on the established level of intensity, few additional cues are needed. If, however, the scene reverses and builds to apology, then cues to indicate a turnaround must be used.

Business

In Chapter Sixteen we discussed the business of a scene in a number of ways. Business helps establish a sense of reality. It creates movement which makes more visually interesting images for the film. Characters are further defined by what they do within a scene. This business of doing relates strongly to subtext. If every action a character takes represents a true portrait of who he is, his action speaks more truth than the dialogue of ten characters telling us how they feel about him.

In *Chinatown*, Gittes reveals his snobbery by pouring cheap booze for Curly, saving his better stuff for his higher class clients. In *Diner*, the way the guys eat and joke about the food while they talk into the night communicates their camaraderie and makes the scene more realistic. In *Citizen Kane*, Susan does jigsaw puzzles to pass away the time, showing her boredom with her life. In *Se7en*, Somerset's meticulous folding of the napkin during the after dinner conversation with Mills and Tracy reveals his fastidious nature.

Atmosphere

Atmosphere also helps to reveal the characters' inner states by reinforcing them. Weather, time of day, nature, all can contribute to creating a mood which reflects the interior world of the characters. Using the external world to mirror the inner emotions felt by the characters helps the audience share in the characters' experiences.

In *Citizen Kane*, when we meet Susan for the first time, rain pours outside her dreary establishment. When Thompson enters, he finds her drunk. The rain serves to heighten her feelings, and ours, of desolation. In both *Rashomon* and *Se7en*, rain plays a large part in creating the oppressive mood dominating the characters and the films.

In *Jerry Maguire*, Jerry's "breakthrough" ("breakdown") happens at night. The nocturnal mood reinforces the dreamlike state Jerry had to be in to create his "Mission Statement." And in *Risky Business*, Joel loses his virginity in a nighttime, dreamlike encounter.

It is interesting to note that in films like *Tootsie* and *Parenthood* rainy days hardly ever intrude upon the stories. Comedies tend to be sunny and light. This is not to say comedies never use rain. In *It Happened One Night*, rain plays a part in the comedy situation, but not really in establishing the mood of the films.

FURTHER READING

An important book to read about subtext is Constantin Stanislavski's *An Actor Prepares*. It gives important insights into how actors work. Additionally, these same methods can be used by screenwriters and directors to discover the emotions motivating characters and thus provide a key to the subtext in a scene.

Thelma and Louise

Thelma and Louise arrived on the cover of *Time Magazine* and at the box office in spring of 1991. Written by Callie Khouri, directed by Ridley Scott who co-produced with Mimi Polk, it tells the story of two women's run from the law after a deadly encounter with a would-be rapist.

Act One begins in Arkansas with Louise (Susan Sarandon), a waitress, and Thelma (Geena Davis), an oppressed housewife, getting ready to go fishing in the mountains for the weekend. Both women are psyched, but Thelma neglects to tell her verbally abusive husband Darryl (Christopher MacDonald). Louise neatly packs while Thelma takes everything but the kitchen sink, including a gun which she turns over to Louise in case they run in to psycho-killers or bears. The two women take off, but Thelma whines and cajoles Louise into finally stopping at a roadside bar for some fun without her husband. Thelma convinces Louise to let her hair down and then she encourages the attention of a slick good old boy, Harlan (Timothy Carhart, 11 minutes into the film, inciting incident). After some dancing and drinking, Louise heads off to the bathroom, saying they are leaving when she comes out. Thelma becomes nauseous from her drinking and dancing and allows Harlan to steer her outside for some fresh air. In the parking lot, Harlan becomes a vicious predator, physically and verbally abusing Thelma while he readies to rape her. Louise arrives with a gun and forces him to stop. He continues to verbally assault them, causing Louise to snap. She shoots and kills Harlan (20 minutes into the film, Act One climax). Thelma and Louise drive off, hysterical with fear. Thelma wants to go to the police, but Louise figures no one will believe them because of the way Thelma was acting all night with Harlan. She hopes no one will connect them to the murder. However, Arkansas State Policeman Hal Slocumb (Harvey Keitel) has been alerted to the body. Questioning witnesses, he finds out about the two women Harlan was hitting on, though no one believes they could be responsible for his death (end of Act One, 26 minutes into the film).

Act Two begins on the road as Louise realizes they need money and checks into a motel to think. She calls her boyfriend Jimmy (Michael Madsen) and asks him to loan her $6700. He thinks there is another man, but she assures him there is not and he agrees to wire her the money. He will send it to Oklahoma City. On the road, Louise reveals she is going to Mexico, Thelma will have to decide if she wants to come.

Thelma meets J. D. (Brad Pitt), a young cowboy who needs a ride, but Louise refuses to give him one. Back home, Slocumb finds Louise's name through her car registration and tries to learn about her. This leads Slocumb to Darryl and he discovers Thelma took a gun with her, the same calibre which killed Harlan. But Darryl refuses to believe Thelma could be mixed up in the trouble. Meanwhile, the women use backroads to avoid state troopers, trying to find the best route to Mexico without going through Texas. They cross paths with J. D. again and Thelma begs and moans until Louise agrees to give him a ride.

When they get to Oklahoma City, Louise goes to pick up her money and discovers Jimmy has brought it himself. Louise tells J. D. to hit the road, gives Thelma the money for safekeeping, then goes to talk to Jimmy in his motel room. Worried about another man, he wants to know what is going on. Louise refuses to tell him and he starts to explode until she tells him she will not tolerate that. Jimmy apologizes, then gives her an engagement ring. He does not want to lose her. But it is too late for them. J. D. turns up at Thelma's room and wins her over easily, even revealing that he is a robber on parole. He demonstrates his criminal technique which turns to their making passionate love. This is contrasted with Louise and Jimmy who realize their relationship is at an end. The next morning, Louise says good-bye to Jimmy in the diner. Thelma shows up just after he leaves, floating on air. She is a different person after her night of passion and Louise is happy Thelma has finally been screwed properly—until she realizes Thelma left J. D. alone in the room with her money. They rush back, but J. D. is gone and so is the $6700 (midpoint, 67 minutes).

Louise is devastated, the money was her only hope. Thelma is apologetic. With nothing else to do, she forces Louise to get going and tells her everything will be all right. Now Thelma goes into a different gear. She robs a market, using J. D.'s technique, but the whole thing is caught on videotape. Slocumb and his FBI counterpart Max (Stephen Tobolowsky) show it to Darryl who is stunned. When Jimmy arrives home, Slocumb picks him up for questioning. Louise starts to realize running was probably not the best response to what she did, but knows now they probably can't even prove Harlan ever touched Thelma. J. D. is caught and questioned by Slocumb and we discover Slocumb is sympathetic to Thelma and Louise's plight. Thelma calls Darryl, but understands immediately his line is bugged and she hangs up. Louise calls back and asks to talk to the man in charge. Slocumb gets on the line. He wants to help her. He knows about Mexico.

Louise hangs up, furious with Thelma for telling J. D. their plans. Louise drives through the night, knowing they have passed the point of no return.

The next day, Thelma and Louise pass a lewd trucker they encountered on the road before and he continues his antics. Thelma figures out that Louise was raped in Texas and that's why she won't enter the state, but Louise refuses to confirm it. A trooper pulls them over for speeding; Thelma pulls a gun on him and locks him in his own trunk, allowing them to get away. At the next rest stop, Louise calls Slocumb again, attempting to convince him the incident was an accident. Slocumb knows what happened to Louise in Texas and wants to help them, but they have to come in. If they do not, they are being charged with murder. Thelma cuts the line, but the FBI trace has worked (Act Two climax). Slocumb convinces Max to let him go with the FBI to protect the women from harm (end of Act Two, 101 minutes into the film).

Back on the road, Thelma worries that Louise is giving up. She thinks Louise has options, but now Thelma has robbed a store. Thelma knows she cannot go back to the lives they have led. Neither one can, they have come to a new level of awareness or consciousness. They encounter the lewd trucker again and this time entice him off the road. They confront him about his behavior, but he just does not get it. At gunpoint, they demand an apology; he refuses to give one. Louise shoots out his tires, but he still won't apologize so the girls shoot his giant silver gasoline tank and it explodes. They drive off, but are spotted by a squad of police cars and followed. They manage to lose them, but wind up lost themselves at the edge of the Grand Canyon. They back up, but now the police have caught up with them, along with the helicopter carrying Slocumb and Max. They are told to surrender, but Louise gathers up the policeman's gun and ammunition, telling Thelma she is not giving up. Slocumb wants to go talk to them, but Max holds him back; they are armed and dangerous. Thelma suggests to Louise that instead of fighting they just keep going. Louise understands her meaning and the two women hug. Louise floors the gas pedal and the car takes off, sailing over the cliff (Act Three climax, 2 hours and 4 minutes).

On the surface, *Thelma and Louise* tells the story about two women who strike back at a violent, sexist world with violence and then go on the lam. There is no denying that the film deals with these issues, but the subtext of the film illustrates an awakening to a new awareness of themselves and their lives. The first act sets up friends Thelma, who is submissive with her husband and naive about life, and Louise, a somewhat suspicious and brittle woman. Thelma is so cowed by her husband she does not even dare tell him about her plans with Louise and leaves him a note instead. Louise, too, has an unsatisfactory relationship with her boyfriend. She has left town without telling Jimmy because she is upset with the direction of their relationship. These are women in dysfunctional relationships, who do not feel in control of their lives and have to resort to deception to try and get what they want.

The crisis with Harlan changes everything. He is the extreme version of masculine power who says to women, "what you want does not matter." It is the same message both women have been getting from their men, now put into a physically abusive context. Empowered by the gun in her hand, Louise snaps. She cannot take Harlan's abuse anymore and shoots him. With this action, Louise crosses a line with society—a male-dominated society that she clearly feels will not support her. Her response is to run and take Thelma with her. But this crisis will be the reason both women wake up to their unfulfilling and unsatisfactory lives.

Once on the run, the Thelma and Louise evolve to new awarenesses of themselves. At first they are both hysterical, but once calmed down, Louise comes up with a plan to get money and head to Mexico. Thelma could decline to go with Louise, if she could think for herself, but she is so used to having someone else do it for her that she goes along with Louise's plan. But there may be more to her decision to stay with Louise than on the surface. Perhaps Thelma can't face going home to Darryl after what just happened. God knows she could never tell Darryl about it and find any comfort in him.

Louise realizes by running she is leaving her old life behind and this gives her a new resolve. She can put her foot down with Jimmy and be honest with him since she is saying good-bye. This puts their relationship on a new ground, but it is too late; it has taken this crisis for Louise to realize her own power. For Thelma, it is after she has been sexually awakened that she begins to change. This awakening makes her realize all the more what she is missing at home and supplies her with additional motivation to rob the market because she does not want to go back. None of these ideas is overtly stated in dialogue, but clearly are the forces motivating the characters' actions.

When Thelma and Louise reach the end of the line, the women have realized that going back to their old lives is no life at all. Instead they choose death over life as it was and life in prison. Louise tells Thelma early in the film, "You get what you settle for," and repeats the line several times. But the line applies to herself as well, though she might have denied it; she settled for what she had with Jimmy which did not make her happy. Now it is too late to settle anymore. They have become too aware of what they have missed by not asserting themselves in their lives and the consequences have grown too great.

The main conflict establishes Thelma and Louise as fugitives with the authorities after them. Subtext helps illuminate why Louise does not trust the system will help her. First, the way she overreacts to Harlan—shooting him dead for a stupid affront—shows Louise's reaction is fueled by a deep-seated anger. Later, Louise refuses to go through Texas to get to Mexico, even though it is the quickest route of escape. Even more, she will not discuss what happened to her there. At this point, the audience realizes Louise was most likely raped and shot Harlan because she identified him with the man who raped her. Whatever happened, it has deeply affected Louise, making her distrustful and unhappy. Near the end of the film, Thelma says what we know already—that Louise must have been raped—and the audience listens hoping for some further illumination. But even now, Louise refuses to admit it. Like Ada in *The Piano*, we do not need to learn exactly what happened; it is enough to know the incident was traumatic.

Another way subtext contributes to understanding why Thelma and Louise will not trust the system is that every able-bodied man they meet along the way is either an outright pig or a cheat. Starting with Darryl who verbally assaults Thelma, to Harlan who physically assaults her, right down to J. D. who steals their money after sweet-talking Thelma, the men they encounter are selfish and conniving. Even Jimmy, who is presented sympathetically, has a moment when he turns abusive and breaks things because Louise will not tell him what's going on. The subtext contained in this moment indicates that Louise's relationship with Jimmy has not been free of violence. Louise, stronger now because she knows the relationship is over, refuses to tolerate his actions and he immediately apologizes. Now they relate more honestly, but ironically it is too late.

The only sympathetic male presented in the film is Slocumb who is truly concerned about the women. But Thelma and Louise never meet him face to face; he is only a voice on the phone and so they fear they cannot trust him, based on how the system treated Louise in Texas.

Subtext is used throughout the scenes. When we meet Darryl he is criticizing Thelma who acts as if his words do not bother her but we see the hurt in her eyes. Later, when Harlan arrives and puts the moves on Thelma, he does not say he's sexually interested in her, but his actions do. When he is assaulting Thelma and she is crying and trying to stop him, his rage mounts. Here the emotions clearly support what is going on. When Louise appears with the gun, Harlan is shocked, but trying to conceal it until his bravado takes over and he insults them.

Another scene loaded with subtext is when the State Trooper (Jason Beghe) pulls them over and takes Louise back to his car. Louise is clearly frightened, but cannot show it. She tries to act calm until she is saved by Thelma. In fact, Louise is so nervous that when Thelma tells her to shoot out the officer's radio, she blasts the commercial radio and Thelma has to tell her specifically to shoot the police radio.

Another aspect of the film subtext handles well is presenting how Louise sees her future. In the aftermath of J. D.'s theft, Thelma takes charge, leaving a devastated Louise in the car while she enters the market to rob it. Louise sees old women staring at her through a trailer window. She holds their look for a moment, then, shaken, glances away and attempts to fix her makeup. She gives up and throws her lipstick out of the car. This one moment subliminally communicates to the audience what Louise sees in her own future: loneliness and old age.

Another scene which hints at change is when Louise trades her jewelry, including the ring Jimmy gave her, to the old man for his hat. The jewelry and ring are personal possessions and can be seen as parts of herself she is casting off, getting rid of as she transforms. She receives in return the old man's cowboy hat which better represents her new persona—outlaw. In another way, the trade also raises the tension for it presages suicide in the way people often give away their personal affects before killing themselves.

Another sequence that adds to the overall meaning of the

film comes late in the second act when Louise drives at night through the canyons. Thelma falls asleep and Louise stops the car. Taken with the desert's nighttime transcendental beauty, she gets out. In this moment, Louise seems at peace, as if she has accepted her fate. In the following scene, Thelma—clearly in an altered state of consciousness from the events, drinking and sleep deprivation—breaks down, both laughing and crying as she recalls the look on Harlan's face and says he deserved what he got. Louise tells her, no, what she did was wrong. In this moment we understand that Louise has come to grips with what she has done, but knows she cannot undo it. She can't go back, but can only go on.

SPECIAL NOTES

In 1991, *Thelma and Louise* rode into theaters and set off a wave of controversy. Many men saw the film as sexist and criticized it for male-bashing. More women responded to heroines' predicament, the characters and the irony of the story. But all who saw it agreed it was an effective example of filmmaking, despite its controversial nature and virtually invented the new genre of female buddy picture/female road picture.

Thelma and Louise is not considered a huge box office hit, grossing a little over $40 million domestically, but it garnered six Academy Award nominations, including two for Best Actress (Geena Davis and Susan Sarandon), Best Director (Ridley Scott) and Best Original Screenplay (for Callie Khouri who won). Reportedly, when Ridley Scott met with Callie Khouri the first time about directing her screenplay, he told her that he knew the ending could not be changed. He understood the film's theme perfectly.

The screenplay is 134 pages long and not dated. There are indications that the screenplay has been revised, but only for minor line changes. Most of the dialogue is contained in this script, although many scenes are shortened. Structurally, the screenplay and the film are very similar, but there are a number of changes. The biggest changes are several scene deletions developing Slocumb in his official and personal capacities. One scene introduces Slocumb's wife as he asks her if she could shoot another person. The scene shows Slocumb trying to understand if Thelma or Louise could actually kill someone. Other scenes in the screenplay show police procedures as they deal with information the audience already knows from watching the two heroines. These scenes play as transitions in the screenplay to help the reader keep tabs on official side of the story, but are not necessary. In film, bringing other characters up to speed with events the audience has already witnessed often feels redundant. Transitions can be simpler and shorter because audiences more quickly comprehend a story told visually. For example, in the film, Jimmy returns from seeing Louise to find the police waiting for him; there is no scene of his police interview. The screenplay plays two police interviews with Jimmy.

In the screenplay, the phones in both Darryl's and Jimmy's homes are tapped and their houses occupied with police; Max is at Darryl's and Slocumb is at Jimmy's. Many of Slocumb's and Max's scenes are played over the phone. The film consolidates these positions, using only Darryl's house and allowing these scenes between Slocumb and Max to play face to face.

There are a few scenes between Thelma and Louise while they are on the road which have been cut or edited. Several of the scenes which play in the film while the women are driving are written in gas stations or convenience stores. A few scenes have been reordered in the middle. A segment in the second half of the film, after Thelma has robbed the convenience store and Slocumb and the others have viewed the video tape of the robbery is followed by Thelma and Louise putting distance between themselves and the crime scene, passing the tanker truck on the road and setting him up. Next, Jimmy arrives home and is picked up by the police. The following scene shows Thelma and Louise at the gas station, Thelma buying provisions while Louise trades her jewelry to an old man for his hat (this scene is not in the screenplay). Next, they are on the road trying to decide if Thelma could say the incident was self-defense and Louise saying no one will believe her. Then J. D. is brought in for questioning with Slocumb. This segment is made up of five separate beats.

In the script, after Slocumb and the other authorities have viewed the tape of Thelma's robbery, Jimmy returns to his apartment and finds police waiting inside. Next, J. D. is picked up on a country road by state troopers. The following scene shows Thelma and Louise driving, putting distance between them and the scene of their last crime. The next scene shows Slocumb questioning Jimmy, then we're back to the women to set up the tanker truck, and then to Jimmy with more questions from

Slocumb about J. D. Another scene shows Thelma and Louise driving, discussing a prison movie and setting up what they think they have to look forward to if caught. A short scene shows J. D. arriving at the State Police building. Then we're back to the women discussing whether Thelma could claim self-defense and Louise saying no one would believe them. Next, J. D. meets Slocumb for questioning. There are ten beats in the script.

The segment in the film is not only reordered but drastically edited and shortened. The order of the film scenes creates a stronger momentum by reducing the amount of intercutting between the separate characters' parts in the story. The editing and reordering of these scenes streamlines and focuses the plot on the two women, where it belongs.

More is made of Louise and Jimmy's relationship in the screenplay than in the film, and several scenes have been changed to make them a little more somber and realistic and a number have been cut. In the script, their scene together in the motel room has them say marriage vows to each other. In the film, Louise knows the relationship is over and they talk about how they first met. There is no sense that they still have a relationship as in the screenplay which even gives the reader the impression that Louise may have told Jimmy what happened before they part. In the script, Louise calls Jimmy before she talks to Slocumb for the last time on the phone. This is not in the film.

Another strong scene in the screenplay which is altered and made stronger in the film plays at a gas station. It has Thelma realize that Louise was raped in Texas before she talks about what happened to Harlan. In the film, the two halves of the scene are inverted and play while they are driving at dawn. In the film scene, Thelma is clearly on the edge, both laughing and crying, as she remembers what happened and how Harlan looked when Louise shot him. This is what leads to her figuring out that Louise was raped in Texas. The scene builds with Louise refusing to confirm Thelma's suspicions, and is followed by the state trooper pulling them over for speeding.

There are a number of other changes. The final chase sequence is filmed differently than it is written in the screenplay. A number of the obstacles are added, including the one which traps a police car under the bridge. The sequence is lengthened by having Thelma and Louise get away briefly, only to find themselves boxed in by the edge of the canyon. The film adds Louise saying she is not giving up as she gets her gun and ammunition before Thelma suggests they just keep going over the cliff. Slocumb gets out of the helicopter (a typo in the scene heading says he's in the helicopter) at the very end, but does not run after the women in the screenplay.

There are a number of character shadings we see in the film which are only suggested in the script. After J. D. steals Louise's money, the film shows Louise is devastated, unable to cope. Thelma takes complete charge in J. D.'s aftermath. In the screenplay, Thelma takes charge in the hotel room, getting them going again, but Louise is more pissed off and alert. She tells Thelma now she will have to sell the ring that Jimmy gave her. Things don't seem so hopeless for her, she just does not want to sell her ring since it symbolizes her marriage to Jimmy (the scene in the screenplay, cut from the film) and Thelma tells her she won't have to. When they are on the road, the screenplay reads as if Louise is driving, not Thelma. When they pull into the parking lot of the convenience store, Louise complains about their cash flow and sits in the car and tries to fix her makeup while Thelma goes inside. The film shows Thelma behind the wheel, smoking like Louise, while Louise sits in a daze. Thelma pulls the car into the parking lot and leaves the shattered Louise. Very slowly, Louise becomes aware of herself sitting there. She tries to pull herself together, but then sees the old ladies watching her. A look of fear overcomes her and she tries to fix her makeup only to give up. Then Thelma comes running out after the robbery. This little but telling bit of business with the old ladies is suggested in a scene later in the script, but cut from the film where Louise admits to her fear of growing old alone. The film uses the brief scene at the right moment and makes more poignant to communicate what it takes two pages of funny dialogue to communicate.

In a scene in the film but not in the screenplay, Louise trades her ring with her other jewelry to the old man for the hat. It makes us think, and rightly so, the ring was not expensive and would not provide Louise with much in the way of money if she pawned it. More important, the relationship signified by the ring is over. This scene, like the one mentioned above, contributes to the mood of the film. Another scene not in the screenplay, but in the film which adds to the overall mood and rhythm, has Louise stopping the car at night in the desert and get out. The quiet of this scene, in contrast to the noise and action of what comes before and after, helps create a feeling of calm in the middle of the storm. Though ambiguous, the scene creates a feeling that Louise has found her center.

Thelma and Louise is a terrific example of how screenwriter, director, cast and crew contribute to making a very good screenplay a terrific film.

BIBLIOGRAPHY

Allen, Woody, *Four Films Of Woody Allen*, Random House, New York. 1982.

Argentini, Paul, *Elements of Style for Screenwriters*, Lone Eagle Publishing, Inc., Los Angeles, California. 1998.

Aristotle, *Poetics*, translated by Richard Janko. Hackett Publishing Company, Indianapolis/Cambridge. 1987.

Armer, Alan A., *Writing the Screenplay*. Wadsworth Publishing Company, Blemont, California. 1993.

Blacker, Irwin R. *The Elements of Screenwriting*. Collier Books, MacMillan Publishers, New York. 1986.

Egri, Lajos, *The Art of Dramatic Writing*. Simon & Schuster, New York. 1960.

E. M. Forster, *Aspects of the Novel*. Harcourt, Brace and World, New York. 1927.

Gasser, John, and Nichols, Dudley, editors, *Great Film Plays, Volume 1 of a New Edition of TWENTY BEST FILM PLAYS*. Crown Publishers, Inc., New York. 1959.

Halperin, Michael, *Writing Great Characters: The Psychology of Character Development in Screenplays*. Lone Eagle Publishing Co., Los Angeles, California. 1996.

Johnson, Lincoln F., *Film: Space, Time, Light and Sound*. Holt, Rinehart and Winston, New York. 1974.

Jung, C. G., *Psychological Types*, a revision by R. F. C. Hull of the translation by H. G. Baynes. Princeton University Press, Princeton, New Jersey. 1971.

Kael, Pauline, *THE CITIZEN KANE BOOK, Raising Kane*. Limelight Editions, New York. 1984.

Kazan, Elia, *A Life.* Anchor Books, New York. 1989.

King, Viki, *How to Write a Movie in 21 Days.* Harper Perennial, New York. 1988.

Lawson, John Howard, *Theory and Technique of Playwriting and Screenwriting.* Garland Publishers, New York. 1985.

Lucey, Paul, *Story Sense.* McGraw-Hill, New York. 1996.

Lumet, Sidney, *Making Pictures.* Knoft, New York. 1995.

Perret, Gene, *How to Write & Sell Your Sense of Humor.* Writer's Digest Books, Cincinnati, Ohio. 1982.

Richie, Donald, editor; *RASHOMON*, Akira Kurosawa, director; Rutgers Films in Print. Rutgers University Press, New Brunswick, CT and London, England. 1987.

Seger, Linda, *Making a Good Script Great.* Dodd, Mead & Company, New York. 1987.

Shaw, Harry, *Concise Dictionary of Literary Terms.* McGraw-Hill Paperbacks, New York. 1972.

Stanislavski, Constantin, *The Actor Prepares,* translated by Elizabeth Reynolds Hapgood. Theater Arts Books, New York. 1948.

APPENDIX:
WHAT SHOULD I RENT TONIGHT?

Deciding what to rent at the video store for the night can be a daunting task, especially when one ventures away from the "Current Releases" shelves. On the box of each video, a blurb invariably advertises that this film is a classic, the best in its genre. How often has this proved true? You can lug along a video guide, but when you don't want to browse through the 20,000 titles to find out what's good, start off with a copy of this list.

Below are over 300 films, from various genres, whose stories are well told and pretty much stand the test of time because of it. This list is broken down into categories for those looking for something specific. Although some films overlap genres (for instance, *Annie Hall* is nonlinear and a romantic comedy; *East of Eden* is a drama, family drama and a coming of age story), I have listed them only their main category. Each category has 10 films. I have included titles other than the obvious choices for each genre, films many missed but are worth viewing. In all cases, I've tried to pick films whose stories hold up regardless of the stars or special effects. It is the integrity of a story—that is, its underlying structure—that best determines how well a movie holds up and continues to feel fresh throughout the decades.

Obviously, each title on this list cannot please everyone. But for each film that is not to your liking, there will be at least ten which will stand the test of time and multiple viewing. Enjoy.

ACTION
Die Hard ('88)
Dirty Harry ('72)
The French Connection ('71)
Guns of Navarone ('61)
The Last of the Mohicans ('92)
Lethal Weapon ('87)
The Professionals ('66)
The Road Warrior ('81)
Runaway Train ('85)
The Seven Samurai
   ('54-Japanese)

ADVENTURE
The Adventures of
   Robin Hood ('38)
Apollo 13 ('95)
The Bounty ('84)
The Crimson Pirate ('52)
Deliverance ('72)
Flight of the Phoenix ('65)
The Man Who Would Be King
   ('75)
Romancing the Stone ('84)
Scaramouche ('52)
The Treasure of the Sierra
   Madre ('48)

BIOGRAPHY
Amadeus ('84)
Bonnie and Clyde ('67)
The Last Emperor ('87)
Lawrence of Arabia ('62)
My Brilliant Career
   ('79-Australian)
My Left Foot ('89)
Patton ('70)
Pride of the Yankees ('42)
Shine ('96)
Spartacus ('60)

BLACK COMEDY
Bullworth ('98)
Clerks ('94)
Dr. Strangelove or: How I
   Learned to Stop Worrying
   and Love the Bomb ('64)
A Face in the Crowd ('57)
Investigation of a Citizen
   Above Suspicion ('70-Italian)
Jamon, Jamon ('92-Spanish)
Network ('76)
Prizzi's Honor ('85)
The War of the Roses ('89)
The Wrong Box ('66)

COMEDY
Arthur ('81)
Back to the Future ('85)
Back to the Future Part III ('90)
Dumb & Dumber ('94)
The Full Monty ('96)
Groundhog Day ('93)
Hail the Conquering Hero ('44)
The Russians are Coming, the
   Russians are Coming ('66)
Some Like It Hot ('59)
Tin Men ('87)
Tootsie ('82)

COMEDY/DRAMA
All About Eve ('50)
As Good as it Gets ('97)
City Lights ('31)
Educating Rita ('83)
Flirting ('90)
Jerry Maguire ('96)
Meet John Doe ('41)
My Life as a Dog ('85-Swedish)
Terms of Endearment ('83)
Turtle Diary ('85)

COMING OF AGE
Breaking Away ('79)
East of Eden ('55)
400 Blows ('59-French)
Gregory's Girl ('81)
King of the Hill ('93)
The Last Picture Show ('71)
Metropolitan ('90)
Rebel Without A Cause ('55)
The Reivers ('69)
A Room with a View ('86)

DRAMA
Another Woman ('88)
Casablanca ('42)
Gentleman's Agreement ('47)
The Grapes of Wrath ('40)
Midnight Cowboy ('69)
One Flew over the Cuckoo's
  Nest ('75)
On the Waterfront ('54)
Rain Man ('88)
Straw Dogs ('71)
The Sundowners ('60)

ENSEMBLE FILMS
The Best Years Of Our Lives
  ('46)
Children of Paradise
  ('45-French)
Day For Night ('73-French)
Diner ('82)
Dinner At Eight ('33)
Grand Hotel ('32)
Husbands and Wives ('92)
Nashville ('75)
A Night to Remember ('58)
Parenthood ('89)

FAMILY
Beauty and the Beast ('91)
The Black Stallion ('79)
E.T.: the Extra-Terrestrial ('82)
The Lion King ('94)
Never Cry Wolf ('83)
Old Yeller ('57)
Time Bandits ('81)
Whistle Down the Wind ('39)
The Wizard of Oz ('39)
The Yearling ('46)

FAMILY DRAMA
Accidental Tourist ('88)
All Fall Down ('62)
Dominque and Eugene ('88)
Five Easy Pieces ('70)
Hud ('63)
Ice Storm ('97)
I Never Sang for My Father
  ('70)
In the Name of the Father ('93)
Mr. and Mrs. Bridge ('90)
A Tree Grows in Brooklyn
  ('45)

FANTASY
Beauty and the Beast
  ('46-French)
Clockwork Orange ('71)
Defending Your Life ('91)
The Ghost and Mrs. Muir ('47)
Gremlins ('84)
Gremlins 2 The New Batch
  ('90)
It's a Wonderful Life ('46)
Metropolis ('25)
The Tin Drum ('79-German)
20,000 Leagues Under the Sea
  ('54)
Wings of Desire
  ('88-West German)

FARCE
All of Me ('84)
Arsenic and Old Lace ('44)
The Bank Dick ('40)
Dirty Rotten Scoundrels ('88)
Duck Soup ('33)
His Girl Friday ('40)
The Producers ('67)
Raising Arizona ('87)
A Shot in the Dark ('64)
To Be or Not to Be ('42)

FILM NOIR
After Dark, My Sweet ('90)
Body Heat ('81)
Crossfire ('47)
The Killer ('89-Hong Kong)
La Balance ('82-French)
Out of the Past ('47)
Sunset Boulevard ('50)
Sweet Smell of Success ('57)
Touch of Evil ('58 — the '98,
    director's cut)
White Heat ('49)

FOREIGN DRAMA
L'Avventura ('60-French/
    Italian)
Amarcord ('74-Italian)
Babette's Feast ('87-Danish)
Death in Venice ('91-Italian)
Fanny and Alexander
    ('83-Swedish)
Jean de Florette ('86-French)
Mamon of the Spring
    ('86-French)
The Man Facing Southeast
    ('86-Argentine)
Mephisto ('81-Hungarian)
Persona ('66-Swedish)
The Return of Martin Guerre
    ('82-French)

HORROR
The Birds ('63)
The Bride of Frankenstein ('35)
Dead Ringers ('88)
The Exorcist ('73)
Frankenstein ('31)
Jaws ('75)
The Innocents ('61)
Poltergeist ('82)
Psycho ('60)
Rosemary's Baby ('68)
The Silence of the Lambs ('91)

LOVE STORIES
The African Queen ('51)
Days of Heaven ('78)
Jou Dou ('89-Chinese/
    Japanese)
Jules and Jim ('61-French)
Out of Sight ('98)
Roman Holiday ('53)
Strictly Ballroom ('92)
Sunrise ('27)
Witness ('85)
Women in Love ('69)

MUSICALS
An American in Paris ('51)
Caberet ('72)
The Commitments ('91)
Funny Girl ('67)
Meet Me in St. Louis ('44)
My Fair Lady ('64)
Oliver! ('68)
The Sound of Music ('65)
The Umbrellas of Cherbourg
    ('64-French)
West Side Story ('61)

MYSTERY
The American Friend ('77)
The Big Sleep ('46)
Charade ('63)
Chinatown ('74)
The Conversation ('74)
Fallen Idol ('48)
Laura ('44)
The List of Adrian Messenger
  ('63)
The Maltese Falcon ('41)
Rebecca ('40)

NONLINEAR FILMS
8 1/2 ('63-Italian)
Annie Hall ('77)
Betrayal ('83)
Citizen Kane ('41)
The Conformist ('71-Italian-
  French-West German)
Living in Oblivion ('95)
Rashomon ('50-Japanese)
Reservoir Dogs ('92)
Two for the Road ('67)
Wild Strawberries
  ('57-Swedish)

PERIOD COMEDY
The Court Jester ('56)
Emma ('96)
The General ('27)
If I Were King ('38)
Impromptu ('91)
Kind Hearts and Coronets ('49)
The Paleface ('48)
Pride and Prejudice ('40)
Sense and Sensibility ('95)
Sirens ('94)

PERIOD DRAMA
The Crucible ('96)
Dangerous Liaisons ('88)
Doctor Zhivago ('65)
Elmer Gantry ('60)
The English Patient ('96)
Gone With the Wind ('39)
Great Expectations ('46)
Remains of the Day ('93)
Tess ('79-French/British)
To Kill a Mockingbird ('62)

POW/PRISON FILMS
The Birdman of Alcatraz ('62)
The Bridge over the River
  Kwai ('57)
Cool Hand Luke ('67)
Dead Man Walking ('95)
The Great Escape ('63)
King Rat ('65)
Midnight Express (78)
Papillon ('73)
The Shawshank Redemption
  ('94)
Stalag 17 ('53)

ROAD MOVIES
Genevieve ('53)
The Hit ('84)
The Last Detail ('73)
Midnight Run ('88)
Paper Moon ('73)
A Perfect World ('93)
The Road to Morocco ('42)
Sullivan's Travels ('41)
Thelma and Louise ('91)
Until the End of the World
  ('91)

ROMANTIC COMEDY
Adam's Rib ('49)
The Awful Truth ('37)
Bull Durham ('88)
It Happened One Night ('34)
The Lady Eve ('41)
Love in the Afternoon ('57)
My Man Godfrey ('36)
Mr. Jealousy ('98)
Touch of Class ('73)
Trouble in Paradise ('32)

SCIENCE FICTION
Alien(s) ('79, '86)
Blade Runner
    ('82—director's cut)
The Fly ('58 & '86)
Independence Day ('96)
Invasion of the Body Snatchers
    ('56, '78)
Planet of the Apes ('68)
Star Wars ('77—original cut)
2001: A Space Odyssey ('68)
Terminator ('84)
Total Recall ('90)

SUSPENSE
Apartment Zero ('88)
The Comfort of Strangers ('91)
The Innocents ('61)
M ('31)
North by Northwest ('59)
Scream ('96)
Se7en ('95)
Shadow of Doubt ('43)
The Silent Partner ('78)
The Third Man ('49)

TRAGIC DRAMA
Billy Budd ('62)
The Earring of Madame De...
    ('53-French/Italian)
The Fugitive ('47)
Last Tango in Paris ('73)
A Man for All Seasons ('66)

Quiz Show ('94)
Ragtime ('81)
Sophie's Choice ('82)
A Streetcar Named Desire ('51)
Tunes of Glory ('60)

WAR FILMS
Battle of Algiers ('66)
Das Boot ('81-German)
From Here to Eternity ('53)
Hell in the Pacific ('68)
The Killing Fields ('84)
Paths of Glory ('57)
The Red Badge of Courage ('51)
Saving Private Ryan ('98)
Sergeant York ('41)
Soldier of Orange ('78-Dutch)

WESTERNS
Dances With Wolves ('90)
High Noon ('52)
Hombre ('67)
The Man Who Shot Liberty
    Valance ('62)
Ride the High Country ('62)
Rio Grande ('50)
The Searchers ('56)
The Shootist ('76)
The Wild Bunch ('69)
Will Penny ('68)

And finally:
GUILTY PLEASURES
Bachelor Party ('84)
Cat People ('82)
Gambit ('66)
The Gauntlet ('77)
Heat ('95)
How to Steal a Million ('66)
Liquid Sky ('83)
Seconds ('66)
The Rocky Horror Picture
    Show ('75)
That Touch of Mink ('62)

INDEX

L

Ladd, Diane 87, 91
Landau, Martin 209
Lassick, Sydney 224
Last of the Mohicans, The 176-182
  Act One 177
    climax 177
  Act Three 178-179
    climax 179
  Act Two 177-178
    climax 178
  action sequence 179-181
  inciting incident 177
  midpoint 178
  scene sequence 181
  theme 179, 182
Last Temptation of Christ, The 150
Lawrence of Arabia 174
Lawson, John Howard 45
Lean, David 253
Les Miserables 61
Lethal Weapon 174, 193
linear understanding 3
Lipnicki, Jonathan 198
Little Big Man 148
Lloyd, Christopher 251
Lorre, Peter 47
Lowry, Hunt 176

M

MacDonald, Christopher 290
MacDowell, Andie 236
Madsen, Michael 155, 290
magnitude 1, 7
main story 7, 13, 19, 24, 26, 108, 159
<u>Making Movies</u> 87
Mandel, Babaloo 145
Mankiewicz, Herman J. 149, 166
Mann, Michael 176, 181
Mark, Laurence 193
Martin, Steve 129
Marty 104
Mason, James 208
Massee, Michael 256
May, Jodhi 177
McQuarrie, Christoper 150
Means, Russell 177
Metropolitan 123
Midnight Cowboy 158
midpoint 29-31, 37, 187
Mifune, Toshiro 155
mini-plots 124, 128, 130, 133-134
  transition between 134-135
momentum, narrative/plot 4, 15, 17-18,
  29-30, 41, 78-79, 86, 89, 199, 205,
  254, 268
  loss of 203
montage 99, 157, 197
Moorehead, Agnes 155
moral dimension 44, 60

Moranis, Rick 129
Moravia, Alberto 150, 168
Mori, Masayuki 153
Morrow, Rob 96
Moschin, Gastone 156
motivation, conscious/unconscious 45, 282
Murray, Bill 116, 236, 239, 268
Mystic forces 9, 10

N

narration 184, 185
Nashville 126, 134
Neame, Ronald 253
Neill, Sam 70
Never Cry Wolf 61
Nichols, Dudley 279
Nicholson, Jack 87, 222
nonlinear
  action for plot framing 152
  plot 149
  structure 148
nonverbal language 271
North by Northwest 207-213
  Act One 208
    climax 208
  Act Three 209-210
    climax 209-210
  Act Two 208-209
    climax 209
  antagonist 210
  inciting incident 208, 210
  main climax 215-219
  main conflict 220
  midpoint 209
  planting 230-232
  plot analysis 207-210
  scene construction 246
  subtext 284, 287

O

Ober, Phillip 208
obstacles 7, 9-15, 17-19, 36-37
  four kinds 9-11
O'Connell, Jerry 196
O'Donnell, Cathy 129
Oldman, Gary 203
One Flew Over the Cuckoo's Nest
  222-228
  Act One 223
    end of 223
  Act Three 224-225
    climax 224
  Act Two 223-224
    end of 224
  antagonist 223, 226
  business 252
  conflict,
    inner 225
    main 223
  dialogue 264, 268-269

OTHER FILM & ENTERTAINMENT BOOKS
FROM LONE EAGLE PUBLISHING. . .

SCREENWRITING

Los Angeles Times
Bestseller List

ELEMENTS OF STYLE FOR SCREENWRITERS

The Essential Manual for Writers of Screenplays
by Paul Argentini

In the grand tradition of Strunk and White's *Elements of Style,* Paul Argentini presents an essential reference master-piece in the art of clear and concise principles of screenplay formatting, structure and style for screenwriters. Argentini explains how to design and format manu-scripts to impress any film school professor, story editor, agent, producer or studio execu-tive. The ultimate quick reference guide to for-matting a screenplay—no book in shorter space, with fewer words, will help screenwrit-ers more than this persistent volume. Includes a playwrite chapter for structure and format and an updated list of literary agent contacts.

PAUL ARGENTINI is a screenwriter, playwright and novelist.

$11.95 ISBN 1-58065-003-1, original trade paper, 5.5 x 8.5, 176 pp.

SECRETS OF SCREENPLAY STRUCTURE

by Linda J. Cowgill

In her new book, Linda Cowgill articulates the concepts of successful screenplay structure in a clear language, based on the study of great films from the thirties to present day. SECRETS OF SCREENPLAY STRUCTURE helps writers under-stand how and why great films work as well as how great form and function can combine to bring a story alive. Cowgill includes many helpful anecdotes, insider strategies, as well as do's and don'ts which will help readers make their writing more professional, and therefore, more marketable.

LINDA J. COWGILL is the author of *Writing Short Films*. She received her Masters in Screenwriting from UCLA after winning several screenwriting awards and fellowships.

$16.95 ISBN 1-58065-004-X, original trade paper, 6 x 9, 336 pp.

GET PUBLISHED! GET PRODUCED!

Tips on how to sell your writing from America's #1 Literary Agent
by Peter Miller

This valuable book tells the reader how to avoid being viewed as a neo-phyte in a business that is notorious for taking advantage of writers. Drawing on over 20 years experience as a top literary agent, Miller offers advice on how to sell your published fiction, structure a nonfiction book proposal, package your book so that it will become a feature film or TV produc-tion, market a screenplay, get an agent, tips on contract negotiation, and more!

PETER MILLER has sold over 800 books on behalf of many best-selling authors, sold book rights for film and TV adap-tation and produced several film and TV projects.

$19.95 ISBN 0-943728-92-4, original trade paper, 6 x 9, 336 pp.

HOW TO ENTER SCREENPLAY CONTESTS. . . AND WIN!

An Insider's Guide to Selling Your Screenplay to Hollywood
by Erik Joseph

There are more than 50 legitimate screenwriting compe-titions across the U.S. Entering such a contest is the best and most affordable way to get your screenplay noticed, optioned, sold, and ultimately produced. Contains comprehensive listings of screenplay contests.

$16.95 ISBN 0-943728-88-6, original trade paper, 6 x 9, 184 pp.

To order or for more information,
call 1-800-FILMBKS (345-6257) or go to www.loneeagle.com

OTHER FILM & ENTERTAINMENT BOOKS FROM LONE EAGLE PUBLISHING. . .

SCREENWRITING

WRITING GREAT CHARACTERS
The Psychology of Character Development
by Michael Halperin, Ph.D.

This valuable book identifies and solves a major problem for writers, creating characters who are so real they literally jump off the page. Halperin has developed an easy to understand, logical system which gives all screenwriters a foolproof and failproof method of developing great characters. WRITING GREAT CHARACTERS is a book for all writers, from the expert who is looking to polish his techniques to the novice who wants to learn the craft from an expert.

MICHAEL J. HALPERIN, Ph.D., has taught screenwriting at UCLA and currently teaches at Loyola Marymount University in Los Angeles, CA. He has written numerous popular television programs and has authored several bestselling computer based interactive media programs. He has given seminars for executives of television and film. He holds a BA in Communications from USC and a Ph.D. in Film Studies from the Union Institute in Cincinnati, Ohio.

$19.95 ISBN 0-943728-79-7, original trade paper, 6 x 9, 208 pp.

WRITING SHORT FILMS
Structure and Content for Screenwriters
by Linda J. Cowgill

Contrasting and comparing the differences and similarities between feature films and short films, WRITING SHORT FILMS offers readers the essential requirements necessary to make their writing crisp, sharp and compelling. Emphasizing characters, structure, dialogue and story, WRITING SHORT FILMS dispels the "magic formula" concept that screenplays can be constructed by anyone with a word processor and a script formatting program. Writing a good screenplay, short or long, is a difficult job. Citing numerous examples from short films as well as feature films, the author teaches strategies to keep a short film on track and writer's block at bay. Chapter headings include The Three Part Nature of Film Structure, Proper Screenplay Format, and Dialogue–The Search for the Perfect Line.

LINDA J. COWGILL received her Masters in Screenwriting from UCLA, after winning several screenwriting awards and Fellowships. She has taught screenwriting seminars at the Boston Film Institute, the American Film Institute, and the prestigious Kennedy Center in Washington, D.C. Currently Ms. Cowgill teaches screenwriting at Loyola Marymount University in Los Angeles. Ms. Cowgill has written over 12 features and teleplays.

$19.95 ISBN 0-943728-80-0, original trade paper, 6 x 9, approx. 250 pp.

TOP SECRETS: SCREENWRITING
by Jurgen Wolff and Kerry Cox

"TOP SECRETS is an authentic stand-out. The combination of biographies, analyses, interviews and actual script samples is a real winner."
–Professor Richard Walter, UCI

"TOP SECRETS provides an
conveys what it takes to b
the craft, the perseverance
–Dr. Linda Seger, Author of M

$21.95 ISBN 0-943728-50-9, origin

142127

To order or for more information,
call 1-800-FILMBKS (345-6257) or go to www.loneeagle.com